JEWISH ENCOUNTERS

Jonathan Rosen, General Editor

Jewish Encounters is a collaboration between Schocken and Next-book, a project devoted to the promotion of Jewish literature, culture, and ideas.

>nextbook

PUBLISHED

FORTHCOMING

Ben-Gurion

SHIMON PERES
IN CONVERSATION WITH DAVID LANDAU

BEN-GURION

A Political Life

NEXTBOOK · SCHOCKEN · NEW YORK

Library of Congress Cataloging-in-Publication Data
Peres, Shimon, [date]
Ben-Gurion : a political life / Shimon Peres, in
conversation with David Landau.
p. cm.
Includes bibliographical references.
ISBN 978-0-8052-4282-9
1. Ben-Gurion, David, 1886–1973. 2. Prime ministers—
Israel—Biography. 3. Zionists—Palestine—Biography.
4. Israel—Politics and government—1948–1967.
I. Landau, David, [date] II. Title.
DS125.3.B37P47 2011 956.9405'2092—dc23 [B] 2011021044

www.schocken.com
Jacket image: David Ben-Gurion,
December 31, 1948, by John Phillips/
Time Life Pictures & Getty Images
Jacket design by Darren Haggar
Printed in the United States of America
First Edition
2 4 6 8 9 7 5 3 1

CONTENTS

A NOTE TO THE READER

As much as the laws of the Talmud, the creation of the State of Israel was the result of argument and debate and compromise. Ben-Gurion not only argued with his ideological opponents on the right and the left, he also argued with members of his own party—and sometimes even with himself. This book, orally produced but hammered through collaboration into written shape, is itself a fusion of memory and history and multiple competing narratives. How else but through dialogue—with myself, with the past, and with my collaborator who, as a lifelong journalist and former editor of *Haaretz*, has his own burning questions for me about Ben-Gurion and his legacy—can a book like this be written? I would even hope that in some sense this book is a dialogue with the future, which will need to choose what of Ben-Gurion's legacy it elects to follow.

In that spirit of dialogue, and even of argument, there are a few places within this book where the questions of David Landau and the answers of Shimon Peres need to stand on their own.

Ben-Gurion

INTRODUCTION

Voyage of Destiny

D avid Ben-Gurion was a mythic figure, the founding father of
Israel and a modern-day prophet, but he was also a real man
who stormed through history on human legs. It was my great
privilege to know him and work with him for many years. This
book is not a memoir of my time with Ben-Gurion, but it is inevitably shaped by my time with him. Since his death in 1973, I have
thought a great deal about the sort of leader he was: visionary and
pragmatic, steeped in Jewish history and yet forward looking and
unsentimental. He is our Washington and our Jefferson, and yet in
some sense our Lincoln too, for the War of Independence in 1948
brought with it a danger of civil war. He seems to me now to be an
emblem not only of the energy that created the State of Israel but
also of the sort of leadership that the country so desperately needs
if it is to find its way to peace and security. Not all of his assump-
tions have been borne out by events. But his historic decision to
accept the partition of the Land of Israel in order to secure the
State of Israel as a Jewish and a democratic state shines forth today
as a beacon of statesmanship and sagacity.

I n order to understand Ben-Gurion, it is necessary to return to
the shtetl in Poland where he was born and which stamped him
deeply with Jewish feeling, Jewish history, and Zionist fervor. But
the place to begin this book is with a boat ride I took from Palestine to Basel in 1946 to attend the first Zionist Congress after the
Holocaust. Moshe Dayan and I were among the delegates from the

Mapai* political party in Eretz Yisrael, though we were much younger than all the others. I represented our youth movement, Ha'noar Ha'oved.

We set out from Haifa on a Polish ship. I found myself sharing a cabin with Mapai veterans Levi Eshkol and Pinhas Lavon. They were old hands at this sort of seafaring, and they insisted that we draw lots for the best bunk, the one right under the porthole. As bad luck would have it, I won. I immediately offered the bunk-with-a-view to Eshkol. He kindly but firmly refused. "No," he said. "You won it fair and square. It's yours." I was all of twenty-three years old and until recently had been used to sleeping on a camp bed in a tent in our fledgling kibbutz, Alumot. When our first child, Zviya, was born a few months earlier, my wife and I graduated to a hut with solid walls. Eshkol, then fifty-one, was a senior and respected official in the Mapai-dominated Yishuv, the pre-state Jewish community in Palestine. At the time of our voyage, he also served as secretary-general of the powerful Tel Aviv Labor Council and as a ranking officer in the Haganah, the Yishuv's clandestine defense force. Ben-Gurion regarded him as a trusted lieutenant.

I was still weakly remonstrating when Lavon chimed in, "Well, if Eshkol won't take it, then, um, I suppose . . ." Lavon was forty-two. As a young man in Polish Galicia, he had founded the pioneering Zionist youth movement Gordonia.† He had served as co-secretary-general of Mapai and was widely seen as one of the party's brightest hopes. Eshkol turned on him with all his bass-voiced vehemence. What kind of Gordonian values were these? What kind of socialist was he if he blithely proposed to rob me of what was mine by right? And on and on. I listened, silent and aghast, to these luminaries of our movement berating each other in the name of our most hallowed principles.

---

*Mapai is an acronym for Mifleget Poalei Eretz Yisrael, or the Land of Israel Workers' Party.

†Gordonia was inspired by the Tolstoyan teachings of the legendary Labor Zionist pioneer A. D. Gordon (1856–1922).

Although still formally a kibbutznik like Eshkol, Lavon was a bit of a dandy. He always left the cabin elegantly and fashionably turned out. I grew ever more aghast as the voyage wore on. I owned two pairs of trousers: khaki work trousers for weekdays and flannels for Shabbat. Interestingly enough, considering what was to happen among us all later,* it was Lavon who got me the job as director-general of the ministry of defense in 1953. As a cabinet minister without portfolio in Ben-Gurion's government, Lavon had occasion to fill in for Ben-Gurion at the defense ministry. (In addition to being prime minister, Ben-Gurion was also defense minister.) I was at the time acting director-general. Lavon said he wanted to give me the permanent appointment.

"I want to appoint Shimon," he told Ben-Gurion.

"Appoint him what?"

"Appoint him director-general."

"But he is director-general."

"No, he's only acting director-general."

Ben-Gurion called me into his office. "Why didn't you tell me?" he asked.

The Basel Congress of 1946 was the scene of high drama, great rhetoric, and fateful decisions. But for me the most memorable moment was when Ben-Gurion's wife, Paula, flustered and fuming, strode into the basement of the convention hall where Mapai was holding its caucus. She marched over to Arieh Bahir of Kibbutz Afikim, a loyal Ben-Gurionist, and said in Yiddish, "*Arieh, er is meshugge gevoren!*" (Arieh, he's gone mad!)

"Where is he?" Arieh asked.

"In the hotel," Paula said.

Bahir turned to me. "Come on, let's go," he said.

We made our way over to the Drei Könige Hotel, which was

---

*The Lavon Affair embittered Ben-Gurion's last years. See pages 158–161 and 184–186.

where Herzl stayed during the First Zionist Congress in 1897 and where that famous picture of him looking pensively out over the Rhine was taken. We climbed the stairs to Ben-Gurion's room and knocked on the door. No answer. Bahir turned the knob and walked in. I followed gingerly behind.

"Shalom, Ben-Gurion!" Arieh said.

Ben-Gurion didn't bother to turn round. He was packing his suitcase, determined to turn his back on Basel. Eventually he asked, "Are you coming with me?"

"Yes," replied Bahir without hesitation. "But where are you going?"

"I am going to create a new Zionist movement," Ben-Gurion said. "Nothing will come of this congress. The leaders are paralyzed by fear and inertia."

I had incredible chutzpah. Ben-Gurion hardly knew me, but I said, "Yes, we'll go with you. But I've got a request: Speak to the delegation this evening." He agreed, and we went back with him to that tension-filled basement.

That congress in Basel was in many ways the defining moment for Zionism and for Ben-Gurion. Our picture of the Shoah, as the Holocaust was called in Hebrew, was complete by then, in all its ghastly details. During World War II the information available had always been only partial and sporadic. We did not have a full picture, in real time, of the magnitude of the disaster that had befallen the Jewish people.

Soon after the war ended, Ben-Gurion had gone to visit the camps—both the Nazi death camps and the displaced-persons camps, where the survivors were being held by the Allied armies. As chairman of the executive of the Jewish Agency for Palestine, he was escorted personally by General Dwight Eisenhower, the supreme allied commander. Eisenhower made a very deep impression on him. All his life, and whatever the tensions that arose between them, Ben-Gurion never stopped praising him. He would on many occasions recall (as Barack Obama did in his speech at Buchenwald in 2009) how Eisenhower had forced the local Germans to visit the liberated camps and see for themselves the piles of corpses and the skeletal survivors. In his speech Obama quoted Eisenhower as saying at the time that he was concerned that humanity would forget what had been done in these places, and he was determined to never let that happen. Ben-Gurion was hugely impressed and moved by this act of Eisenhower's, both for its humanitarian quality and for its historic significance.

Ben-Gurion returned to Jerusalem shocked to his core, both by what he had seen in the camps and by a more thorough understanding of how the reaction of the rest of the world had contributed to the fate of Europe's Jews. Not only had the Allies failed to save them; not only had they failed to bomb the death camps or the railway lines; but British warships had kept the gates of Palestine shut to any Jews who managed to escape from the European hell. His conclusion was stark and unequivocal: We must have our independent state at once.

That was the underlying issue of conflict at the congress: *le'altar*, to establish a state immediately, as Ben-Gurion demanded; or to wait, as Chaim Weizmann, the venerable president of the World Zionist Organization, advocated. To Ben-Gurion, the Biltmore Program* had meant partition of Palestine into a Jewish state and an Arab state. He was absolutely as clear as day about that. And now *le'altar* meant put this into effect immediately. But there lay the problem: Both the right and the left opposed parti-

*The Biltmore Program was adopted by an Extraordinary Zionist conference held at the Biltmore Hotel in New York City on May 11, 1942, at which Ben-Gurion was present. It declared, "The new world order that will follow victory cannot be established on foundations of peace, justice and equality, unless the problem of Jewish homelessness is finally solved. The Conference urges: 1. That the gates of Palestine be opened to Jewish immigration; 2. That the Jewish Agency be vested with control of immigration into Palestine and with the necessary authority for up-building the country, including the development of its unoccupied and uncultivated lands; 3. That Palestine be established as a Jewish Commonwealth integrated into the structure of the new democratic world."

tion. Today it is almost incomprehensible, but at that time Yitzhak Tabenkin, the leader of the left-wing Siah Bet,* opposed the immediate establishment of an independent Jewish state on a portion of the British Mandate. He preferred an international mandate over the whole land. He thought the most important thing was to preserve *shleimut haaretz* (the integrity of Eretz Yisrael), even if we weren't independent. In the meantime, he reasoned, we would bring in immigrants, build new settlements, and continue creating facts on the ground until a state came into being somehow, in the undefined future. Ben-Gurion replied that without a state we would not be able to open the gates of Palestine to immigrants, including the Holocaust survivors clamoring to get in.

Tabenkin's ideological orientation was to the "world of tomorrow"—meaning universal socialism, as preached by the Soviet Union. That's also hard to comprehend now. He once assured me that Lenin was the greatest statesman of the twentieth century. In some of the kibbutzim of the Hakibbutz Hameuchad confederation, there were pictures of Stalin hanging on the walls, as there were in some of the kibbutzim of Hashomer Hatzair, the Mapam-affiliated pioneering movement. Mapam's leader, Meir Ya'ari, preferred a binational, Jewish-Arab state to partition. Moshe Sneh, who was nominally a General Zionist and whom Ben-Gurion had

---

*Siah Bet, or Faction B, began in 1937 as a group of disaffected workers within Ben-Gurion's Mapai. They railed against what they said were the dictatorial methods of the party machine and corruption in the Histadrut, the trade union federation, also controlled by Mapai. In elections in the Tel Aviv branch of the party, they won more than 50 percent of the vote. They later linked up with Hakibbutz Hameuchad, led by Yitzhak Tabenkin, a group of flourishing kibbutzim more hawkish in outlook than the Mapai mainstream, yet at the same time more left-wing than the mainstream. Ben-Gurion fought them implacably, demanding obedience to party discipline and rejecting their counterclaims for pluralism within Mapai. In 1944 the rivalry led to a split. Siah Bet seceded and formed a new party, Ahdut HaAvoda. In 1948 Ahdut HaAvoda merged with Hashomer Hatzair to form the farther-left Mapam. Ahdut HaAvoda broke with Mapam in 1954 and remained independent until 1965, when it linked with Mapai again in the newly named Labor Alignment.

installed as the commander of the Haganah, was also inclining toward Communism by this time.* Sneh's analysis was that Russia would win the Cold War and would ultimately therefore control the Middle East. The only one who got it right was David Ben-Gurion. He had said early on during World War II, better a state on part of the land than the whole land and no state.

But the opposition to Ben-Gurion wasn't only from the political parties on the left and from the Revisionist and religious parties on the right. It also came from within his own party. The so-called Gush, the tough Mapai machine politicians, were with Ben-Gurion, including people like Shraga Netzer and his wife, Dvora. But many people in Mapai supported Weizmann, who still looked to Great Britain, despite everything, to support the Zionist cause. Eshkol, as usual, was in the middle. Golda Meir was initially against partition. It was she who had chaired that crucial session in that Basel basement. She ran it with an iron hand. But in the end she sided with Ben-Gurion. By dawn the party was with him.

The third and crowning phase of Ben-Gurion's remarkable career of Jewish leadership was at hand. For thirteen years, from 1922 to 1935, as secretary-general of the Histadrut, he had built up and led the Labor Zionist camp in the Yishuv. For the next thirteen years, as chairman of the Jewish Agency Executive, he had led the fight for immigration and independence, both at home and on the world stage. Now he was about to embark on thirteen[†] extraordinary years of constructing and consolidating the Jewish state, in war and in peace.

---

*Sneh (1909–1972) later went on to become leader of Maki, the Arab-Jewish Communist Party.
†Ben-Gurion's tenure as prime minister, from 1948 to 1963, was interrupted by a two-year break, in 1954–55, during which time Moshe Sharett served as prime minister.

1

Beginnings

Ben-Gurion once told me he decided to learn Hebrew at
the age of three. "Why did you waste so much time?" I
asked him.

David Ben-Gurion was born David Gruen on October 16, 1886,
in Plonsk, a town in north-central Poland with a Jewish
presence that went back to the sixteenth century. He grew to
manhood immersed in that brief but radiant phenomenon in our
people's history that might be called "shtetl Zionism." When he
was a teenager, his father, Avigdor Gruen, wrote to Theodor
Herzl, the Zionist visionary, asking his advice on his gifted youngster's education. Herzl, busy organizing his Zionist movement, apparently didn't find the time to write back. How could he know
that in less than fifty years this promising lad would be the man
whose iron will would translate his dreams into reality?

As in so many of the towns and villages of the Pale of Settlement,[*]
most of the people in Plonsk (which was forty-five miles from Warsaw) were Jewish. As the nineteenth century wore on, many were
touched by the winds of modernity and emancipation and by the
Haskalah,[†] which blew across Europe from west to east, changing

[*]The Pale was a swath of territory in the western Russian Empire where
permanent Jewish residence was permitted. It included much of present-day
Lithuania, Belarus, Poland, Bessarabia, and Ukraine and parts of western
Russia, but it excluded some of the major cities within that area.

[†] The Haskalah, literally "Enlightenment," was a loose movement of intellectuals promoting secular learning and modern modes of studying Jewish
texts.

the centuries-old pattern of life in the ancient Jewish communities. A minority channeled their newly acquired intellectual energies into the revival of Hebrew language and literature. Among these was Zvi Arye Gruen, David's grandfather and a formative influence on his young life. Zvi Arye was among the first in the district to join the Hovevei Tzion (literally "Lovers of Zion"), a movement founded in the early 1880s that encouraged agricultural settlement in Palestine.

Avigdor was a sort of unofficial attorney-at-law—a familiar figure in the Pale at that time—who helped people with their legal problems. He was among the first in Plonsk to set aside the more traditional Jewish garb in favor of the frock coat and winged collar that suited his profession. The Gruens, though not rich, were a comfortable family. But they were stricken by tragedy when David, an introspective boy, was only eleven: his mother, Sheindel, whom he doted on, died in childbirth. It was her eleventh confinement. Five of the children lived: three boys, of whom David was the youngest, and two girls. David now grew even closer to his father. There was one episode of tension—common to many Jewish families at the time—when the young David, after his bar mitzvah, refused to continue putting on his *tefilin*.* But it didn't last.

At fourteen David founded his first party—not a political party, but rather an ideological society of like-minded boys in Plonsk that he named Ezra, after the biblical scribe who led the return of the Israelites from the Babylonian exile in the fifth century B.C.E. The boys studied Hebrew and discussed the weighty issues of the day affecting the Jewish people. Chief among them was what was called within the Zionist movement "territorialism," which was the idea, supported at first even by Herzl himself, that the Jews make do with a territory of their own somewhere

---

**Tefilin are phylacteries, or black leather boxes containing parchment scrolls with handwritten passages from the Bible. Males over thirteen are required to don them each morning at the start of prayers.

other than in Palestine, perhaps in British-administered Uganda. This would be at the very least an interim solution, to help the Jews escape the steadily worsening threat of rampant European anti-Semitism.

The young members of Ezra were dismayed and outraged at the idea. Sitting on the banks of the River Plonka that ran through Plonsk, David and his comrades drafted their response to the Uganda Plan, which had been submitted to the 1903 Sixth Zionist Congress in Basel. "We have reached the conclusion," they asserted, "that the way to fight Ugandism is to make *aliyah*."* They were not yet adults, but their thinking at that time would inform and shape their entire adult lives. For Ben-Gurion, this brisk dismissal of Zionist rhetoric in favor of Zionist action was a theme that was to recur countless times in his speeches and writings. For him, Zionism was what Jews did in Eretz Yisrael, not what they or others said or did elsewhere.

Soon afterward David became involved in Zionist politics proper. Despite the sense of almost personal bereavement that he and his friends felt at the death of Herzl in 1904 at the young age of forty-four, David threw his energies into founding and running the Plonsk branch of the fledgling Poalei Zion, a socialist-Zionist party. He was supposed to be spending his time now in Warsaw, studying engineering. But the restrictions and quotas on Jewish students imposed by the czarist regime made it hard for him to gain admittance to a reputable college. Back home, he led the fight against the Bund† in Plonsk and the surrounding region, persuading the boys and girls of his own generation to give their hearts to the Zionist cause. His own heart was totally committed, though part of it had also been given to the willowy Rachel Nelkin, stepdaughter of another prominent Zionist and scholar of the Haskalah in Plonsk, Reb Simcha Eizik. They had grown up together, but

*Aliyah, literally "ascent," is the Hebrew term for immigration to Eretz Yisrael.

†The Bund was a Jewish socialist party advocating cultural and social autonomy in the Diaspora.

only now, upon his return from Warsaw, was David suddenly and powerfully struck by Rachel's dark beauty. "In Plonsk people were very conservative," he recalled many years later. "A boy and girl couldn't walk out alone. But I walked out with Rachel, and we caused a storm!"

In 1906 they joined a large group of young people from Plonsk planning aliyah. Rachel's mother came with them, carefully chaperoning her daughter on the voyage to shield her honor from David's ardor. On September 7 they disembarked in Jaffa. "My Dear Ones," David wrote on his first postcard home. "Hurrah. Today at the ninth hour I alighted on the shore of Jaffa . . . We're going to Petah Tikva. I'll write in more detail from there. I wasn't ill on the journey even once! I'm feeling well, full of courage, and full of faith."

Though I was born more than a generation after Ben-Gurion, I too experienced as a boy both shtetl life and shtetl Zionism. In our little town, Vishneva, there were no Gentiles. We would see them only on Wednesday, market day, when they came to sell the produce from their farms. Like Ben-Gurion, I too was deeply loved and deeply influenced by my grandfather, Reb Zvi Meltzer. He taught me my first Bible stories. An alumnus of the famous Volozhin yeshiva, he later introduced me to the Talmud. I remember going to the train station, sometimes with him and sometimes with others from our shtetl, to say farewell to groups leaving for Eretz Yisrael.

Of the thousand-odd Jewish families in Vishneva, almost half went on aliyah before the Holocaust. In my mother's family all four of her sisters, together with their husbands and children, made it to Eretz Yisrael. But my beloved and revered grandfather stayed behind and was burned alive in his synagogue by the Nazi Einsatzgruppen. I will never forget his words to me on the station platform when my mother, my brother, and I set out for Palestine. (My father, Yitzhak Persky, had gone on ahead and established himself in Tel Aviv before bringing us over.) My *zeide* embraced me and said, "My child, one thing above all else: Always be a Jew."

Looking back on that period of profound agitation and dramatic change in Jewish history, the period that produced Ben-Gurion and a whole generation of pioneers, I would say, first, that the Jewish people is a fighting people. The Jews' greatest contribution to history is dissatisfaction! We're a nation born to be discontented. Whatever exists we believe can be changed for the better. The Jews represent permanent revolution in the world. However small a nation we may be, we are the flag-bearers of revolution.

The State of Israel is part of that revolution, part of an ancient ethos that demands that we be a "treasured people" and a "light unto the nations." The Jews of Europe at the turn of the last century were faced, essentially, with two options: assimilation or Zionism. In Western Europe—in France, Germany, and Italy—the majority of the Jews inclined toward assimilation. In Eastern Europe they inclined toward Zionism. The great debate was catalyzed by the Dreyfus Affair.* Later, the main protagonists were Communists and Social Democrats. But the question remained the same: Why are the Jews so hated? And what can we do about it? The two sides provided different answers. The Communists said, we have to change the world; the Zionists said, we have to change the Jews. The Communists saw the world divided by class, race, and religion, with the Jews as victims on all counts. Herzl said that we have to change the Jewish condition wherein the Jews have no state of their own—no land, no agriculture, no army. All that makes them strange and different. Ben-Gurion took up this theme of Jewish uniqueness. He would often stress the Jewish people's singularity in its religion and in its unparalleled and incom-

---

*Alfred Dreyfus, a Jewish officer in the French Army, was wrongly convicted of treason in 1894 and sentenced to life imprisonment on Devil's Island in French Guiana. Those who struggled to exonerate him found themselves engaged in a battle that had anti-Semitic undertones that affected large sections of the French establishment. Theodor Herzl covered the trial as a journalist, an experience that inspired his embrace of Zionism.

parable history. To counter anti-Semitism, Zionism posited, the Jews have to change themselves and, hence, how the world sees them.

These were the two broad trends shaping the Jewish world in 1906 as Ben-Gurion made his journey to Palestine. In addition, the young people were rebelling against their parents' world. Many saw the older generation as provincial, narrow-minded, and hidebound by outmoded traditions.

When their ship docked, David and his friends made their way on foot from Jaffa to Petah Tikva, which was then a Jewish agricultural village some eight miles away. There they joined other young Second Aliyah* pioneers vying daily with local Arab laborers for poorly paid jobs in the fields and orchards of the Jewish farmers.

Even in those very early years—the dawn of organized Zionist settlement on the land—the Zionist movement as well as the individual pioneers were already preoccupied with two issues of principle. One was *avodah Ivrit*, or Hebrew labor, the social imperative for Jews to work their own lands or hire other Jews to work them. The fear was that the Zionist aliyah would become like the British presence in India, with the natives (in this case, the Arabs) doing the work. *Avodah Ivrit* was the ideological and rhetorical bulwark against nativism. The second principle was *geulat hakarka:* literally "redemption of the soil," the political imperative to buy up tracts of land and not occupy them by force.

People ask me what Ben-Gurion would have thought about *avo-*

---

*In Zionist parlance, the First Aliyah was the wave of immigrants, mainly farming families, who came to Eretz Yisrael between 1882 and the turn of the century; the Second Aliyah were mainly young socialist pioneers, like Ben-Gurion, who came before World War I; the Third Aliyah arrived in the immediate postwar years; the Fourth Aliyah were mainly bourgeois families who arrived in the 1920s; and the Fifth Aliyah were refugees, mainly from Germany, who came in the 1930s.

dah Ivrit today, especially given that Israel employs many foreign workers from around the globe, in agriculture, construction, and paramedical care. But physical work as such is no longer a matter of principle, because muscles aren't what matter anymore; what matters is brainpower. There's not much human labor required on the land today, what with the mechanization of agriculture and, more important, with the huge changes that have come about in the use of land. For instance, there used to be a quarter-million *dunams*[*] of citrus groves in the area around Ness Ziona and Reho-vot.[†] In the early years of the state, they brought in $100 million a year in hard currency and were considered, rightly, a major export industry. Now the orange trees have been largely uprooted. On a 400-*dunam* corner of the former orchards, there's a science and technology park that brings in $4 *billion* a year.

It's amusing, and also perhaps heartening, to recall that the two great exports of Israel in the early years were actually oranges and false teeth. All over the world Israeli diplomats were required to help sell false teeth. It sounds funny, I know. Yitzhak Navon and Yaakov Tsur[‡] were in Argentina once, meeting with Juan Peron. Their main goal was to sell him false teeth! And oranges.

Young David Gruen had had no training or experience in agricultural work and found it hard going at first. After just a fortnight he was felled by the malaria that made life so miserable for so many of the pioneers. A doctor who examined him quietly suggested that he might do well to consider returning home. He had clearly misjudged his patient. "For weeks, the whole country prayed for rain," David wrote to his father in December 1906.

When the rain comes, the oranges are picked, so there's work. That's not the only blessing it brings us workers: when

---

[*]One *dunam* equals 1,000 square meters.

[†]Ness Ziona and Rehovot were two early Zionist villages in the center of the country.

[‡]Navon was Ben-Gurion's long-serving secretary and subsequently the fifth president of Israel. Tsur was a senior diplomat.

the rain comes the malaria stops. At the end of Heshvan the skies to the west darkened with clouds. Gradually they spread . . . The parched earth swallowed or, more accurately, sucked in the liquid treasure that the skies emptied down on it for two whole weeks . . . In the morning, in groups of ten or a dozen, we young men and women go out to the orchards to pick the oranges. This is one of the easiest and pleasantest tasks.

Rachel, not a natural laborer, much to David's chagrin, had dropped out of the group by now. And she fell in love with somebody else.

David went on to describe in detail, in flowing Hebrew and with occasional Yiddish terms thrown in for clarity, the techniques for harvesting oranges and his own prowess and progress in moving up the ranks of pickers. Lunch, he wrote, was bread, eggs, halvah, and oranges. Sometimes there were sardines too. "Some people eat olives and tomatoes," he added, supplying in parentheses the Yiddish word for tomatoes, *pomadoren*, in case his father was unfamiliar with the Hebrew *agvaniot*. "But I haven't got used to eating this sort of food yet." He signed off, "With greetings from Zion." Clearly he was in his element.

Yet David did not stay long in Petah Tikva. He moved on to Kfar Sava, another farming village nearby, and then on to the famous winery at Rishon LeZion, founded by the French Baron Edmond de Rothschild, the major philanthropic backer of many of the First Aliyah settlements. About a year after his aliyah, David moved to the Galilee, where he found work, pleasure, and peace of mind in the village of Sejera, near Mount Tabor. All the farmhands in this small settlement were Jewish. "I get up at half past four in the morning," he reported to his father in February 1908,

and go to the cowshed to feed "my" animals. Then I brew up some tea and have my breakfast. At first light, I take my "flock"—two pairs of oxen, two cows, two calves, and a donkey—over to the trough to drink. The sun's still not up, and

I'm harnessing the yoke on my oxen, putting the bag of seed on the donkey, getting my cattle-prodder ready [a detailed description of this implement appears here in parentheses], and heading for the field, where I plow steadily all day long. How easy and pleasant plowing is! . . . The oxen plod slowly ahead, like important burghers, and I have all the time in the world to think and to dream. And how can one not think when one is walking and plowing the land of Eretz Yisrael, and when all around other Jews are plowing their land in their own country? This land that you tread on, this land that reveals itself in all its rich shades and magic charm . . . isn't this experience itself a dream? . . . At four I'm back home. I feed and water the oxen, muck out the cowshed, and clean up—and then I'm free for myself! I spend the evenings reading, writing, partying with friends (there are some twenty Hebrew workers here), or busy with public work.

Despite his pride and self-assurance, others at Sejera appear to have been less appreciative of David's bucolic abilities. Some recalled the time he was so engrossed in his newspaper while plowing that he failed to notice that the oxen had plodded right out of the field and headed off to pasture elsewhere. David himself gave voice, in letters to his friends, to the loneliness that sometimes assailed him up in Sejera, a small settlement surrounded by Arab villages, some of them hostile. Later he moved farther north, to Kinneret and Menahemia, then returned to Sejera, where he witnessed at first hand the shooting of one of the Jewish guards by Arab marauders.

In one of his early articles in the newspaper of the Poalei Zion Party, which was called *Ha'achdut* (literally "Unity"), David plunged into the issue that would preoccupy him for so much of his time as leader of the nation: defense. He pointedly compared the Turkish authorities' lackadaisical attitude toward the murder of Jewish farmers by Arabs to their stern efficiency in pursuing and punishing the killers of a German resident of Haifa. But his criticism was aimed not so much at the Turks as at the fledgling Yishuv itself.

Who is to blame if not the Hebrew public, which reacts apathetically to the murder of one of its own? When a German is killed, all the Germans immediately bombard the Turkish authorities, the German consul, and the Emperor himself with their vigorous demands for protection of their persons and their property and for punishment of the miscreants. And they, the Germans, do not rest until they obtain firm assurances . . . Whereas in our villages there have been assaults, brawls, armed attacks, and six murders, and what have we done to protect our persons and property? Nothing!

We Jews don't have a foreign government to come to our aid. But precisely because we don't, precisely because our existence and our future depend on ourselves alone, we absolutely must be more active politically, always on guard to assert our national and political interests and to demand our legal rights from the central government in Constantinople.

2

Young Turk

In his heart Ben-Gurion felt from a very young age that he
was destined to lead. But he never said it. And he never
would say it.

When David Gruen wrote his article on defense in September 1910, the need to "demand our legal rights" in Constantinople had been on his mind for some time. He felt that the
tiny Yishuv needed someone to represent it at the policy-making
level within the Ottoman Empire, especially now, after the Young
Turk revolution in 1908, when minorities were being allowed representation in the Turkish parliament. Perhaps he was the man.
He was troubled by the thought, as he recalled later, that

> nowhere in the world is the Jewish community so disengaged
> from the political life, from the people, and from the lan-
> guage of the country in which it lives, than here in Eretz
> Yisrael . . . Even though we are so much more advanced in
> our education than the native population here, we lag far be-
> hind them in terms of political activism . . . Our political
> alienation and political ignorance weaken our efforts to es-
> tablish ourselves in the Land.

In his heart, he knew by this time that his own contribution to
the Zionist enterprise could be greater than tilling the soil and
mucking out the cowshed—though he never stopped praising,
indeed almost venerating, agricultural workers. "Settling the
land—that is the only real Zionism," he wrote to his father in

February 1909 from the village of Kinneret in the Galilee, after a
brief trip back home. "The rest is just self-delusion, idle chatter,
and time-wasting."

In a long letter home later that year, he considered the pros and
cons of the whole family coming out to the Galilee to farm the land
while he himself would pursue his legal education and political
aspirations on behalf of the Yishuv. "There's no purpose in life in
Plonsk," he wrote. The family was in danger of dispersion, as one
sibling after another sought a better life elsewhere. "Wouldn't it be
better therefore if all of us settled here?" The Jewish Colonization
Association* was distributing plots of 250 *dunams* with a farmhouse,
barns, an initial inventory of cattle and seed, and a grant of 2,500
francs. "So I thought I would take one next year for our family, for
'colonization,' as it's called here." As for their fears of hardships,
which some of the family had expressed, they weren't to worry.
"I've suffered them—on your behalf, too." And now there weren't
any more hardships.

We, the first-comers, lived a "barefooted" life. We were inex-
perienced, lonely, had no homes and no suitable food. We suffered a little. But now, life here is no harder than in Russia . . .

As to myself, I have no desire to remain a peasant . . . I
despise land ownership, which makes one rich and at the
same time makes one enslaved. I love freedom, freedom of
body and soul. But there's a deeper reason. There is much
work to be done in Eretz Yisrael. Every Hebrew person in
Eretz Yisrael who feels and understands that he can make a
contribution to the revival of our land . . . has the duty to
make that contribution . . . That's why I would like to study
law, in Constantinople or in Plonsk, in order to prepare for
the work that I feel myself capable of doing. I don't know if it

*This fund for assisting the early settlers was established in the late nine-
teenth century by the philanthropist Baron Maurice de Hirsch; it was later
taken over by Baron Edmond de Rothschild and known as the Palestine Jewish Colonization Association, or PICA.

will be possible . . . If the future of our family requires that I become a farmer, then I'll do my duty and become a farmer.

Meanwhile he became an editor. Poalei Zion voted him onto the editorial board of *Ha'achdut*, which meant living and working in Jerusalem. A famous photograph from this time shows him sitting with the other editors, including Yosef Haim Brenner, who had recently made aliyah and was already regarded as the foremost Hebrew writer in the Yishuv, and Yitzhak Ben-Zvi. Ben-Gurion went on to forge a bond of close, lifelong friendship with Ben-Zvi and his wife, Rachel Yannait.

It was for his articles in *Ha'achdut* that he first took on the pen name Ben-Gurion, which quickly became the name he went by. "The Hebrew Yishuv will be built by the Hebrew worker or it won't be built at all," he wrote forcefully. Time and again he insisted in his articles that the pioneers in Palestine, and not the armchair Zionists back in the Diaspora, must be the ones to decide the future of Zionism. This led to tensions when he and Ben-Zvi traveled to Vienna in 1911 to represent the Palestinian branch at a world conference of Poalei Zion. The two of them were accused of separatism by the twenty-three other delegates from Russia, the United States, England, Bulgaria, Austria, and Romania. Ben-Gurion and Ben-Zvi compounded their guilt by advocating a united front of all Hebrew Palestinian workers, whether they were members of Poalei Zion, or of the rival party, Hapoal Hatzair, or not members of any party at all. This was close to heresy in the eyes of the party loyalists from the Diaspora.

The Gruen family did not, after all, make aliyah at that time, and Avigdor, fortunately for his son, was prepared to subsidize David's legal studies. "If you can send me money quickly," David wrote in August 1911, "I'll go straight to Salonika without wasting any further time." In the ancient Greek port city, which was then under Turkish rule, he proposed to study the Turkish language prior to entering law school in Constantinople. "Your advice to me to set aside all my other affairs and focus solely on my studies is completely superfluous. I know as well as you that until I'm a student at the university I must do nothing other than study." He had already decided to drop all his public and political work for the duration of his language course, "for I know that later I'll pay it back sevenfold. So don't worry about me wasting time. My studies are intended to facilitate my work, which is the essence of my life and my soul's soul . . . I shan't be wasting a minute." In another letter he asked his father to make sure the money for his upkeep arrived regularly, "for otherwise I could find myself in Salonika facing very great difficulties indeed."

Avigdor apparently lived up to his commitment, and David spent a year in Salonika studying hard. He was pleased to see, he wrote, that the Jews of the city worked hard too at physical labor. Among them, famously, were the stevedores at the port.* His landlord was a local Jew, and at his table, David wrote, he celebrated "a kosher Passover in every detail and regulation, as I never did in Eretz Yisrael." But the Sephardic foods and smells were not the foods and smells of home, and he missed "the family warmth of Plonsk and the comradely and ideological warmth of Eretz Yisrael."

Having mastered Turkish, Ben-Gurion moved on to Constantinople where, in 1912, together with his friends Yitzhak Ben-Zvi and Yisrael Shochat, he embarked on his legal studies. The well-known photograph of Ben-Gurion and Ben-Zvi dressed in Turkish tarbooshes was no mere posing for the camera. Ben-Gurion believed that the Yishuv's basic political interest lay in nurturing its loyalty to Turkey. He saw his own future role, inter alia, as a faithful and efficacious conduit of political communication between the imperial government in Constantinople and the Jews returning to settle and rebuild the far-off province.

The young men's studies were disrupted somewhat by the out-

---

*Salonika's approximately 70,000 Jews accounted for half the city's population at that time and much of its commercial life. The port closed down on Shabbat and during Jewish festivals. More than 90 percent of the Jewish population would be murdered by the Nazis.

break, in October 1912, of what later became known as the First Balkan War. Turkey did badly against an array of Balkan states and emerged stripped of almost all her remaining European territories. Ben-Gurion followed events with insight and prescience. "Maybe this war will end soon," he wrote to his father in November 1912 (it ended the following May), "and maybe we face a large-scale European war. In any case it's clear that we are on the cusp of huge historical events that will completely change the politics of Europe."

"You can imagine how turbulent life is here," he wrote. "Food prices are rising sharply. Bread is in short supply. It's pretty impossible in this atmosphere to study or to do any cerebral work. The university is gradually filling up with wounded from the war front. There seems no chance of it reopening soon." He sailed back to Palestine to wait out the conflict. "If it turns out that the university won't reopen this entire academic year I think I'll go to Damascus to study Arabic in order not to waste valuable time." In fact, the university reopened in March, and Ben-Gurion was back in class in April.

Another letter to Avigdor from that period shows that David's temporary dislocation and pursuit of a bourgeois profession had in no way cooled his Zionist and socialist ardor.

> About [his brother] Avraham's idea of selling lottery tickets in Eretz Yisrael, I can only express my total deprecation of it. Better he should stay in Plonsk and not bring such "business ventures" into Eretz Yisrael. Let him engage in it in Poland; Eretz Yisrael needs other kinds of "businesses." If he thinks that to be redeemed it is enough simply to change one's place of residence from the Diaspora to Eretz Yisrael without repudiating all the dirt and sordidness that has stuck to us in the Diaspora—all the "airiness,"* all the abnormal and ugly and unnatural lifestyles that we wallowed in in the ghetto—then

---

*A *luftmensch* (literally "man of air," Yiddish) is an impractical, contemplative person having no definite business or income.

he is absolutely wrong! Eretz Yisrael is not just a geographical concept. Eretz Yisrael must be a process of repairing and purifying our lives, changing our values in the loftiest sense of the term. If we merely bring the life of the ghetto into Eretz Yisrael, then what's the difference if we live that life here or live it there?

In the summer of 1913 Ben-Gurion attended a Zionist congress in Vienna, then returned to Constantinople for another intensive phase of studies. This time he was disturbed by illness and by a worrying but thankfully brief interruption in his father's remittances. He spent Passover of 1914 with his family in Poland. "Shalom to you, my very dear ones!" he wrote to them from Odessa, on his way back to Constantinople.

Thank you for the pleasant moments I've spent with you. Years may pass before we see each other again, and we can only pine for each other across the cruel expanses that separate us. And perhaps that day will come at last when we can all unite, never to be separated again   in our Land. Goodbye and *lehitra'ot* [until we meet again]. Your David.

In August 1914, after excelling in his end-of-year exams, Ben-Gurion sailed back with Ben-Zvi to Palestine for their summer vacation. They learned that war had broken out in Europe when the ship suddenly changed course and headed full speed for Alexandria. The captain had received the news on wireless telegraph and, fearing German warships off the Palestine coast, sought safety under the guns of the Royal Navy. Once they did get back to Palestine, they found the Yishuv in a state of distracted anxiety. Zionist leaders abroad, dispersed among the fighting nations, were at odds over where the movement's allegiance should best lie. Chaim Weizmann,* working in his chemistry laboratory for the

---

*Weizmann (1874–1952) was a Russian-born, German- and Swiss-educated chemist who moved to Britain early in the century and quickly rose to a leadership role in the British and international Zionist movements.

British war effort, wanted young men in Palestine to enlist in the Allied cause. Two other Russian-born Zionists, Vladimir (in Hebrew, Ze'ev) Jabotinsky and Josef Trumpeldor,* both now in Egypt, campaigned for the creation of a Jewish legion to fight as part of the British Army. Ben-Gurion and Ben-Zvi stuck to their pro-Ottoman guns and joined an Ottomanization Committee that the Yishuv set up in Jerusalem. But it didn't help them. All Zionists were suspect in the eyes of the beleaguered Turkish regime. *Ha'achdut* was closed down, and Ben-Gurion and Ben-Zvi were incarcerated in the Kishle jail, inside the Jaffa Gate of the Old City of Jerusalem, in preparation for their deportation to Alexandria. From their cell, they penned an appeal in florid Turkish to Jamal Pasha, the supreme military commander of Syria and Palestine.

> We have heard that at Your Excellency's orders we are to be expelled from Turkish soil and forbidden from continuing our studies at the Ottoman University, all this on the grounds of our membership in a purportedly secret society inimical to the welfare and interests of the motherland . . . We have never been members of a secret society, as we made clear during our interrogation. We are members of a section of the Zionist organization called Poalei Zion, which defends workers' interests. Poalei Zion, like the Zionist organization itself, is not secret. All its activities are open and public, and it does nothing it needs to hide . . . It was out of the love we have felt from our earliest youth toward the Ottoman Empire— which distinguished itself throughout history by its humane attitude toward the Jewish People—that eight years ago we left Russia, which is well known for its persecution of the Jews, and came here to live as sons of the homeland. We are tied not only to this Land, which is dear and holy to us, but also to the Ottoman Empire, which has given refuge to our

---

*Jabotinsky (1880–1940) was a journalist, writer, and Zionist leader who later founded the Revisionist Zionist movement. Trumpeldor (1880–1920) was a decorated czarist officer who joined the Zionist movement.

people for hundreds of years. By going to Constantinople to study . . . we linked our own personal futures to the Ottoman regime, to the Ottoman legal system, and to the Ottoman language . . . When universal conscription was announced, we duly registered to defend the motherland alongside all the other subjects of the empire.

They sent off their letter by registered mail but received no reply. Ben-Zvi went to find out why. (The conditions of their incarceration were not especially onerous, it seems—they came and went with relative freedom.) Ben-Zvi takes up the story:

As I turned to leave through the gate I saw Jamal Pasha walking with his adjutant. Someone approached him and greeted him, so I did the same. He turned to me.

JAMAL PASHA: What are you doing here?

BEN-ZVI: It's about our appeal. We haven't got an answer.

JAMAL PASHA: I knew it. You're the same two. I threw your letter away. You're Poalei Zion. There's no place for Poalei Zion in this country. You want to establish a sovereign Jewish state in Palestine. You can't stay here as long as you espouse those views.

BEN-ZVI: God forbid. We absolutely do not espouse such views . . .

JAMAL PASHA: I have ruled that you are to be deported.

BEN-ZVI: I would like to see the ruling.

JAMAL PASHA: I've torn up your appeal. Do you understand me?

BEN-ZVI: Well, we are going. But nevertheless, we remain tied and committed to the Ottoman cause, and we'll work as hard as we can to get back.

JAMAL PASHA: You can work as hard as you like, but you won't succeed. As long as you hold those opinions of yours, you won't come back here.

3

Union Boss

Ben-Gurion never wrote a *petek*.*

Jamal Pasha turned out to be more prescient than his two deport-ees, who now joined thousands of other Jewish exiles from Pales-tine waiting out the war in Alexandria. They did change their opinions eventually, returning to Eretz Yisrael in the uniform of the British Army. But that was years away, after the two of them would spend time in America, to which they sailed from Alexan-dria in April 1915. Once they reached New York, they quickly got rid of their tarbooshes and Turkish-style mustaches and set about the grueling and often thankless work of winning hearts and minds for the movement.

"No one can yet determine what the outcome of the World War will be," they conceded in Circular No. 18 of the Poalei Zion Cen-tral Committee, New York, which was published in Yiddish and English in June 1915. It was a first, tentative admission that perhaps the Turks would not win after all, and that the Zionist movement might best serve its own interests by aligning itself elsewhere.

> [P]ossibly the result will not be favorable, but we dare not under any circumstances refuse to proclaim and demand the minimal rights which will guarantee us freedom of immigra-tion, colonization, cultural development and participation in all the political and public institutions in the land.

---

*A *petek* is an "old-boy-network" note. To write a *petek* is to use one's influ-ence to obtain a favor for someone.

Now we need fresh forces and new people, a new army of workers who can move quickly into Eretz Yisrael as soon as the war comes to an end. This army must now be mobilized so that it is ready to travel to and work in Eretz Yisrael at a moment's notice. The first example must be shown by our own comrades, especially those who have already given thought to their personal lives by tying them to Eretz Yisrael.

Though he wrote of an "army," Ben-Gurion did not support, at this stage, the calls for a Jewish fighting force to be raised as part of the Allied war effort. The land, he believed, must be conquered by the toil and sweat of Jewish pioneers, not by force of arms. But here too, as with the Ottomanization in which he had invested such time and effort, Ben-Gurion was not hidebound in his thinking, but sensible and pragmatic. After the Balfour Declaration* in November 1917, he too favored the creation of the Jewish Legion. And six months later he joined it, going up to Canada to swear allegiance to the British Crown and begin his military training.

By this time Ben-Gurion was a married man. He had tried, without much conviction, to persuade Rachel Nelkin by mail to leave her husband and children in Palestine and join him in America, but unsurprisingly, he was turned down. Sometime later, in 1916, he met a nurse named Paulina Munbaz, known as Paula.

---

*The British government issued the Balfour Declaration over the signature of the foreign secretary, Lord Balfour, after much lobbying by Weizmann and his colleagues in the Zionist movement. The text read as follows: "Dear Lord Rothschild, I have much pleasure in conveying to you, on behalf of His Majesty's government, the following declaration of sympathy with Jewish Zionist aspirations which has been submitted to, and approved by, the Cabinet. 'His Majesty's Government views with favour the establishment in Palestine of a national home for the Jewish people, and will use their best endeavours to facilitate the achievement of this object, it being clearly understood that nothing shall be done which may prejudice the civil and religious rights of existing non-Jewish communities in Palestine, or the rights and political status enjoyed by Jews in any other country.' I should be grateful if you would bring this declaration to the knowledge of the Zionist Federation. Yours sincerely, Arthur James Balfour."

Russian-born and Yiddish-speaking like himself, she was by some accounts a member of Poalei Zion, but by her own account was not a particularly ardent Zionist. Nevertheless they married in December 1917 in a civil ceremony, with a view to making their lives in Eretz Yisrael after the war.

As a young man in Ben-Gurion's bureau, I was once privy to the couple's reminiscing about their life together in America. Like everything else about them, it was unique. During his time as prime minister, Ben-Gurion sometimes vacationed with Paula in Tiberias, and sometimes I would have to go up there to see him on defense ministry business. He would always receive me kindly. One time he, Paula, and I were having lunch at his hotel, the Galei Kinneret. As usual, his mind was miles away from the food in front of him and the small talk around him.

PAULA: Look how he eats.

PERES: Paula, you married him. What are you complaining about?

PAULA: *Ma yesh?* [What's your problem?]

PERES: *Ma yesh?* Who'd have married you apart from him!

PAULA: *Chanfan!* [Flatterer!] You're pandering to him.

PERES: Why am I a *chanfan*? Was anyone else courting you?

PAULA: *Tippesh!* [Idiot!]

PERES: So who was?

PAULA: Trotsky!

Ben-Gurion remained completely oblivious throughout this tart exchange. After the meal we walked a little in the garden, and I asked him if there really had been something serious between Trotsky and Paula.

BEN-GURION: *Ma pitom!* [No way!]

PERES: So what was she saying?

BEN-GURION: Trotsky came to New York to give a lecture,

and Paula said, Let's go and hear him. He doesn't interest me, I said, you go yourself. When she returned, I asked her, How was Trotsky? And she said, I think he's fallen for me. What leads you to that conclusion? I asked. He never took his eyes off me throughout the lecture, she said. Where did you sit? I asked. In the middle of the front row, she said.

From his British Army boot camp in Canada, the unlikely thirty-two-year-old Private Ben-Gurion inundated his new bride with passionate letters of longing and love. Longing and love for her but also for Eretz Yisrael, which seemed nearer now that the British Army, under General Edmund Allenby, was moving up from Egypt to take Palestine from the Turks. Allenby effectively accomplished it thanks largely to the collapse of the defending Turkish forces, before Ben-Gurion and his comrades-in-arms actually reached the front.

Ben-Gurion's unit of the Jewish Legion eventually marched into Palestine from Egypt in December 1918, after the war was officially over. Unable, therefore, to distinguish himself in military prowess, Ben-Gurion, by now a corporal, plunged straight back into his foremost field of distinction—Zionist affairs. This unmartial activism set him on collision course with his commanding officer, and he was finally deprived of his corporal's stripes. It was a demotion he suffered willingly, in the national interest. His aim, right from the outset, was to bring about a merger of the two main workers' parties, his own Poalei Zion and the less radical Hapoal Hatzair.

While still in Cairo, he had thrashed this out with Berl Katznelson, a fellow member of the Jewish Legion who was growing into the role of principal ideologue of the Labor Zionist movement. Katznelson, one year younger than Ben-Gurion, became his closest friend and mentor. Katznelson agreed to the merger, but back in Tel Aviv the Hapoal Hatzair leader, Yosef Sprinzak, did not. Nevertheless, after much arcane and ultimately unsuccessful negotiation, Ben-Gurion and Katznelson convened what they called a "general congress of workers." With the enthusiastic acclaim of the eighty-one delegates (who did not, however, include representatives of Hapoal Hatzair), they announced the creation of Ahdut HaAvoda, the United Labor Party. It would take another decade before Sprinzak's resistance finally gave way to Ben-Gurion's single-minded determination and a truly united Labor movement, called Mapai, came into being in Eretz Yisrael. But as near-hegemonic as it became in the political and economic life of the Yishuv, it would be plagued, as we shall see, by dissension and defections.

When Ben-Gurion went to war, he left Paula in America, pregnant with their first child. It was a girl, whom they named Geula. "In spite of the fact that she looks like you, she is so pretty," Paula informed him. Ben-Gurion was hugely excited, but Paula was worried about how they were going to get by. "I will supply eggs and milk," he wrote, "not only for drinking but for bathing our baby . . . I promise you, my Paula, that Geula will have all the comforts that exist in Brooklyn and the Bronx, at least until she wants to go to the Metropolitan Opera." When they were at last reunited in Eretz Yisrael, in November 1919, Ben-Gurion determined that "without any father's prejudices, she is one of the nicest, most attractive, charming, beautiful, and bright little girls I have ever seen."

But they were soon off again. In the spring of 1920 Ahdut HaAvoda sent Ben-Gurion to London, to run the office of the World Poalei Zion organization and to forge links between the Yishuv's fledgling labor movement and the increasingly important British Labor Party. The little family set up home in a small apartment in Maida Vale, a suburb not far from the lively West End and the city center. And the summer of that year marked the arrival of a son, Amos. Ben-Gurion went to work each day on the Underground. He did not much enjoy life as a Zionist functionary in the

Diaspora. Nor did he enjoy the London weather. "You always live in cold, monotonous fog," he wrote to Rachel Yannait. "I've got to be here at least a year," he wrote to his father in October, apparently without enthusiasm.

Ben-Gurion's plans changed peremptorily with the outbreak of widespread Arab rioting in Palestine in May 1921—the first violent insurrection against the Balfour Declaration and the Zionist enterprise. The riots left forty-seven Jews dead and scores more injured. Among the fatalities was the writer Yosef Haim Brenner, who was murdered near his solitary house between Jaffa and Tel Aviv.

Brenner was one of the most famous writers in Palestine at the time and probably the most influential too. He was consciously attempting to forge a new Hebrew literature to go with the new politics that Labor Zionists like Ben-Gurion were laboring to create. A Second Aliyah figure like Ben-Gurion, he had remained in Palestine during the First World War, though he was expelled from Tel Aviv to the countryside with thousands of others as the Turks sought to assert their flagging rule over the war-torn country. Brenner's vision was far darker than the pragmatic optimism of Ben-Gurion. His masterpiece, the novel *Breakdown and Bereavement*, was the book Franz Kafka chose to read in a futile attempt to learn Hebrew. The manner of his death—he had refused to be evacuated because there was no room in the rescue car for his companions—made him a Zionist martyr. From a widely admired writer in life he became an iconic, prophetlike figure in death, especially venerated within the socialist youth movements.

Herbert Samuel, the Jewish and pro-Zionist former home secretary whom the British government (which had been awarded a mandate over the former Ottoman territories of Palestine and Iraq by the League of Nations at the San Remo Conference in Italy in 1920) had appointed high commissioner of Palestine, suspended immigration in the wake of the violence in May 1921. When it was resumed a year later, it was under the terms of a white paper issued by the colonial secretary, Winston Churchill, which limited the future rate of immigration to the "economic absorptive capacity" of the country. The same white paper sheared off Transjordan from western Palestine and made it a Hashemite emirate under Emir Abdullah. The British were juggling the various and contradictory promises they had spread around the Middle East region during the war. Their behavior introduced a note of disillusionment and suspicion into the Zionists' dealings with them. Some, especially in America, went so far as to accuse the British openly of betraying the Balfour Declaration.

For Ben-Gurion and his comrades, all this merely underscored the need for patient, diligent building and settlement of the homeland. "The terrible crisis now affecting the Zionist movement," he wrote to Avigdor from a meeting of the Zionist Actions Committee in Prague in July 1921, "is opening the eyes of both the leaders and the rank-and-file to see what we [the workers in Eretz Yisrael] realized long ago: That without steady, vigorous work in many different economic areas in Eretz Yisrael there is no solid basis for all our diplomatic successes."

Ben-Gurion had taken his young family to Plonsk in March 1921 to visit with his father. He planned for them to spend the summer there while he worked in Tel Aviv. He had booked a cheap ride home aboard a ship chartered to carry young immigrants from Trieste to Palestine. When news of the riots reached him, he left immediately for Vienna, en route, as he hoped, to Palestine. But once there he learned that the charter vessel was stuck in Trieste because of the high commissioner's clampdown on immigration. He had no money to buy a regular ticket, so he remained in Europe until the Prague meeting in July.

Writing to his father from the Zionist Actions Committee meeting, Ben-Gurion described in detail the kind of prosaic project that he believed was vital for the diligent, bottom-up growth of the Yishuv.

> The Jews in Palestine have at their disposal some 11,000 building plots in Jaffa, Jerusalem, Haifa, Tiberias. The mini-

mum sum required to build a house of two rooms, a kitchen and a hall is 200 pounds . . . A mortgage bank is being founded now which will lend home-purchasers sixty percent of the money. They want to start on five hundred homes immediately . . . The success of this conference lies in the fact that the Zionists have finally shaken off their kowtowing to the rich men . . . the illusion that the millionaires will build the homeland.

Ben-Gurion eventually reached Palestine in August and immediately threw himself into the creation of a new, supraparty workers' organization—the Histadrut. From the very start, the new organization was envisaged both as a federation of trade unions and as the owner and operator, on behalf of the workers, of agricultural, industrial, and commercial concerns. The Histadrut would also apply to the government to receive and distribute among its members public works projects. Initially, Ben-Gurion saw the Histadrut as even more all-embracing than this: "an egalitarian commune of all the workers of Palestine under military discipline . . . taking over all the farms and urban cooperatives, the wholesale supplies of the entire working community." But key colleagues, including Ben-Zvi and Katznelson, shot down these "Bolshevik" excesses.

Some 4,400 workers joined up at first—not a large number, even in the context of the 65,000-odd Jews who lived in Palestine at that time. Ben-Gurion's membership card was number three. But soon enough, as secretary-general, he became the number one man in the new organization. Under his leadership, the Histadrut grew to become a major force in the life of the Yishuv and the Zionist movement. His co-secretary-general, David Zakkai, who left in 1925 to edit the Histadrut-owned newspaper *Davar*, recalled later, "After Ben-Gurion joined the secretariat, the organization took on a new lease of life. More activism, visits to workplaces, resolution of labor disputes on the basis of *avodah Ivrit* [Jews employing Jews], resolution of wage problems. He was good to work with. He worked hard and for long hours and he encouraged those around him to work that way, too."

At first the work was grueling and the secretary-general's pay pitifully low. Ben-Gurion sent most of it to Plonsk, to Paula and his father. Paula's visit to Plonsk, extended due to the riots and their aftermath, was not a success. David's American wife got on badly with Avigdor's second wife and apparently with Avigdor too. She found living conditions in the little Polish town too unsophisticated, and they in turn found her spoiled and demanding. Nevertheless, Paula and the children stayed in Plonsk for more than a year before Ben-Gurion brought them back to Palestine.

Ben-Gurion's own relations with Avigdor and the rest of the family deteriorated around this time, in part because of his stolid refusal to help them come on aliyah. Avigdor, now eager to make the move, seems to have expected his up-and-coming son to facilitate his immigration. But Ben-Gurion was distinctly unforthcoming. It was only years later, in July 1924, that he put his concerns down on paper, in a letter explaining how strict and stern he felt he must be with himself and his loved ones, how firmly he had to distance himself from pulling strings or, as it was known in the Yishuv, using *protektzia.*

I know, my dear father, that you relate to me by now with some suspicion [in the matter of the family's aliyah]. But I assure you again most faithfully that my hope and my longing to see you settled in the Land have in no way diminished. Not for a single day. It will be the greatest festival-day for me when I can welcome you to our country. If I were employed in the private sector and were not connected to a public movement weighed down by responsibilities and cares, I could have facilitated your coming to Eretz Yisrael long ago. I would have exerted my every effort to make it happen. But the burden that I bear exhausts all my thoughts and all my efforts, and denies me all my personal freedom. I have neither the ability nor the authority to do what I want to do, how I want to do it. I can do only what is required of me for the benefit of the Movement. At this time, I cannot properly fulfill my obligations to my wife and children, nor to you, Father. And that is the reason—the one and only reason—that has delayed me until now in acting to bring about your aliyah.

Ben-Gurion went on to suggest that Avigdor sell his house. This would bring in some three or four hundred pounds, he estimated, which would enable him to live in Palestine for a year at least. During that time, he hoped that Avigdor would find work

and perhaps build a house, together with [David's sister] Rivka . . . I hope you will find work to suit your abilities and your knowledge. I need to take this opportunity to explain to you a paradoxical situation so that you understand things aright. My position in the country is such that every public institution, both of the Histadrut and of the Zionist Organization, is open to me and would gladly respond to my request to provide employment for anyone I ask. But that is precisely the inhibition that prevents me from using my influence for anyone close to me. I fight constantly in Eretz Yisrael against the accepted system of *protektzia*, both in our own movement and in the Zionist movement in general. And I have an almost physical aversion towards making use of it myself, even when it would be entirely legitimate to do so. What I can do for a total stranger, I can't do for my own kith and kin. I don't want people to look at someone dear to me and think to themselves that he got his job thanks to my influence.

As far as Rivka was concerned, Ben-Gurion wrote, "If she can somehow pull together the sum of five or six hundred pounds she can come on aliyah and will be able to settle successfully. I'll send her the requisite papers as soon as she tells me she's ready to leave." As regards Avraham (his brother) coming,

I remain opposed to it, as I explained in my previous letter. My advice is that he send Yisraelchik [Avraham's son, who did make aliyah in 1925] and if Sheindele [Avraham's daughter] knows Hebrew well, then her, too. She should learn to type, and if possible bookkeeping as well. Then she'll be able to find work. When his two children are settled, and not before that, it will be possible to consider Avraham's own aliyah.*

Avigdor made aliyah about a year after receiving this letter and settled in Haifa, where he worked as an accountant in the Histadrut-owned construction company, Solel Boneh.

I can confirm from my own personal experience that Ben-Gurion never wrote a *petek* to recommend employment or some other benefit for anyone. Political critics accused him of fostering a regime in which such notes held sway. But there was a great deal of tendentious exaggeration in this. There was a certain air of intimacy, almost familylike, in the main institutions of government and business before the state was established and in the state's early years. But that did not mean, and it is inaccurate to say, that the people in power deliberately froze out people who were not members of the dominant political party and instead handed out jobs only to their own people. That is a *bobbe mayseh*, an old wives' tale. I do not believe that people were given positions of authority on the basis of their political affiliation. Ben-Gurion himself appointed people who weren't members of his political party. And on occasion, he threw out people who were.

As secretary of the fledgling Histadrut, Ben-Gurion lived a life of penury in a rented room in Jerusalem. He had moved the nascent trade union federation to the holy city for "national rea-

---

*Another sister, Feigele (Zippora), lost her husband in a shooting, and Ben-Gurion helped her and her two children make aliyah. He also helped another son of Avraham, Binyamin, with his aliyah. And he sent money to help pay for Sheindele's studies. She was his favorite niece, but alone among all his nieces and nephews, she remained in Poland and perished in the Holocaust.

sons." Even on his austere budget, he often had to borrow money to make ends meet. He also began indulging himself, despite his financial straits, in a new and costly pastime—buying books. By March 1922 he listed 775 volumes in his collection: 340 in English, 219 in German, 140 in Hebrew, 29 in French, 13 in Arabic, 7 in Russian, 7 in Latin, 2 in Greek, 2 in Turkish, and 15 assorted dictionaries. He was trying to learn Spanish too, in order to read Cervantes in the original.

Throughout his life Ben-Gurion read widely and deeply in whatever field he was engaged at the time. Thus, as Histadrut chief, he read Marxist literature and books on mass psychology. He told me he had read all forty volumes of Lenin's writings! Later, as chairman of the Jewish Agency Executive, he would focus his reading on Jewish history and the history and geography of Palestine. He himself, together with Ben-Zvi, had written a book in Yiddish on the history and geography of Palestine while they were in America. When the clouds of war gathered over Eretz Yisrael, he switched to military histories and biographies. He particularly admired Thucydides. He claimed he'd read through *The History of the Peloponnesian War* sixteen times, and he made us all read it too. As statehood approached, he turned to the ancient Greek political philosophers—in the original Greek—because he felt that they best understood the concept that he called *mamlachtiyut*,* and also because he believed passionately that statesmen should be intellectuals, imbibing and imparting the noblest human values.

Ben-Gurion's Bolshevist leanings were forever laid to rest during a lengthy visit to the Soviet Union in the summer of 1923, as the Palestinian representative to an agricultural fair in Moscow. "We discovered Russia," he wrote in his diary on the voyage home. "Russia, floundering in the fire of rebellion and revolutionary tyranny. The land of deep conflicts and contradictions, which calls for

---

Mamlachtiyut is often translated, inadequately, as "raison d'état." A better definition, closer to Ben-Gurion's intention, would be "unity despite difference." *Mamlachtiyut* seeks to draw the line where party and political differences should give way to the overriding needs of the national agenda.

worldwide civil war to give power to the proletariat and denies its own workers all rights as men, citizens or class."

Russia's deep contradictions affected Ben-Gurion's own attitudes and policies. On the one hand, he wanted to foster close ties between the Histadrut and the Soviet state. On the other hand, he viscerally hated dictatorship and was painfully conscious of the murderous inhumanity of the Soviet system and the inherent anti-Semitism still prevalent in Russia. This sojourn in the Soviet Union and his experience almost two decades later in London during the blitz were perhaps the two most formative experiences in his life on foreign soil. In the one he saw close up the depredations of dictatorship upon the human spirit. In the other he witnessed a mature and deep-rooted parliamentary democracy survive intact during the most grievous tribulations.

Compounding the contradictions, Ben-Gurion saw Lenin as a great man. He admired him above all for his single-mindedness and his clear-eyed view of history. "There is integrity in his soul, he disdains any inhibitions, he is faithful to his aim, he knows neither concessions nor leniency, he will crawl through the mire to obtain his objective." On his return to Palestine, he took to wearing Lenin-like neomilitary clothes, an apparent expression of his bewitchment. His deep reverence for Lenin did not carry over to Stalin, however, to whom he would refer privately in later years as "just a hot-blooded Georgian." Trotsky too emerged shrunken in his eyes from any comparison to the great Lenin. This I learned, unforgettably, in my own first meeting with him. I was at the time a young activist in Ha'noar Ha'oved, and I had the chutzpah to ask the chairman of the Jewish Agency Executive for a lift in his car from Tel Aviv to Haifa. Breathlessly, I prepared the sparkling questions with which I was going to pepper our leader en route, demonstrating my cleverness. In actual fact, Ben-Gurion sat in silence all the way up the coastal road, and I didn't dare open my mouth. As we approached the outskirts of Haifa, he suddenly said, "You know, Trotsky was no statesman."

Almost struck dumb with self-consciousness, I muttered, "Why is that?"

"Because of his concept of no war—no peace," Ben-Gurion replied. "That's not statesmanship. That's some sort of Jewish invention. A statesman must decide, one way or the other: to go for peace and pay the price, or to make war, knowing what the risks and dangers are. Lenin was Trotsky's inferior in terms of intellect, but he became the leader of Russia because he was decisive. He decided on peace and paid the heavy price that peace required." I knew vaguely then, and much more clearly soon after, that Ben-Gurion was mulling in his mind his own imminent, unavoidable confrontation with history. Would he seize the moment, *le'altar*, Lenin-like, to create the Jewish state? Or would he allow himself to be persuaded by his "Trotskyite" colleagues to defer the decision for more propitious times?

Shalom Geula, shalom Amos, from Abba in Moscow," Ben-Gurion wrote home in September 1923. "Speak to Ima only in Ivrit. I will buy you nice toys." He was not much more effusive to Paula: "Please tell Zakkai to send me *The Manchester Guardian*. I know nothing of what's going on in the world outside Russia. I kiss you and the children." A month later, still in Moscow, he wrote,

> My visit to Russia has been more successful, on the whole, than I could have expected. I know you have suffered a bit, but believe me, my dear, that it was not in vain. I shall have to stay here another fortnight, and I hope during that time to receive the exit visa for [Paula's sister] Fanya. I haven't been able to visit Minsk and see the rest of your family. But at least I'll bring one of your sisters. Be healthy and happy.

That same week he wrote again: "I've sent home five parcels with sixty books, most of them about trade union issues in Russia and the revolutionary movement." And a month later: "I'm very happy to inform you that Fanya's got her entry visa to Palestine . . . I've bought you a nice samovar and I hope you'll like it. Fanya will bring it. I paid three pounds for it. In a few days I'll get an entry visa to Germany. My visit here has been very satisfactory in all respects. I long to embrace you and kiss the dear children."

Ben-Gurion tried, but the fact is he did not give much time to family life. He spent long periods traveling abroad, alone. And even at home he was busy around the clock with his work. He devoted hours to writing in his diary, meticulously recording the events of his day that he regarded as significant. "We grew up at home as though we had no father," Geula recalled as an adult. But Ben-Gurion was a man of one idea, to create a state. Everything else was secondary. He was like a rock, and he never moved from his fixed purpose. When he rose in the morning, what he saw before him was—a state. Creating a Jewish state in Eretz Yisrael. And when he went to bed at night—the same. Even after he had created the state, he never saw it as created but as in the ongoing process of creation. And he continued to be wholly preoccupied with it. It was his destiny.

Paula was different. For Paula, the family came first. Her children were the greatest children ever. Amos was the best son, and she couldn't bear other people troubling him. But she did always behave nicely toward me. And she liked my wife, Sonia. She would often invite her over.

The mid-1920s saw a surge in aliyah, but also a marked change in the kind of Jews who were coming. The Polish government had imposed on its people severe economic restrictions that particularly affected Jews. As a result, thousands sought to leave. With the gates of the United States now closed to mass immigration, Eretz Yisrael became a destination not only for idealists and youngsters but also for middle-class people who sought to transfer their bourgeois, urban lifestyles to Tel Aviv and Haifa. About

35,000 immigrants had come from Russia and Eastern Europe during the years 1919–23, most of them young people and many of them members of Zionist youth movements. An additional 65,000 arrived between 1924 and 1927, but these were mainly older people, tradesmen and professionals, most of them not natural supporters of Ahdut HaAvoda or of the Histadrut.

Ben-Gurion's initial reaction, and that of his close colleagues, was one of classic class struggle: socialists against capitalists, overlaid with a layer of Zionist passion.

We have fought and shall continue to fight against those who fall into the delusion that this great and difficult task—the realization of Zionism—can be accomplished solely by a profit-making joint stock company . . . If there is a fantasy that lacks foundation, it is the empty notion that by means of the pursuit of profit, it will be possible to accomplish this unprofitable undertaking—assembling a dispersed people with no roots in labor, and getting it absorbed into a desolate, impoverished land.

Exacerbating the intense rivalry that now developed between the left and the right in Eretz Yisrael and within the Zionist movement was the fact that the right now had a very attractive and resonant spokesman in the person of Ze'ev Jabotinsky.

The Fourth Aliyah, as this latest wave of newcomers was called, spurred a new rush of building, manufacturing, trade, and business. Fashionably dressed men and women, coffee shops, and tea dances straight out of the salons and main streets of Warsaw and Bucharest began to appear on the sun-drenched boulevards of Tel Aviv—much to the disgust of the khaki-clad worker-pioneers for whom Ben-Gurion was a hero. And they indulged in a vindictive display of self-righteousness when the prosperity proved to be just a brief bubble that gave way to a sustained period of recession. Many of the newcomers gave up and left. "The middle class came—and failed," Ben-Gurion wrote. "It had to fail because it wanted to continue in Palestine using the same means by which Jews gained their livelihood in the Diaspora; it did not understand that Palestine is not like Poland."

Meanwhile, on the international organizational front, Ben-Gurion put into effect long-held plans to create a Zionist organization consisting exclusively of socialists, which would compete directly with the World Zionist Organization. He had spent years doggedly persuading his dubious and reluctant colleagues that this was the way forward. Eventually, he won them over, only to lose interest almost immediately as a new, much more ambitious, and much more relevant goal swung into view: domination by the Labor Zionists of the World Zionist Organization itself.

The catalyst that made this possible—and that thrust Ben-Gurion onto the world stage—was a double crisis that erupted in 1929: between the Jews of Palestine and their Arab neighbors, and between the Zionist movement and its British patrons. In August 1929 Arab violence broke out in Jerusalem and quickly spread to other cities. There had been tension and clashes at the Western Wall dating from 1928, when temporary partitions between male and female worshippers erected for Yom Kippur were deemed "new construction" by Arab religious leaders. The British sent in riot police and tensions simmered through August 1929, when the mufti of Jerusalem spread rumors that Jews intended to occupy the al-Aqsa Mosque.

On Tisha B'Av,* which fell that year on August 15, Jewish followers of Jabotinsky marched to the wall, proclaiming Jewish sovereignty. Several days before, in Zurich, Jabotinsky had given a fiery, maximalist speech at the Sixteenth Zionist Congress, demanding exclusive Jewish sovereignty over the whole of original Palestine—that is, the land on both sides of the Jordan River. Though Jabotinsky represented a minority and his policies were

---

*The ninth day of the month of Av was the day on which the Temple in Jerusalem was destroyed, first by the Babylonians in 586 B.C.E. and then by the Romans in 70 C.E.

never adopted, the congress did adopt Weizmann's plan for a dramatic broadening of the Jewish Agency for Palestine to embrace non-Zionist Jewish organizations, which were mainly in the United States. To the Arabs it seemed that the Jewish star was in the ascendant. On August 16 a young Jew was stabbed to death in the Bukharan Quarter of Jerusalem. His funeral became a political demonstration that further inflamed passions. On August 22 three Jews and three Arabs were killed in rioting in Jerusalem after Muslim prayers on the Temple Mount. The next day the tiny, centuries-old Jewish community in Hebron was decimated by jihadist murderers. Sixty-seven Jews were killed there; the rest, 435 souls, fled the city.

In all, more than 130 Jews were killed across the country before British troops were able to bring the situation under control. Again, the British reaction was to clamp down on the growth of the Yishuv. A commission of inquiry set up by the colonial secretary, Lord Passfield, recommended restrictions on Jewish immigration and land purchases. In October 1930 Passfield published a white paper adopting these recommendations. British policy was clearly veering away from the original meaning and intent of the Balfour Declaration. The Passfield White Paper interpreted the Mandate as imposing upon Britain equal obligations to the Jews and the Arabs of Palestine.

Weizmann resigned the presidency of the World Zionist Organization in protest and anguish at the British betrayal. Within the movement and in world Jewry as a whole, there was bitterness against the British, but there were loud recriminations against Weizmann too. He was seen as too close to the Whitehall mandarins, too trusting of them, and—by some—too obsequious.

Ben-Gurion, in a paroxysm of rage, called for rebellion against Great Britain. The greatest rocks, he asserted at a Mapai conference, crumbled before a small quantity of explosives. The Yishuv had within it that explosive energy needed to "destroy this bloody empire." If the British were seeking to appease the Muslims in

India at the expense of the Jews in Palestine, they would "quickly learn what Jewish youth are capable of . . . Fear for yourself, mighty British Empire!"

Soon, however, under the withering criticism of his colleagues, Ben-Gurion regained his sagacity and agreed the next day that it might be wiser to prune from the protocol some of his more intemperate phrases. He began thinking about an intensive political campaign, directed principally at sympathetic sentiment within the British Labor Party, which might bring about a change of policy. Still, he warned, if the British Empire persisted "in deploying all its might to prevent us from coming to the Land and working in it" then no one should expect young Jewish people to stand by "with their arms folded."

Ben-Gurion now brought to fruition his plans for a separate, socialist Zionist movement, convening in Berlin in September 1930 the First World Congress for Labor Palestine. Nearly a quarter of a million membership cards for the new organization were purchased in America, Europe, and Palestine—better than the organizers had hoped. The congress attracted a strong showing of eminent socialists from all over the world, alongside 196 Labor Zionist delegates from nineteen countries. Ben-Gurion, the keynote speaker, set out the movement's vision: "A Jewish state, a laboring society, Jewish-Arab cooperation." Ben-Gurion reported to his father after the congress that "the foundations have been laid for a world-wide movement focused around the Palestine labor movement."

In practice, however, these ambitions were quickly overtaken by the unfolding Zionist drama. In February 1931 the British prime minister, Ramsay MacDonald, effectively abrogated the Passfield White Paper. Writing to Weizmann (who had, meanwhile, resumed the presidency of the World Zionist Organization) in response to the massive Jewish outcry, he stressed his government's abiding commitment to the Mandate and reversed the limitations on immigration and land purchase. Immigration, he pledged, would be based on an objectively economic, and not political, interpretation of the country's "economic absorptive capacity." A new high commissioner, Sir Arthur Grenfell Wauchope, was appointed soon afterward, and he was to prove sympathetic to the Zionist cause. Weizmann's own standing in the movement, however, was not wholly restored. The party with which he was associated, the General Zionists, declined in strength in advance of the Seventeenth Zionist Congress, held in Basel in July 1931. The two strongest forces now were Ben-Gurion's Mapai, with 29 percent of the delegates, and Jabotinsky's Revisionists, with 21.

4

Onward and Upward

Ben-Gurion thought the Jewish people lacked statesmen
and that this was a key reason for its long history of
disasters.

Weizmann observed Mapai's growing strength on the world
Zionist stage and acknowledged its basic sympathy with
his own moderate policies, as opposed to Jabotinsky's stridency
and radicalism. He tried to woo Ben-Gurion into an alliance with
his General Zionist Party, sending him secretly from the congress
on a mission to meet with Prime Minister Ramsay MacDonald.
Together with the historian Lewis Namier, a high official of the
Zionist Executive, Ben-Gurion flew to London and met with Mac-
Donald at the British prime minister's country residence, Che-
quers.

Ben-Gurion came away impressed with MacDonald's support
for Zionist goals. This was the message he brought back with him
to Basel, but it did not suffice to stanch the tide of hostile opinion
against Weizmann. In a majority vote, he was replaced as president by the distinguished Hebrew author and longtime Zionist
activist Nahum Sokolov. This, even though the congress resolved
by majority to support Weizmann's policies and reject those
advocated by Jabotinsky. Mapai, with two of the five seats on the
Zionist Executive, emerged as the most powerful group in the
movement. The Revisionists were discomfited and began plotting
their eventual secession.

Ben-Gurion realized now that the World Zionist Organization

itself was within his reach. From an almost marginal group, he had led the Palestine Labor movement, flanked by its sister parties abroad, to a position of prominence and a prospect of dominance on the world Zionist stage.

Back home in Tel Aviv, he began markedly moderating his dogmatic leftist rhetoric, seeking to position himself as a more centrist, national leader rather than solely a socialist or unionist one. Some of his less agile comrades were taken aback when he urged his party to develop a policy "not only for pioneers, but for all sections of the population, including private capital." He explained to colleagues, patiently and repeatedly, that Mapai needed now to set its sights higher and wider than its traditional constituency. It needed to see itself, and persuade others to see it, as the central political force leading the Yishuv and the Zionist movement.

The evolution of Ben-Gurion's political and diplomatic persona at this time—from worker, pioneer, and union boss to national leader and statesman—was in sync with the ongoing development of his unique Zionist–social democratic weltanschauung. While he drew encouragement from the international socialist fellowship, Ben-Gurion was always loath to use the word *socialist* to describe his own ideology and his own party. One reason for this was his intense loathing of dictatorship; *socialist* carried with it associations with Marxist dictatorships for much of the twentieth century.

Beyond that, Ben-Gurion believed that Labor Zionism was an original movement with an original, profoundly Jewish philosophy. His point of departure was the Bible. He felt that centuries of Diaspora life had seriously eroded the pristine Jewish values embodied in the texts of the great biblical prophets. For him, Isaiah's "And they shall beat their swords into plowshares" represented the quintessential Jewish political message. And Amos encapsulated Judaism's clarion call to humanity for social justice and compassion with his "Thus saith the Lord: Shall I turn away punishment for the three and the four crimes of Israel? Because they sell the righteous for silver, and the needy for a pair of shoes."

Why, he would say, do we need Marx or Lenin or Léon Blum, or even the British Labor Party (which he deeply admired), when we have our own glorious heritage of social justice from thousands of years ago?

In Ben-Gurion's view—the view of a Jew who lived history and was conscious of making history—the re-creation of national independence after a two-thousand-year hiatus ought to restore the Jewish people to the period when their prophets were their ideologues. It should enable them to transcend their long and sterile years of Diaspora, with all its social and spiritual ills, and leap back in time to that golden age. We do not need to ape revolutionary socialism, Ben-Gurion taught, and we do not need to ape evolutionary socialism. Instead, we must strive to relive and reapply our own authentic teachings, which were originally conceived on this ancient land.

The renaissance of Jewish culture and of the Hebrew language were inseparable parts of Ben-Gurion's Zionist and socialist worldview:

> Whereas the Jewish worker in the Diaspora, in his spiritual poverty, turned his back on all the cultural treasures that his people had created over the centuries and instead made Yiddishism his intellectual ideal, the new Hebrew worker in Eretz Yisrael has made himself the heir, the true owner, of all the cultural assets of his people. Prime among these is the vessel that holds all the treasures within it—the language.

In his cultural outlook Ben-Gurion was deeply at one with Berl Katznelson, whom he admired and loved dearly. Katznelson was revered throughout the movement as an intellectual and moral compass. "Throughout the generations we were persecuted and exiled," Katznelson wrote, admonishing the young pioneers against nationalistic hubris. "We learned not only the pain of exile and subjugation, but also contempt for tyranny. Was that only a case of sour grapes? Are we now nurturing the dream of slaves who wish to reign?"

Katznelson was, in a ritual sense, more religious than Ben-Gurion; he fasted on Yom Kippur and on Tisha B'Av, for example, and would not eat pork, or eat bread on Passover. But Katznelson, like Ben-Gurion, did not approve of the institution of the rabbinate. He regarded it as an alien, hierarchical structure. Both of them saw Judaism as a faith but not as a *dat*, which is the modern Hebrew word for "religion" but originally meant "verdict" or "rule." For them, Judaism was not a clerical establishment or hierarchical church. Their Judaism comprised the Promised Land, the Hebrew language, the vision of the biblical prophets, the belief in the one God, the concept of *tikkun olam*, and the concept of *am olam*, which was the special responsibility of the Jewish people.*

Tikkun olam meant for Ben-Gurion social responsibility. He spoke not of equality but rather of solidarity. People are not born equal, he would say; therefore pretending they are isn't true, and Ben-Gurion valued truth above all else. However, the strong in society must help the weak. One of the meanings of *am olam* for Ben-Gurion—and in this he was inspired by the great Greek philosophers as well as the biblical prophets—was that above politics there has to be a philosophy, a moral criterion that governs a nation's behavior.

To drum up support for the Labor Zionists at the next Zionist congress, Ben-Gurion set out in March 1933 on a months-long whistle-stop tour of Jewish communities throughout Eastern Europe. He knew full well that his rival Jabotinsky was a popular and moving orator, a master of many languages with a maximalist message that appealed to many people as the tides of political extremism began to sweep through Europe. The Revisionist youth

---

Tikkun olam means literally "repairing of the world," or living according to the universal values of social justice. *Am olam* means literally "the people of the world" or "the people of eternity." There is a wordplay here: the word *olam* has both spatial and temporal connotations; it means "universal" but also "eternal."

movement, Betar, took on the mien and paraphernalia of other far-right groups. This instilled pride and won popularity among some Jewish circles. Ben-Gurion did not mince his words, directly comparing his rival's concepts to fascism and referring to Jabotinsky himself as "Il Duce." Both leaders needed burly guards to protect them at public meetings and to keep hecklers from the other side from physically assaulting them.

In Warsaw the Revisionists threw two stink bombs into the theater where Ben-Gurion was scheduled to speak, and as he wrote to Paula in April, "we needed two hours to clean the air." Still, he started his speech on time and spoke for an hour amid respectful silence until he touched on "the incitement against the workers in the Polish Jewish press." As he described it to Paula,

> I said, "Directing this incitement is a man who seeks to be the Zionist dictator." Something very heavy landed next to me and I was covered in yellow stuff. Pandemonium broke out. Everyone thought it was a bomb. It turned out that a Betar girl student had thrown a bottle full of sand from the gallery. If it had landed on my head I'd have been settled good and proper. She was arrested and I carried on talking. Afterwards the Betarim attacked the *halutzim* [labor pioneers]. The communists joined in on the side of the Revisionists and a free-for-all ensued. But our boys are strong in Warsaw and the Betarim got what was coming to them.

This overheated political atmosphere came very close to exploding into serious internecine violence, if not outright civil strife, within the Yishuv following the murder on June 16, 1933, of Haim Arlosoroff, the young and promising chairman of the Jewish Agency's political department and a rising luminary in Mapai ranks. He was shot dead while walking along the Tel Aviv beachfront, having just returned from Europe, where he negotiated an agreement with the new Nazi regime in Germany for the transfer of the assets of German Jews immigrating to Palestine. Rightist commentators had excoriated him for this deal, and the immediate suspicion on the left was that the right had assassinated him. Three known rightists were arrested on suspicion of planning and perpetrating the murder. They were all eventually acquitted for lack of evidence.* "I can't agree with what you wrote me," Ben-Gurion wrote to Geula, then fifteen, from Warsaw,

> that you can't believe the Revisionists are capable of murder. I'm afraid they absolutely are capable. They're not only capable, they did it. Obviously not every Revisionist would do such a thing. The great majority would leave the party if they knew the full truth. But . . . the leaders, Jabotinsky, Abba Ahimeir, and others, educate their youth to kill.

The backlash of horror and outrage that swept through Palestine and the Jewish world doubtless increased Labor's margin of victory over the Revisionists in the mid-July election for the Zionist Congress: Labor won nearly 45 percent, its rival barely 16. When Ben-Gurion, now age forty-eight, mounted the rostrum at the Eighteenth Zionist Congress in Prague, he was greeted with prolonged applause. He was voted onto the Zionist Executive, although he insisted that it be for only two years and that he retain his role as secretary-general of the Histadrut. The two years extended to fifteen, at which time he left to head the newly formed government of the newly formed State of Israel. He kept his position at the Histadrut until 1935, when he was elected chairman of the Zionist Executive and of the executive committee of the Jewish Agency for Palestine and had to devote all his energies to those demanding positions.†

It was at this Eighteenth Zionist Congress that the Revisionists finally seceded, setting up a rival Zionist organization that never

---

*A judicial commission of inquiry set up almost fifty years later by Prime Minister Menachem Begin, Jabotinsky's political heir, posthumously cleared the suspected perpetrators.

†See the Appendix for an overview of the complex web of Jewish organizations, unions, and political parties that somehow morphed into the functioning apparatus of a state.

really gained much traction. Before that, because of the continuing tension and the violence in the Yishuv between Laborites and Revisionists, Ben-Gurion and Jabotinsky made a sustained but secret effort to resolve their conflict. The intermediary who brought them together, in London, was Pinhas Rutenberg. He had been a senior figure in the pre-Communist Kerensky government in Russia. Now he was head of the Palestine Electric Corporation and one of the most original and dynamic figures in the Yishuv's economic infrastructure. A close friend of Jabotinsky, he was also an admirer of Ben-Gurion.

By Ben-Gurion's own account, their first conversation surprised both leaders by its frankness and civility, and by the remarkable degree of agreement that seemed to exist between them on many key issues. Ben-Gurion later described Jabotinsky, "greatly aroused," as suggesting that if they did reach an agreement, they should mark it with some "grandiose project." Ben-Gurion suggested a settlement project. Jabotinsky said he wasn't opposed to a settlement, but that it was not something in which all the people could take part. In Ben-Gurion's account, Jabotinsky proposed " 'a giant mass project with every Jew taking part.' 'What kind of project?' I asked. And he said, 'A petition . . . You do not comprehend the value of a demonstration and a formulation. The word, the formula, they possess enormous strength.' I sensed that, here, we had come to the fundamental conflict."

But the talks continued for a month, with both men maintaining complete secrecy. On their last night of negotiation they stayed up till dawn, drafting and signing two agreements, one ending the violence between the activists of the two camps in Eretz Yisrael and the other regulating relations between the Histadrut and the Revisionists' rival trade union. What remained to be achieved was a third, "great agreement," providing for cooperation between their two political parties within the World Zionist Organization. For that they both needed the consent of their respective memberships, to whom they now proposed to report. Before departing from London, they wrote to each other, promising that even if things didn't work out and the agreements fell through, they would remain friends. "Whatever happens, I grasp your hand in esteem," Ben-Gurion wrote. "I am moved to the depths of my being," Jabotinsky replied. "I grasp your hand in genuine friendship."

Ben-Gurion returned to a storm of protest and dissent within his camp. His senior colleagues and many grassroots Laborites protested vehemently, as did much of the Yishuv's press. Unfazed, Ben-Gurion went back for more secret talks with Jabotinsky on the third agreement. This time the party intervened in advance, strictly instructing him not to sign anything without the prior approval of Mapai's central committee. The draft agreement he submitted was voted down. Ben-Gurion's argument that he had negotiated not as representative of Mapai but as a member of the Zionist Executive was given short shrift. He was flatly overruled, though there was no move, nor even any thought, of ousting him as leader. The two men renewed their written pledges of personal friendship. But as relations between their two movements began again to deteriorate, their friendship too faded, and soon they were back hurling insults at one another in speeches and in print.

Jabotinsky died of a heart attack in the United States in 1940 and was buried in a cemetery in New York. In his will he wrote that he wanted to be buried in Eretz Yisrael, but only by order of a sovereign Jewish government. But as prime minister, Ben-Gurion refused to give that order. "I don't see any need or purpose in bringing 'bones' on aliyah," Ben-Gurion wrote in 1959 "as a friend" to his old comrade Yitzhak Ben-Zvi, who was then president of Israel. "We urgently need living Jews, not dead ones." He had made two exceptions, he said, for Herzl and Baron Edmond de Rothschild. But there were "hundreds, perhaps thousands, of great men who had died abroad. Are we going to bring all their bones to the homeland?" He didn't know if the purported will was authentic, but in any case, he was against anyone posthumously "ordering" the government to take any action. He then entered into a long and detailed argument about Jabotinsky's historical role over the years. Eshkol, when he became prime minister in 1963, brushed all this aside and ordered Jabotinsky's reinterment in Eretz Yisrael. It took place at the national cemetery on Mount Herzl in Jerusalem in 1964 with full honors.

Throughout his life Ben-Gurion thought the Jewish people lacked statesmen, and that this was a key reason for our long history of disasters. We are a nation, he often said, with a wealth of prophets but a dearth of statesmen. He saw himself as a national leader from very early on, when he was still in his twenties. But he probably never articulated that thinking in words, even to himself. He didn't think in terms of titles. In his heart, yes, he felt he was destined to lead. I once asked him when he had realized this. "When I looked around and found that I had no one to ask," he replied. But he never referred to himself as a "leader"—unlike Jabotinsky, who positively reveled in the title. Ben-Gurion never shrank from making difficult political decisions; he had the courage and the will not to defer. But he didn't think about what title he would receive as a result of having made them.

By the same token, the first-person singular rarely appeared in his speeches or writings—especially when things were going well. He used *I* only when talking about something that had failed. When something succeeded, it was *we* or *Israel*. As he described it, "I" retreated from the Sinai desert after the 1956 Kadesh campaign, but "the IDF"* won the war. His title was unimportant to him; he was focused on the substance of what needed to be done. I remember when he appointed Moshe Dayan chief of staff of the IDF, in 1953. I was in the room, and Ben-Gurion said he had a personal request to put to the new chief of staff. He wanted to join the paratroopers. In other words, he wanted do the required series of jumps from airplanes. Dayan said, "You want to be a paratrooper? So, I'm your commander. I command you to be something else: be prime minister!"

As for Jabotinsky, despite their written professions of mutual

*The IDF is the Israel Defense Forces, i.e., the Israeli armed forces.

regard, Ben-Gurion's opinion of him in later years was dismissive, almost contemptuous. Jabotinsky's standing in many people's minds has been enhanced by the widely held image of him as a prophet of doom in the pre–World War II years, warning Jewish communities and the Zionist establishment that the clouds of destruction were gathering. This image has been reinforced by accusations in some political and academic circles that the Zionist establishment—both in Eretz Yisrael and in the Diaspora—did not foresee the horrors that were to come and did not warn of their advent. The record shows, however, that while Ben-Gurion warned in 1934, with uncanny accuracy, that the entire Jewish people was in danger, Jabotinsky poured scorn on Hitler's simplistic writings. In a speech to the Histadrut in January of that year, Ben-Gurion said:

> The tragedy that has struck the Jews of Germany has not struck them alone. Hitler's regime endangers Jews everywhere . . . because he regards them as the bearers of the ideals of justice, peace, and freedom, and therefore an obstacle to his plan to make the German race rulers of the world. Hitler's regime cannot exist for very long before embarking on a war of revenge against France, Poland, and Czechoslovakia, and other neighboring countries where Germans live, or against vast Soviet Russia. Germany will not go to war today because she is not prepared. However, she is preparing. I don't want to be a prophet, but it does appear that the danger of war today is as great as it was in 1914 . . . What will be our [the Yishuv's] strength and importance here [in Palestine] when disaster strikes the world? This terrible day may be only four or five years away. In the meantime, we must double our numbers. The size of the Yishuv may determine its fate.

Jabotinsky, on the other hand, assured people in 1933 that he had "read *Mein Kampf*, and my impression is that it is simple stuff, without talent . . . simplistic, prosaic ideas. But Hitler's no fool. He knows how to bring examples from life, from history."

Ben-Gurion was not especially impressed by Jabotinsky's mind, despite his obvious intellectual gifts. He viewed Jabotinsky as a strange phenomenon: a man of hollow rhetoric who was in love with making speeches. (Years later he adopted the same critical attitude toward Menachem Begin.) For Jabotinsky, it seemed to Ben-Gurion, the medium was the total message. He was greatly under the influence of Josef Pilsudski.* The Revisionists revered Pilsudski, and they were equally impressed by the uniforms and the pomp and circumstance surrounding him. They thought well of Mussolini too, going so far as to send a naval unit to be trained in Italy. Shlomo Erel, later commander of the Israeli Navy, was trained there.

Still, Ben-Gurion sometimes mentioned that he thought it was a mistake that the party hadn't endorsed the agreement he reached with Jabotinsky. He thought he could do business with him. Despite their designations as leaders of the "left" and "right," they were not in fact all that far apart on social issues. Jabotinsky's socioeconomic thinking was not capitalist in the doctrinaire sense. In fact, he believed it was the duty of the state to provide all its citizens, free of charge, with five fundamental services: housing, food, clothing, health care, and education.†

B en-Gurion, like Jabotinsky, was intimately involved in Diaspora life. But the difference was that Ben-Gurion involved himself exclusively with Jews, while Jabotinsky sought to become a part of the general sociopolitical culture of that era, the period of nationalist renaissance.

One of the most important things to understand about Ben-

---

*Marshal Josef Pilsudski led Poland to independence in 1918, commanded Polish forces in the war against Soviet Russia (1919–23), and led the country again from 1926 to 1935.
†In Hebrew he called these the five *mems: ma'on* (housing), *mazon* (food), *malbush* (clothing), *marpeh* (health care), and *moreh* (teacher, meaning education).

Gurion—something that isn't really known about him today—is his insistence on the return of the Jewish people to the sources of Jewishness. Jabotinsky, like Herzl, wanted us to be like the other nations of the world. Ben-Gurion wanted us to be as we were before the Diaspora spoiled us. He lived the Bible. Jabotinsky and Herzl were steeped in foreign languages. Ben-Gurion knew other languages, but they weren't *his* language. He took his Zionism from the Bible; other political philosophies were foreign and alien.

I don't want to create the impression that Ben-Gurion was in favor of cutting the Jewish people off from the rest of the world. But he believed the core values of *am olam* and *tikkun olam* needed to originate from within us and were not to be acquired by copying others. That was the difference between Ben-Gurion and Jabotinsky/Herzl. He was constantly going back to Jewish sources, while they were entranced by the world around them. They wanted the Jews to have a state of their own like the rest of the world, which at that time was not a global, interdependent community of nations but a world of xenophobic nation-states.

Ben-Gurion remained intimately connected to the Bible and retained his faith in its primacy for his entire life. Long after the establishment of the state, in the 1960s, I was in Paris with Ben-Gurion at a dinner hosted by Georges Pompidou, who was Charles de Gaulle's prime minister at the time. I was doing the social rounds when I was summoned by a uniformed and bemedaled official to a "secret meeting" in a side room. I went in and saw the entire French cabinet, including Maurice Couve de Murville, the foreign minister, sitting there with Ben-Gurion and with Walter Eytan, our ambassador.

In France most of the Catholics had little knowledge of the Jewish people, while the Protestants were steeped in the Bible. Couve was a Protestant. He had also been ambassador to Egypt. "Monsieur le President du Conseil," he said to Ben-Gurion, "could you please explain to us your theory about the Exodus." I thought I'd fall through the floor. Ben-Gurion lit up like a bonfire. He started lecturing about the meaning of the Hebrew word *ribbo*, which is generally translated as "ten thousand." But he insisted that it could also mean "family." So there weren't necessarily sixty times ten thousand Israelites leaving Egypt in the Exodus, but just sixty families. He went on to analyze the word *elef*, which means "a thousand" in Hebrew but also "a family," and the word *alma*, which means "a girl." Is it the same as *betula*, "a virgin"? Couve says yes; Ben-Gurion says no.

It's the word *family* here that feels significant. This wasn't a mere linguistic exercise for him; the exchange captures his sense of the Bible as a living document about a family—his family.

B
en-Gurion's gradual assumption of the role of Zionist states-man and policy maker prompted him to seek direct dialogue with authentic and authoritative Arab spokesmen. In 1934 he embarked on a series of meetings with Musa Alami, a prominent, Cambridge-educated Palestinian politician who served for a time as an attorney in the Mandatory administration.

With great charm but total frankness, Alami spurned Ben-Gurion's talk of the benefits that the Zionist enterprise had brought to Palestinian Arabs. "I prefer the country to be poor and desolate, even for a hundred years," he said, "until we Arabs are capable, alone, of developing it and making it flourish." Nevertheless, Alami was prepared to listen to Ben-Gurion's vision of a federative framework embracing Palestine, Iraq, and other Arab states. "Even if the Arabs of Palestine constitute a minority," Ben-Gurion suggested, "they will not have a minority status because they will be linked to millions of Arabs in the neighboring countries."

At first Ben-Gurion spoke of incorporating Transjordan into the putative Jewish state, but in subsequent discussions with Alami he indicated that this was not his final position. Despite Alami's opening statement, Ben-Gurion continued to dwell on the beneficial contribution that the Zionist project could bring to Palestine and to the region as a whole. The talks were important beyond the specific schemes discussed because they enabled Ben-Gurion to reassure Alami, and through him the Palestinian Arab community, that the Jews had no designs on the Haram al-Sharif, the Temple Mount in Jerusalem, which has been a Muslim holy precinct since the seventh century. Alami reported all this back to Haj Amin al-Husseini, the mufti of Jerusalem and foremost Palestinian nationalist leader at the time.

Ben-Gurion had thought long and hard about the "Arab problem." He understood how central it would be in the realization of Zionism's goals. As early as 1921 he had warned against the illusion prevalent among some Zionists that "Eretz Yisrael is an empty country and we can do whatever we wish without taking into account its inhabitants." During his Bolshevik period, Ben-Gurion spoke a good deal about the common class interest of the Jewish and the Arab worker and suggested that this might somehow enable them to transcend their national differences. The 1929 riots put an end to such fanciful thinking. It was becoming ever more clear that demography—the question of which side was the majority—would be critical in determining the ultimate outcome of the conflict. "Herein lies the true conflict, the political conflict between us and the Arabs," he said late in 1929. "Both we and they want to be the majority."

Ben-Gurion's attempt to persuade Alami that neither nation need rule over the other, regardless of which was larger, was no improvised polemic. He had been wrestling with that dialectic for years. Back in 1924 he asserted at an Ahdut HaAvoda conference that the only real meaning of the Zionist idea was statehood.

> Zionism is the desire for a Jewish state, the desire for a country, and the desire to rule over that country. But when we say rule over a country, we do not, of course, mean rule over others. We have no intention, no desire, and no need to rule over others. When we say a state we mean two things: That others shall not rule over us, and that anarchy shall not rule over us. We want to rule over ourselves.

The Arabs of Palestine had the same right of self-determination as the Jews, Ben-Gurion maintained. "We do not dream of denying them that right or diminishing it," he continued.

> We demand the same national autonomy for the Arabs as we demand for ourselves. But we do not accept their right *to rule over the land*, to the extent that the land has not been built up by them and it awaits its builders. They do not have the right to forbid it being built, to forbid the resurrection of its ruins, the development of its resources, the expansion of its cultivated areas, the advancement of its culture, the increase of its laboring settlements.

There were many other meetings with Arab interlocutors during the 1930s and after, in Palestine, in Geneva, and in London. Ben-Gurion was later to incorporate his records of them in a book entitled *My Talks with Arab Leaders*,[*] one of the many he published. It makes for fascinating but sad reading. In a meeting in 1937 with Fuad Bey Hamza, an important adviser to King Abdul Aziz of Saudi Arabia, the "demographic issue" was set squarely on the table. "The question of aliyah was the key political issue for the Arabs of Palestine, and not merely an economic issue," Fuad said. (The report of this conversation published in Ben-Gurion's book was written up at the time by Eliahu Eilat, a senior Jewish Agency diplomat who accompanied Ben-Gurion and took notes.)

> The Jews aspire to be the majority. So what benefit will accrue to the Arabs from the economic prosperity that the aliyah brings on its train if, at the end of the day, they become a minority and lose control of Palestine? Whoever heard of a nation that voluntarily forgoes its control, by dint of its majority status, over its own territory? Mr. Ben-Gurion's contention that a political system can be established in which neither side rules over the other, regardless of the demographic balance between them, is impractical. Today, when

[*]Tel Aviv: Am Oved, 1967 (Hebrew).

the Jews are in the minority, they propose this. But when they become a majority, and today's leaders are replaced by other leaders, it will be entirely natural for them to act in light of the demographic situation that then prevails and to cast off the commitments they gave previously, when the Jewish Yishuv was in the minority.

Ben-Gurion argued that Palestinian Arabs' rights would be ensured not only by their agreement with the Jews but by the fact that they were surrounded by, and closely linked to, the Arab states neighboring Palestine. "Here Fuad observed," Ben-Gurion wrote,

> that for the time being the Arab world was divided into several states and there was no knowing when a confederation would come into being that would dismantle the walls that divide between the Arabs of Syria, of Iraq, of Saudi Arabia and of Palestine . . . And as for the historic rights of the Jews to Palestine, Fuad remarked, on that basis one could make a case for the rights of the Arabs to Spain.

Ben-Gurion replied that Spain had been conquered by the Arabs; it was not the birthplace of the Arabs' culture and their national identity. Palestine, by contrast, was "the birthplace of the Jewish nation and the cradle of its culture." Ben-Gurion went on to recall at length how at the turn of the century, the Russian Zionists had rejected the Uganda Plan and insisted that the restored homeland be in Palestine, even though their community was oppressed and needed a place of refuge. Subsequently, he pointed out, the Zionists had appeared together with the Emir Feisal at the 1919 Versailles Peace Conference "as friends and partners, not as adversaries. The Jewish people," he continued, "were an important force in the world, and they could be of assistance to the Arab people in many areas . . . The Arabs ought not to scorn such assistance."

A year later, at a meeting in London with Musa Husseini, a prominent Palestinian Arab, Ben-Gurion was warned categorically that if the Jews set up a sovereign state, the Arabs would make war on it. A Jewish state wedged into the Middle East, said Husseini, would be seen as an imperialist pawn and an impediment to Arab unity. There was definitely no room for the six million Jewish immigrants that Weizmann had talked about. The only way forward, therefore, was to agree on a demographic ceiling: no more than one-third of the population of Palestine could be Jews. Some Arab states might be prepared to take in some Jewish refugees who could not be absorbed in Palestine, Husseini suggested. But that could happen only after all foreign rule ended and Palestine became a sovereign Arab state, one of a federation of states that would extend to North Africa. What was there to ensure that the Arabs would protect the rights of the Jewish minority? The answer, said Husseini, lay in history: No Arab country had persecuted its Jews. The violence that had erupted in Palestine was a case of self-defense. If there was an agreement, it would cease.

5

What Could He Do?

Then, there was no shouting. Then, everything was subordinated to one thing only: winning the war.

B y this time, early in 1938, bloody violence had been erupting in Palestine in waves for close to two years, and Ben-Gurion was working with Haganah commanders on plans for defending the Yishuv while at the same time imposing upon them a policy of restraint (*havlaga*, in Hebrew) that dictated no indiscriminate retaliation even for acts of wanton terrorism perpetrated against Jews.

Violence had broken out again in April 1936, in what the Arabs dubbed their Revolt against the British. But it was aimed equally at the Jews, whose Yishuv was growing by leaps and bounds. Refugees streamed in from Germany and from central European countries threatened by Nazi Germany's territorial ambitions. Between 1930 and 1936 the Yishuv doubled in size, from 200,000 to 400,000. Aliyah in 1935 alone was more than 66,000. The Arab violence was directed above all at getting the British to stop or drastically slow down this torrent of Jewish refugees. It worked. By mid-1936 British officials were once again contemplating a temporary halt to immigration, this despite weeks of intensive lobbying efforts in London by Weizmann and Ben-Gurion to rally support in government and political circles for the Zionist cause.

Compounding his suspicions of British appeasement of the Arabs, Ben-Gurion was horrified to learn that Weizmann, in a secret conversation with the prime minister of Iraq, had indicated that he could countenance restrictions on aliyah. Weizmann made matters worse when the colonial secretary, William Ormsby-Gore, asked the two of them about the idea of a temporary suspension of immigration during the visit to Palestine of a Royal Commission of Inquiry into the Palestine Problem, which the British now proposed to set up. Weizmann answered equivocally. Ben-Gurion left that meeting "broken, dejected, and depressed as I have never been before." As far as he was concerned, Weizmann could no longer be trusted to advocate the Zionist position.

Weizmann made matters even worse, in Ben-Gurion's view, by equivocating again on the question of aliyah in his in camera testimony before this British commission, which was headed by Lord Peel and took evidence in Palestine in November 1936. In public, Weizmann spoke forcefully of the Jewish people's ever-more-urgent need to keep Palestine open to aliyah. "I spoke of six million Jews," he writes in his memoirs,

> (a bitter and unconscious prophecy of the number extermi-
> nated not long after by Hitler) pent up in places where they
> are not wanted and for whom the world is divided into places
> where they cannot live and places which they may not
> enter . . . There should be one place in the world, in God's
> wide world, where we could live and express ourselves in ac-
> cordance with our own character and make our contribu-
> tions to civilization in our own way and through our own
> channels.

Ben-Gurion was full of praise for him. But in camera, as Ben-Gurion learned unofficially, Weizmann spoke very differently—of a maximum of one million Jews who would come to Palestine over a period of "twenty-five or thirty years." Ben-Gurion resigned as chairman of the Jewish Agency shortly thereafter. "After long and bitter reflection," he wrote to Weizmann, "it has become clear to me that in questions of Zionist policy, my ideas do not coincide with yours."

The resignation was quickly rescinded as, under pressure from all sides, the two leaders agreed to bury the hatchet and try again to work together. But there was never much love lost between them, even though Ben-Gurion wrote to Weizmann later in 1937, "All my life I have loved you . . . I have loved you with all my heart and soul." Weizmann was to mention Ben-Gurion precisely twice in his six-hundred-page autobiography,* the first time in his recounting of events that took place in 1947. Before then, in Weizmann's book, Ben-Gurion did not exist.

Ben-Gurion really did have profound respect and even admiration for Weizmann. He never made light of Weizmann's abilities or his international standing. But he came to differ with him deeply on the fundamentals of Zionist diplomacy. In Ben-Gurion's view, Weizmann was too dependent on Britain. That was why he had difficulty adopting an independent policy for the Zionist movement that would mean resisting Britain and cutting loose from Whitehall. In many other ways too they were opposites, for whom collaboration did not come naturally. They were neither personal friends nor ideological comrades. Weizmann's Eurocentric world and his political outlook were very different from Ben-Gurion's socialist worldview. And this was, of course, a very ideological era; everything was grounded in ideology. Their personalities were incompatible too. Weizmann was not a compulsive, almost obsessive Hebraist like Ben-Gurion. He knew Hebrew, of course, but his main language was Yiddish, followed by English, and only then by Hebrew.

But very soon after the crisis between them, they were fighting shoulder to shoulder in favor of a proposal, first broached by the Peel Commission, that now tore the World Zionist Organization apart: the partition of Palestine into a Jewish state and an Arab

---

Trial and Error (London: Hamish Hamilton, 1949).

state. Both leaders, despite their differences, saw this proposal for what it clearly proved to be with the passage of time: an opportunity, however imperfect, to realize the Zionist dream, however partially. Above all, they knew it was their only chance to save Europe's Jews from the gathering cataclysm. "The opponents of partition are living in a fool's paradise," Ben-Gurion wrote to Moshe Sharett.* He told his party he was "moved to the depths of my heart . . . by the great and wonderful redeeming vision of a Jewish state."

The borders envisaged by the Peel Commission were tiny and cramped: less than one quarter of western Palestine was to be in Jewish hands, with the Arabs taking most of the rest for their state and the British retaining certain sensitive swaths under their "protectorate." The Jewish state would comprise the Galilee, the Jezreel Valley, and the coastal plain.

In a letter to his son, Amos, Ben-Gurion confided that he did not necessarily see this as the last word:

> A partial Jewish state is not the end, but only the beginning . . . We shall bring into the state all the Jews it is possible to bring . . . and then I am certain that we will not be prevented from settling in other parts of the country, either by mutual agreement with our Arab neighbors or by some other means. Our ability to penetrate the country will increase if there is a state. Our strength vis-à-vis the Arabs will increase. I am not in favor of war. [But if] the Arabs say "Better the Negev remain barren than the Jews settle there," we shall have to speak to them in a different language.

At the Twentieth Zionist Congress, which was held in Zurich in August 1937, the pro-partition camp was assailed from both sides: from the right wing and the religious, joining together with

---

*Moshe Sharett (originally Shertok, 1894–1965) was head of the Jewish Agency's political department (1933–48), Israel's foreign minister (1948–56), and prime minister between Ben-Gurion's two terms in office (1953–55).

the American delegation and the socialist Greater Israel stalwarts; and from the far-left labor movements that favored a single, binational Jewish-Arab state. "I know that God promised Palestine to the children of Israel," Weizmann argued with a group of Orthodox friends.

I believe the boundaries were wider than the ones now proposed . . . If God will keep His promise to His people in His own time, our business as poor humans, who live in a difficult age, is to save as much as we can of the remnants of Israel. By adopting this project we can save more of them than by continuing the Mandatory policy.

The upshot of a hard-fought and emotional battle was a compromise. The congress rejected the Peel Commission's specific partition plan as "unacceptable." But it empowered the executive "to enter into negotiations with a view to ascertaining the precise terms of His Majesty's Government for the proposed establishment of a Jewish state." The executive was not empowered, however, to accept such terms—only to bring them before a newly elected congress to decide.

Whether because of the Zionists' hesitations or because of the Arab leaders' flat rejection of the plan,* the British now backed away from their own partition idea and moved instead to impose drastic restrictions on immigration. The monthly quota was cut to one thousand. Ben-Gurion spoke of preparing the Yishuv to revolt. But he agreed, without expectations and without illusions, to take part, alongside Weizmann, as heads of a Jewish delegation to what might be called in today's jargon a "proximity peace conference," convened by the British government at St. James's Palace in London. Prime Minister Neville Chamberlain and members of his government hosted the Jews and the Arabs (there were high-ranking Arab representatives from Palestine and from the neigh-

---

*Emir Abdullah of Transjordan was the only Arab leader who welcomed the plan.

boring countries) separately at a formal opening session on February 7, 1939. They did not encounter each other then or at the subsequent sessions of the conference. The British shuttled between the two delegations. The negotiations led nowhere. The Chamberlain government, Weizmann wrote later, "was determined to placate the Arabs just as they were placating Hitler." At a small, unofficial session that the British arranged between top Jewish and Arab delegates early in March, Weizmann once again began to backslide on aliyah, but Ben-Gurion and Sharett intervened forcefully and made it clear that they, not he, spoke for the Jewish Agency on this matter and that they were not prepared to agree to slow down the pace of immigration.

The British response was to impose a truly draconian showdown, in the form of a new white paper. Britain's "perfidious plan," as Ben-Gurion called it, provided for just 75,000 Jewish immigrants to enter Palestine over the next five years. Immigration after that would be contingent on Arab consent. Jews would be forbidden to purchase land in some 95 percent of the country. Within ten years Palestine would become an independent country, possibly with separate cantons for Jews and with the Jews' minority rights guaranteed. The Jewish delegation to the conference rejected the white paper unanimously.

Back in Palestine, Ben-Gurion drew up plans for a countrywide campaign of civil disobedience. He ordered the Haganah to create "special action squads" of well-trained fighters whose job would be to harass the British military authorities, as well as to carry out targeted reprisals against the Arabs and to punish Jewish informers. Separately, he put into place plans to assist large-scale illegal immigration, using force of arms if necessary to bring people ashore. Not all his militant thinking was supported by his own close party colleagues, but the principle was accepted: The Jews of Palestine, now close to half a million strong, were going to fight the British Empire for their right to retain the national home that Britain had promised and then reneged on.

The Twenty-first Zionist Congress was held in August 1939 in

Geneva. Weizmann wrote that they convened "under the shadow of the White Paper, which threatened the destruction of the National Home, and under the shadow of a war, which threatened the destruction of all human liberties, perhaps of humanity itself." Ben-Gurion spoke, in the Labor Zionist caucus, of the need for armed struggle against Great Britain. The Molotov-Ribbentrop Pact was signed on August 22, and the pall of disaster that hung over the congress became almost palpable. As Ben-Gurion made his way home, Germany invaded Poland. He immediately ordered the Haganah to call off military action against the British forces and to disband the special action squads. He coined the slogan that has entered the annals of Jewish history: "We must help the British in their war as though there were no White Paper, and we must resist the White Paper as though there were no war."

An early incident was far from auspicious. The British police raided a Haganah commanders' course, and the army surrounded one group of forty-three participants, trying to make its getaway on foot, and arrested them. They were tried and, on October 30, 1939, sentenced to long terms of imprisonment.* When Ben-Gurion tried to intercede with the British military commander, General Evelyn Barker, the general suggested sourly that instead of being called Haganah ("defense" in Hebrew), the Yishuv's no-longer-secret military force should more aptly be named "attack."

In February 1940 the British government announced that the recommendations of the white paper on land purchase were now going into effect. "We are no longer citizens with equal rights in our own country," Ben-Gurion declared the next day. "We have been deprived of the right to the soil of our homeland." As chairman of the Zionist Executive and in the absence of its president (Weizmann, who was in Britain), Ben-Gurion had to represent the Yishuv before the British authorities. He could no longer do so, he said, and was resigning forthwith. This took his colleagues by sur-

---

*These terms were commuted later, and the whole group was released in February 1941. Among them was Moshe Dayan.

prise. They were divided over his demand for an activist response: a countrywide strike and militant demonstrations planned and led by the Haganah. But they gave him his way, and a wave of Jewish unrest swept the country. Two Jewish demonstrators, in Jerusalem and Haifa, were beaten to death by police truncheons. Their funerals provoked further violence.

The divisions within the leadership now deepened. Ben-Gurion's militancy ran into broad opposition both in the Zionist Executive and within his own party. On April 18, 1940, at a meeting of the Zionist Actions Committee (a body within the Zionist Organization, broader than the Executive), Ben-Gurion insisted that there was "only one hope left now for Zionism—if it becomes fighting Zionism. A Zionism of mere words is pointless." But he stood almost alone. Berl Katznelson gave him hesitant support; most of the others voiced outright opposition. Some argued that violent action against the British simply strengthened Hitler. Tel Aviv's civic leaders warned that draconian measures by the police could leave hundreds dead and wounded in the town. Ben-Gurion promptly announced his resignation again, and although a large majority of the Actions Committee rejected it, he left it hanging in the air and embarked, by seaplane, for what was to be a ten-month trip to Britain and America.

He took his case to Weizmann and the rest of the Zionist leadership in London, and predictably, they rebuffed him too. But now he witnessed from close up the dramatic events during the spring and summer of 1940 as the "phony war" gave way to a series of desperate reverses, first in Norway, then in the Low Countries, and finally in France itself, where the Nazi blitzkrieg swept all before it. Zionist activism against the beleaguered British Empire could no longer be a serious option, as Ben-Gurion himself now admitted.

Winston Churchill, a lifelong friend of Zionism, took office as prime minister in May 1940. But Ben-Gurion never believed the white paper policy would be abrogated during the war: Britain had too much to lose by angering the Arabs. Unlike the Jews, as

Ben-Gurion once pointed out, the Arabs had the option of siding with Germany against the Allies, as some Arab leaders openly threatened to do. The mufti of Jerusalem, Haj Amin el-Husseini, spent the war years in Germany as an enthusiastic and welcome ally of Hitler.

Ben-Gurion's experiences alongside ordinary Londoners during the Battle of Britain served as a profound lesson for him in what a united nation, determinedly led, could withstand and achieve. He was to apply it at the Yishuv's moment of decision, in May 1948. And he wrote about it later on: "I recalled the men and women of London during the blitz. And I told myself, 'I have seen what a people is capable of achieving in the hour of supreme trial. I have seen their spirit touched by nobility . . . This is what the Jewish people can do.' We did it." He wrote of Churchill's

> unique combination of qualities—magnetic leadership, powerful eloquence, contagious courage . . . a deep sense of history and an unshakeable faith in the destiny of his people. I think . . . that if not for Churchill, England would have gone down . . . History would have been quite different if there had been no Churchill.

He would never have written or said that of himself, of course. But I say it without reservation: Our own history would have been quite different had there been no Ben-Gurion. I have never met a man with such inner strength and determination. I truly believe that without Ben-Gurion the State of Israel would not have come into being. I cannot think of anyone else who could have done what he did. As with Churchill, all the other details of his life and long career shrink into insignificance alongside the decisions he made at crucial junctures in Israel's history. His decision to accept the fundamental concept of two states for two nations despite all the opposition and hesitations on our own side—that was a historic choice and a critical act of leadership.

And the truth is that the people around him understood the irreplaceable value of his leadership for the Zionist cause. Many of them didn't like him. Some were afraid of him. But they were more afraid of being left without him. That's why, time and again, he would resign! Whenever he resigned, they voted for him to come back—even his opponents did so. They said he was an autocrat, but they voted for him. They left to him all the fateful decision making, and he never shrank from making the decisions.

B ut that's getting ahead of the story. Ben-Gurion left Britain for the United States in the fall of 1940 in a somber mood. A long sojourn in New York did little to relieve his sense of isolation. The American Zionist leadership, like their confreres in Jerusalem and London, were against a policy of active militancy against Great Britain at its time of heroic struggle, almost alone, against Hitler. "Does the fate of millions of their kin in Europe concern Jewry in America less than the fate of England affects the people of America?" Ben-Gurion wrote bitterly as he made his way back to Palestine early in 1941. Because of the Battle of the Atlantic he had to take the long way round: a Clipper seaplane from San Francisco via Honolulu to Australia, then on to Indonesia, Singapore, Siam, India, Iraq, and finally Palestine. It took a month.

He returned with a clear vision of what the Zionist movement must strive for in the context of the convulsion that now gripped most of the globe:

> It is essential to make the maximum effort during the war and immediately after it to find a full and fundamental solution to the Jewish problem by transferring millions of Jews to Palestine and establishing it as a Jewish Commonwealth, an equal member of the family of nations that will be established after the war.

An important adjunct to this vision was the creation by the Allies of a Jewish division to fight the Nazis, preferably in the Middle Eastern theater. Weizmann had pursued this idea since the outbreak of the war, thus far with scant success. Churchill and Foreign Secretary Anthony Eden had given assurances, but other elements in the British government and armed forces had effectively blocked it. Ben-Gurion also put it to his colleagues in Palestine: The age of British dominance in world affairs was now perforce over. Britain, even victorious, would emerge from the war much weakened. America would become—was already becoming—the preeminent focus of power. By the same token, the disaster that had overtaken European Jewry meant that the major center of Jewish influence would henceforth be in America. The Zionist movement must adjust its sights accordingly.

He set off in June 1941 for another visit to America, again by way of London. He joined Weizmann in his efforts to move the British government on the Jewish division, but they were once again spurned. This further stiffened Ben-Gurion's resolve to campaign vigorously and unequivocally in the United States, among the Jews and in policy-making circles, *against* the continuation of the British Mandate after the war and in favor of the immediate establishment of an independent Jewish state in Palestine. If this meant a break with Weizmann, then so be it.

Weizmann, for his part, published an article in the January 1941 issue of *Foreign Affairs* calling for the establishment of a Jewish commonwealth in Palestine after the war. Their dispute was not over the goal but over the means to achieve it. Weizmann was in no way prepared to throw over decades of patient collaboration with Britain. His lifelong belief was in the gradual, dogged progress of Zionism toward its goal. He had no faith in instant solutions—whether they were the chimerical "charter" for Palestine that Herzl had promised to deliver from the Great Powers forty years earlier, or Ben-Gurion's push toward a rupture with Great Britain.

Ben-Gurion diligently lobbied for his view among American Zionists. In May 1942 a national Zionist conference was held in the old Biltmore Hotel in Manhattan. Given the enforced wartime suspension of Zionist congresses, this was to be an important gathering. Weizmann made a powerful opening speech, but the Biltmore Conference was Ben-Gurion's moment. He had been working on his proposals for months. The conference, he urged, must reiterate the original significance of the Balfour Declaration as President Wilson had interpreted it back in 1919: Palestine was to be a Jewish commonwealth. The conference must insist too on the right of the Jewish Agency to administer aliyah and land purchase. Ben-Gurion dwelt at length on the need to ensure equal rights for all in the envisioned commonwealth: "autonomy for all the communities, Jews and Arabs, in their internal affairs—education, religion, and so forth." He went on to say, "Whether Eretz Yisrael will remain a separate political entity or will be joined to a wider unit, such a Middle Eastern federation, the British Commonwealth, an Anglo-American union, or some other union—that will depend on circumstances and conditions that we will not determine and that are unpredictable now . . . We will all be part of a new world and a new world order which, we hope, will arise after our victory in this war."

The Biltmore Program,* passed unanimously the next day with only the left-wing Hashomer Hatzair delegate abstaining,† closely followed Ben-Gurion's main points. For Ben-Gurion, it was a historic turning point in the annals of Zionism. The program, subsequently adopted by the Zionist Actions Committee in Jerusalem as the movement's official policy, meant for him the prospect of breaking away from British tutelage after the war and striking out—if necessary, in active defiance of Britain—to achieve the immediate immigration of up to two million European refugees and the declaration of Jewish statehood. He did not know, he reported ominously to the Actions Committee, if there would in fact be millions of Jews left in Europe after the war. But it was important that the Zionist movement present now to the world, and

---

*For the text, see the footnote on page 7.
†The left-wing Hashomer Hatzair favored a binational Jewish-Arab state.

especially to America, a comprehensive plan for the solution of the Jewish question. "The Great Powers are not going to quarrel with anyone over little plans for bringing in 20,000 immigrants over ten years . . . They might argue with the Arabs if we put before them a plan that solves the problem of millions of Jewish survivors, if, that is, Hitler has not killed them."

The boundaries of the putative state were shrouded in deliberate vagueness. The words used in the program, "Palestine be established as a Jewish Commonwealth," could certainly be taken to mean all of Palestine, not Palestine partitioned. This made it possible for those opposed to partition to support it. At the same time, the words "the Jewish Agency be vested with control of immigration" implied that statehood would not come immediately, leaving it possible for moderates and Weizmannists to support it too.

Weizmann, however, was disdainful. Such a "fuss" had been made of Biltmore, he wrote. In fact it was

just a resolution, like the hundred and one resolutions usually passed at great meetings . . . It embodies . . . the chief points as laid down in my article in *Foreign Affairs*. But B.-G. [conveys] the idea that it is a triumph of his policy, as against my moderate formulation of the same aims, and he injected into it all his own extreme views.

There now followed a period of open and ugly sparring between the two men. Ben-Gurion, still in America, accused Weizmann of acting "entirely on your own" and insisted that he was "not empowered to do so." At a leadership meeting called to sort out the dispute, he flung these allegations in Weizmann's face in front of the others. "Dr. Weizmann can render invaluable service in concerted action; he can do incalculable harm when he acts alone . . . He wants to seem reasonable to an Englishman." The Zionist Executive had always attached someone else to Weizmann when he went into diplomatic meetings, Ben-Gurion hurtfully disclosed. "This system worked more or less until the war."

Weizmann replied in fury that it was up to the leadership to decide if he needed "a kashrut supervisor." What Ben-Gurion was doing to him was "reminiscent of purges . . . an act of political assassination . . . I shall act as I did," he pledged. "I shall not swerve, because I think that is the right way. I shall be collegial. If in most cases I choose to see people alone, or sometimes go with another, that must be left to my discretion . . . Ben-Gurion's presence here [in the United States] has been an irritant and a source of disruption almost from the day of his arrival eight months ago."

Most of those present were embarrassed by the ruthlessness of Ben-Gurion's attack on the grand old man of Zionism, and they were relieved when Ben-Gurion returned to Palestine shortly thereafter. But the feud continued by cable and mail. In Palestine, despite the near-unanimous endorsement of the Biltmore Program by the Actions Committee and despite the broad agreement with Ben-Gurion's vision, many key leaders were also uncomfortable with the attempt to sideline Weizmann. In June 1943 Weizmann was back in London, meeting with members of the British government on his own again. Ben-Gurion fumed. The leadership in Jerusalem repeatedly invited Weizmann to come to Palestine for policy discussions. He refused. Ben-Gurion resigned. Once again Berl Katznelson and the others had to work on him to rescind his resignation, while at the same time bringing pressure to bear on Weizmann in London to ease the tensions betweem the two men.

Significantly too, despite the effort to blur the wording of the Biltmore Program on the crucial issue of borders (and despite the near-unanimous adoption of the program), the antipartition Siah Bet dissenters inside Ben-Gurion's Mapai read it—rightly—as implying partition, and they began, belatedly, to balk. Led by the hard-line Yitzhak Tabenkin, they seceded from Mapai in May 1944 to form their own separate party. They chose the name of the original Ben-Gurion–Tabenkin–Katznelson alliance from the early 1920s—Ahdut HaAvoda.

These various political and personal struggles over what was to happen once the war ended took place against the backdrop of the raging global conflict and the horror felt by both Palestinian and Diaspora Jews as the details of Hitler's destruction of European Jewry began to trickle out. After the British defeat of the German army in North Africa at the Battle of El Alamein in the fall of 1942, the threat of Nazi invasion that had been hanging over the Yishuv was effectively lifted. But at the same time news reports of the atrocities being perpetrated by the Nazis against the Jews in occupied Europe began to appear.

Sixteen women with British-Palestinian citizenship who had been trapped in Poland at the outbreak of the war now returned home, exchanged for German POWs. They told of ghettoes and mass killings, death camps and rumors of a "final solution." In America, a small group of activists led by Peter Bergson, a Palestinian Revisionist whose real name was Hillel Kook, campaigned relentlessly for the Jewish leadership, and especially the Zionists, to focus their efforts on immediate rescue prospects rather than on postwar plans for Palestine. In subsequent decades this tragic controversy continued to reverberate both in Israel and in the Diaspora, among historians and also among politicians. It haunts us even today, and it is fitting that the first of the verbatim exchanges between David Landau and me is on this vexed subject. To debate the issue is to ask what price Israel paid for its single-minded drive to statehood, what Israel owes Diaspora Jewry, what the tiny pre-state collective was actually capable of accomplishing, and how the complex legacy of guilt, responsibility, heroism, and sacrifice continues to shape the country today.

DAVID LANDAU: Ben-Gurion was accused of not doing enough, even of not caring enough about the carnage being wrought in Nazi-occupied Europe. Some even accused him of cynically exploiting the Holocaust in his single-minded pursuit of the Zionist goal of independence.

SHIMON PERES: That is all arrant nonsense. Ben-Gurion, like

Jabotinsky, had made his political career in Poland hardly less than in Eretz Yisrael. They both lived it. They knew it intimately. It's absurd to say he didn't care. During the war we didn't know the facts. We knew only that the Germans were persecuting the Jews. There wasn't a full picture of concentration camps and gas chambers. We didn't know the scope. The reports were partial. We knew a little about the Warsaw Ghetto uprising. But everything was unclear. For instance, I didn't know what had happened to my family. Until after the war we didn't have a full conception of the scope of the catastrophe.

DAVID LANDAU: How do you relate to the subsequent controversy—it's not about you, of course, you were too young to be held responsible—but about Ben-Gurion and the other leaders?

SHIMON PERES: They didn't know. There was no clear picture. The Jews abroad, the World Jewish Congress and others, didn't know much either. The mass killing didn't begin until 1942. Only toward the end did more complete information begin to seep through.

DAVID LANDAU: The accusation is that they didn't want to know.

SHIMON PERES: That's rubbish. Rubbish!! But let's go down to earth: What could they have done?

DAVID LANDAU: You've told me of your weekly Sunday-evening conversations with Berl Katznelson toward the end of his life.* You said how privileged you felt as a youngster to spend that quality time with him. Anita Shapira, in her biography of Berl,† writes that he was tortured inside himself regarding the policy of the leadership on the Holocaust. And regarding the youth of Palestine. He accused himself, and Ben-Gurion too, of raising a generation—you were one of the brightest stars of that genera-

---

*Katznelson died in August 1944.

†*Berl: The Biography of a Socialist Zionist: Berl Katznelson, 1887–1944* (New York: Cambridge University Press, 1984).

tion—that was alienated from its Jewish roots, incapable of expressing or even feeling solidarity with the victims of the Holocaust. Did this come through in those Sunday-evening meetings you had with him?

SHIMON PERES: I remember Shapira's book, of course. I didn't entirely agree with the way she depicted the early Berl. That wasn't how it was.

DAVID LANDAU: That part of his life was before your time.

SHIMON PERES: But I looked at it and I saw . . . *Ce n'est pas serieux.*

DAVID LANDAU: Let me read some quotes from the later part of the book. "Berl saw with what apathy the Yishuv received the reports of the Holocaust and how easily it moved on to other things . . . 'This indifference to our agony—it's frightening,' he wrote. 'The youth in Palestine had grown up detached from the Jewish people and from its suffering . . . A new tribe of Jews had grown up in Eretz Yisrael, with qualities of its own but without roots in the history of its people, alien to the instinctive Jewish feeling that all Jews are responsible for one another.' "

Berl blamed himself as much as anyone else, Shapira says. He felt toward the end of his life that the classic Zionist doctrine of *shlilat hagolah* [deprecating the Diaspora], which originally meant negating the old-style modes of the Jewish life in the Diaspora, had come to mean, among some of the teachers and their pupils in Palestine, a negation of the Jewish people who lived in the Diaspora.

SHIMON PERES: Yes, I heard that sort of thing from Berl. But Berl was very critical; he educated by means of criticism. Berl was a teacher, whereas Ben-Gurion was a leader. You can't compare the two.

DAVID LANDAU: But wasn't he being critical of Ben-Gurion? Reading Shapira, the impression is that Berl felt Ben-Gurion and the whole leadership echelon were repressing, in the psychological sense, what was happening in Europe. There's the famous scene that she describes, when they're taking leave of the parachutists,* and each one defines the mission as he sees it. Eliahu Golomb† says, "Teach the Jews to fight." Ben-Gurion says, "Teach the Jews that *Eretz Yisrael* is their country and their fortress." Berl says, "Save Jews. All the rest is for later. If there are no Jews left, *Eretz Yisrael* and the Zionist homeland will not survive, either."

SHIMON PERES: That doesn't surprise me. But it doesn't contradict the other things I've said. Berl's most important article was *Bizchut Hamevucha Uvignut Hatiyach* [In Support of Confusion and Against Cover-up]. He preferred complexity to synthesis. He believed in constructive criticism. He wasn't criticizing the youth in the quotes you read; he was criticizing their ignorance. He held a famous monthlong seminar at Ben-Shemen in 1940 for selected youngsters from around the country and another in Haifa in 1944, shortly before his death. He wanted to educate them. Ben-Gurion supported that. But both of them opposed the *Golah* and *galutiyut*—the Diaspora as a condition and Diasporic behavior as a mind-set. *Shlilat hagolah* didn't mean, for Ben-Gurion, turning his back on the Jews of the Diaspora. He wanted to save the Jews. He didn't hate the *Golah;* he hated *galutiyut.* He saw *galutiyut* as a proclivity to compromise, to bend with the winds of fate. He felt the *Golah* had eroded the values of the Jewish people, that they'd become too supple and supine. He hated concepts like *Hashem yerachem* and *Dina demalchuta dina.*‡

---

*Twenty-six young Jewish Palestinians, all of European origin, volunteered to parachute into Nazi-occupied Europe to help Jews there. The British selected them from a pool of 250 volunteers assembled by the Yishuv. Trained during 1943, they were eventually dropped into Hungary and other occupied countries. Fourteen of them managed to link up with local partisans; twelve were captured, and seven of those twelve were executed, among them the young poet Hannah Senesh.

†Golomb was the head of the Haganah. He died in 1945, at the age of fifty-two.

‡*Hashem yerachem* means literally "God will have mercy." It was the quintessence of Diasporic Jewish fatalism, in Ben-Gurion's view. *Dina demalchuta dina*

DAVID LANDAU: In a book of conversations with you* that came out more than a decade ago, you make an incredibly arresting—if not shocking—statement about the victims of the Holocaust: "We disagreed with the way they were living, so we disagreed with the way they were dying."

SHIMON PERES: I regret that choice of words. What I really wanted to express was how deeply I resented the way they were murdered—because we didn't have a state to save them. The image of Jews being taken like sheep to the slaughter has haunted me all my life. The words I used didn't bring out the depth and the starkness of what I wanted to say. But let's go back to my question: What could Ben-Gurion do?

DAVID LANDAU: You say "do," and I say "speak."

SHIMON PERES: Ben-Gurion's most famous aphorism was "It's not important what the goyim say; what's important is what the Jews do." Declarations for their own sake seemed pointless to him. For Ben-Gurion, words were for arguments, for debating. Most of his speeches were polemical, to persuade people. But Ben-Gurion knew there is a limit to the effectiveness of words. They have power, as weapons of confrontation, but not as a substitute for policy. Words are not policy. His entire story was a story of action, what was later called, half mockingly, "another goat and another *dunam*." Goats and *dunams*, not words and phrases.

DAVID LANDAU: The speech he gave in 1934, laying out the terrible future like a prophecy—

SHIMON PERES: He laid out all of it.

DAVID LANDAU: And yet from then on, he virtually fell silent.

SHIMON PERES: What could he have done?

DAVID LANDAU: He could have raised the heavens. Shouted. The Zionist movement, with all its weakness, was the most united

means literally "The law of the land is the law," signifying, in Ben-Gurion's view, a spineless readiness to accede to Gentile demands.

*Shimon Peres and Robert Little, *For the Future of Israel* (Baltimore: Johns Hopkins University Press, 1998).

and best-organized group in the American Jewish community. Ben-Gurion spent many months in America during the war. But instead of channeling this strength into getting the U.S. government and the Allies to rescue Jews, he focused entirely on Zionist diplomacy.

SHIMON PERES: The Americans entered the war relatively late. Roosevelt's actively pro-British policy—Lend-Lease, etc.— was not all that popular. There was strong isolationist opinion. The Jews couldn't come out against Roosevelt because the priority was to smash Hitler. The situation was full of contradictions.

DAVID LANDAU: The critics' contention is that the entire focus of the Zionist movement, even after 1942, after the facts were known, was to promote the Jewish state—

SHIMON PERES: No, also to promote the war effort. The effort was to defeat Hitler. Don't forget that. Roosevelt needed support. The Jews wanted him to help Britain finish off Hitler. The way to overcome Hitler was to defeat him, and so to save the Jews. Defeating Hitler was the aim, and everyone was mobilized for this effort. This was the supreme policy.

DAVID LANDAU: There were Jews in America, albeit not accepted by the Jewish or Zionist establishment, who believed that it was possible both to support the war effort and to urge the administration and the Congress to invest in rescue.

SHIMON PERES: The Bergsonites. What did they achieve? Nothing. Getting a Jewish state was by no means to be taken for granted.

DAVID LANDAU: But it wasn't the immediate goal—

SHIMON PERES: That was our only chance of saving Jews.

DAVID LANDAU: That's the nub of the argument.

SHIMON PERES: I don't think so. And I repeat: We did not have the full picture. The gas chambers, the extent of the murder.

DAVID LANDAU: You didn't have the full picture. But Ben-Gurion knew very well, in detail, what was happening.

SHIMON PERES: When?

DAVID LANDAU: From November 1942. The U.S. State Department withheld the information during the summer of 1942, until it all burst forth. There was even a day of national mourning in the Yishuv.

SHIMON PERES: Yes, but nevertheless there was still no real conception of what was happening. There were fragmentary items of information, not clear, not collated. The extent of the disaster became clear to us only after the war ended. Our minds were not conditioned to comprehend such a thing. It was unprecedented. There was nothing to compare it to. We were not capable psychologically or intellectually of imagining such a thing. What Hitler imagined, we could not imagine. That is why we did not comprehend the enormity of the Holocaust. That's my opinion.

DAVID LANDAU: The critics would say that you too were the victim of the deliberate policy of the Jewish Agency, headed by Ben-Gurion, to lower the profile of the available information.

SHIMON PERES: Why would he do that?

DAVID LANDAU: I don't know.

SHIMON PERES: It doesn't make sense. A number of refugees arrived during the war and told their accounts, and we were shocked to the depths of our being. We had no idea.

DAVID LANDAU: Yes. You had no idea. But Ben-Gurion and Sharett did have. When you learned years later about Rudolf Kastner,* didn't you think the leadership of the Yishuv could have acted with more energy and a greater sense of urgency to stir public opinion in the United States? In effect, there was collaboration between the Yishuv and the British to close the gates

---

*Kastner was a Zionist leader in Hungary during the war who worked out a deal to rescue 1,684 Jews who would otherwise have been deported to Auschwitz. He was later accused of having collaborated with the Nazis. An Israeli judge, in a libel action brought by the Israeli government and Kastner in 1955, excoriated him for "selling his soul to the devil." Kastner was assassinated in Tel Aviv in 1957. He was vindicated posthumously in an appeal to the Supreme Court in 1958.

to Hungarian Jewry. The British incarcerated Joel Brand* and suppressed the information—

SHIMON PERES: Don't forget there was heavy censorship. They wouldn't even permit publication of Churchill's illness. Nothing. There was no atmosphere of free protest. And don't forget that until Alamein there was a real danger that Rommel would sweep through the entire Middle East, Palestine included. Everything was subordinated to defeating Hitler. And there was no room for any other voice. Anyway I don't much believe in voices. If you would have raised your voice, what would you have had the Americans do?

DAVID LANDAU: If the United States had set up the War Refugee Board† at an earlier stage, perhaps they could have—

SHIMON PERES: Yes, but again, their whole mind-set was given over to their two wars: against Japan and against Germany and Italy. In peacetime it's hard to imagine and hard to judge what it was like in wartime. Today you can shout. Then, there was no shouting. Then, everything was subordinated to one thing only: winning the war. The censorship would not permit anything else. True, Ben-Gurion spent a long time in America. He wanted us to emerge at least with a state from this thing. In Washington they were against a Jewish state—in particular, James Forrestal and Dean Acheson.‡

DAVID LANDAU: But why are you preoccupied with the Jewish

---

*Brand was an aide to Kastner, sent by the Nazis from occupied Hungary to offer the Allies a "blood for trucks" deal.

†Established by President Roosevelt in January 1944, this U.S. government agency was designed to aid civilian victims of the Nazis. It was created largely through the efforts of Roosevelt's treasury secretary, Henry Morgenthau, Jr. Roosevelt stressed that it was urgent "that action be taken at once to forestall the plan of the Nazis to exterminate all the Jews and other persecuted minorities in Europe."

‡Forrestal served as secretary of the navy (1944–47) and secretary of defense (1947–49). Acheson served as assistant secretary of state under Roosevelt and secretary of state under Truman.

state in 1944 and 1945, while the potential citizens of this Jewish state are being slaughtered? Neutral states around the Reich could have been pressured—

SHIMON PERES: Forget about the neutrals. They were totally cynical. Ben-Gurion didn't give up hope of rescue; he just didn't see how it would be possible to save these people. Shouting wouldn't have helped. I still think, today, that shouting would not have helped.

DAVID LANDAU: Even regarding Hungarian Jewry in 1944? Half a million Hungarian Jews were killed.

SHIMON PERES: I know. But I say to you again, during the war there was only one consideration—and that was Churchill's directive—to win! All other considerations were subordinate. They didn't even want to bomb the rail line to Auschwitz—

DAVID LANDAU: On the grounds that anything that diverts from the war effort—

SHIMON PERES: Yes.

DAVID LANDAU: You are not supposed to accept that.

SHIMON PERES: So I don't accept it! So what? The fact that I don't accept it doesn't change the reality!! I'm not the supreme commander of the Allied forces. They were guided solely by what was required by the war effort; no other consideration.

DAVID LANDAU: But you had the power to influence them.

SHIMON PERES: At that time we didn't have the power to influence anyone. And if we did, our power of influence was to hit Hitler, time and time again. To destroy him. Our power, such as it was, was to strengthen the coalition to defeat Hitler. That would have saved the Jews more than everything else. If Hitler had been defeated earlier, many lives would have been saved. That was the focus.

DAVID LANDAU: That would be an overwhelming argument were it not for the fact that Ben-Gurion devoted so much effort to persuading the U.S. Congress to endorse, in effect, the Biltmore Program. Why was he, why was the Zionist Organization, devoting their time and effort to getting the Congress to adopt the goal of setting up a Jewish state after the war? For that they had power and influence?

SHIMON PERES: No, not for that, either! It was touch-and-go right to the end. Truman decided at the last moment. He wasn't in favor of a Jewish state until the last moment. We had to try to ensure that it came about. I do not accept this allegation against Ben-Gurion of cynicism, not in the slightest degree. The man was not cynical. He felt that these were the priorities, and they were immutable at the time, and that was that.

6

Fateful Hour

The moment the partition option ended—it ended. There was a new ballgame. . . . To him, it was against morality and against political wisdom to rule over another nation.

The war's end found Ben-Gurion in London again, and he wandered the streets, mingling with the jubilant crowds but thinking his own dark thoughts. In his diary he wrote, "Rejoice not, O Israel, unto exultation, like the peoples" (Hosea 9:1). "I knew what had happened to us in the war," he recorded later.

The six million Jews of Europe, whom Dr. Weizmann had told the Royal Commission needed a Jewish state and were capable of building it, were no longer among the living. But there were still masses of Jews who needed a state. Moreover, when the British left the country we would have to face the Arab armies. Therefore, we had to prepare ourselves to confront that danger, which meant first and foremost acquiring of all types of weapons . . . Clearly with the end of the war the United States would dismantle a large part of its arms industry. An effort must be made to obtain the necessary machinery from that source. On May 15, 1945, I left London for the U.S.

Relations with the British were raw, partly due to a wave of terrorist attacks mounted by the two rightist undergrounds, the Etzel, affiliated with the Revisionist Party, and the breakaway

Lehi.* Etzel, also known as the Irgun, was led by Menachem Begin, the former leader of the Betar youth movement in Poland. It blew up British intelligence installations, attacked police stations, and killed British personnel. These operations won admiration among significant sections of the Yishuv. Lehi's bank robberies and killings of Jewish "collaborators" were less popular. But the dissident groups' worst excess was the murder, by Lehi, in Cairo late in 1944, of the British resident minister in the Middle East, Lord Moyne, an official of cabinet rank and a personal friend of Churchill. The Zionist establishment reacted with horror and outrage, and Ben-Gurion personally directed a Haganah campaign to crack down on the dissidents and actively hand over militants to the British for deportation. This four-month manhunt became known as the *saison*, or hunting season. Many Etzel and Lehi men were deported, but Begin himself was not captured, the organization was not broken, and it lived on to fight another day.

The tension with Great Britain came at a particularly inopportune time because the government in London had finally come around, at least partially, to Zionist importuning to create a Jewish fighting force within the British Army. The Jewish Brigade saw action in Italy and Germany. After the hostilities ended, its units were to play an important role in organizing the Jewish survivors and helping some of them embark on illegal immigration to Palestine. Ben-Gurion was to put the military experience acquired by the Jewish soldiers from Palestine to good use when he built the Israel Defense Forces after independence.

There had also been indications in London, toward the end of the war, that Churchill's government was giving renewed consideration to a partition plan for Palestine after the war. More recently, however, the Zionists had been disappointed when the prime minister deferred sine die a scheduled meeting with Weizmann. Ben-Gurion told his colleagues in New York, and also the

*Etzel is an acronym for Irgun Tzvai Leumi (National Military Organization). Lehi is an acronym for Lohamei Herut Yisrael (For Israel's Liberty).

media there, that there would be one final effort to terminate the Mandate and achieve statehood peaceably. But if the British persisted in applying the white paper policy, the outlook was for armed struggle by the Yishuv against the Mandatory government. Meanwhile Ben-Gurion turned his attention to the armed struggle that he regarded as inevitable once the British had been eased or forced out of Palestine—the struggle for survival against the neighboring Arab states. Together with Henry Montor, director of the United Jewish Appeal in the United States, Ben-Gurion drew up a list of seventeen "Jews who could be depended upon" from around the country. He invited them all to the New York home of his friend Rudolf Sonneborn on Sunday, July 1, 1945, at 9:30 A.M., "to discuss a very important matter. All arrived on time," he wrote in his diary. Also present were Eliezer Kaplan, the treasurer of the Jewish Agency; Meyer Weisgal, Weizmann's close aide; and Reuven Shiloah, an important aide to Ben-Gurion.

"I told the participants that I felt the British would be leaving Eretz Yisrael in a year or two," Ben-Gurion wrote in his diary,

and that the neighboring Arab states would then send in their armies to conquer the country and destroy the Jews living there . . . I was certain we would be able to repel them, I said, if only we had the necessary weapons . . . A Jewish arms industry must be established in good time . . . The necessary machinery could now be purchased cheaply. Even so, hundreds of thousands of dollars were needed.

The meeting went on until late afternoon. All the participants pledged their discreet and active help. "That was the best Zionist meeting I have ever had in the United States," he wrote. He left Yaakov Dori, the future IDF chief of staff, and Chaim Slavin, head of the Haganah's tiny arms-manufacturing project, in New York to work on the purchase and shipment of the required machinery. Remarkably, as Ben-Gurion himself writes, the British authorities did not open or impound any of it.

Sailing on the *Queen Elizabeth* to Britain, along with American Zionist leaders, for the first postwar international Zionist conference there, Ben-Gurion learned that Churchill had been ousted by the British electorate; Labor was returned to power by a landslide. There was much rejoicing among the Zionists. The British Labor Party had been steadfast during the war in its support for the Jewish national home. A report by the party's national executive committee in 1944 recommended, embarrassingly for the Zionists, that the Arabs of Palestine "be encouraged to move out as the Jews move in. Let them be compensated handsomely for their land, and their settlement elsewhere be carefully organized and generously financed."

Ben-Gurion, presciently, stayed skeptical. "The assumption that a party in power resembles a party in opposition is not proven," he remarked. "If Britain retains the White Paper regime indefinitely, we will fight her."

His fight with Weizmann, meanwhile, had narrowed, but also sharpened, into one of timetable. "Palestine as a Jewish state should be one of the fruits of victory," Weizmann began his speech at the conference. "And with God's help it shall be!" But he still believed in gradualism and eschewed Ben-Gurion's demand for *le'altar*, independence forthwith, and the threat of armed activism to achieve it.

It soon became clear that Ben-Gurion's skepticism about the new Labor government was warranted. Clement Attlee, the prime minister, and Ernest Bevin, the foreign secretary, continued to base their Palestine policy on the prewar white paper. They resisted a demand from the new American president, Harry Truman, to permit 100,000 Holocaust refugees to enter the country at once.

Ben-Gurion flew from London to Paris on October 1, 1945, and gave coded orders to the Haganah to launch an armed uprising. Signing his cable "Avi Amos" (father of Amos), he instructed that the two dissident groups, Etzel and Lehi, be invited to join in a

Hebrew resistance movement, "but on condition that they accept a unified command and total discipline." On November 1 the first joint action took place: railroads were blown up at 153 points around the country, and coastal cutters that were used to chase illegal immigrant ships were damaged in Jaffa port.

Ben-Gurion was back in London when Bevin, at a press conference, spoke infamously of his anxiety "lest the Jews in Europe over-emphasize their racial status . . . If the Jews, who have suffered so much, try to push to the head of the queue, there is a danger of a renewed anti-Semitic reaction throughout Europe." For Jews everywhere, these words, directed at the Holocaust refugees in the displaced-persons camps, *were* a renewed anti-Semitic reaction.

"I want to address a few words to Bevin and his colleagues," Ben-Gurion said in his response.

We, the Jews of the Land of Israel, do not want to be killed. We wish to live. In defiance of the ideology of Hitler and his disciples in various lands, we believe that we Jews, like Englishmen and others, also have the right to live, as individuals and as a people. But we too, like the English, have something that is more precious than life. And I want to tell Bevin and his colleagues that we are prepared to be killed but not to concede three things: freedom of Jewish immigration, our right to rebuild the wilderness of our homeland, and the political independence of our people in its homeland.

The violence in Palestine intensified, and the British intensified their response, promulgating draconian emergency regulations and sending in the crack Sixth Airborne Division to enforce them. Curfews and searches were the order of the day. Death sentences were handed down for involvement in the underground forces. In March the Anglo-American Commission of Inquiry took evidence from all sides. The Hebrew Resistance Movement ceased its activities while the commission was in the country. "I saw the blitz in London," Ben-Gurion told the commission in his testimony. "I saw the Englishman whose land and liberty is dearer than his life. Why do you presume that we are not like you?"

His testimony was less convincing, even in the eyes of sympathetic commission members, when he doggedly refused to admit to any connection with the Haganah, or even to being aware of the existence of such an organization. He apparently feared that the authorities were intent on dismantling the Jewish Agency and might use evidence of a link between it and the illegal paramilitary organization as legal grounds to do so. Ben-Gurion met privately at his home in Tel Aviv with a key commission member, the British socialist Richard Crossman. He warned him not to confuse the Yishuv with a Diasporic Jewish community. The Jews of Palestine would fight to the death for their collective national rights.

While the Anglo-American Commission's recommendations, published on May 1, 1946, did not endorse the Zionist demand for statehood—they called in effect for an indefinite extension of the Mandate—they did urge the annulment of the white paper restrictions on land purchase. And even more dramatically, they urged the admission as rapidly as possible of 100,000 refugees.

There was rejoicing in the displaced-persons camps in occupied Germany and Austria, but it was short-lived, as was a flare-up of the Ben-Gurion–Weizmann rift, this time over whether the recommendations were to be welcomed or rejected. The British government, despite a prior commitment to accept the commission's recommendations if they were unanimous, now said it could not implement them so long as armed groups continued to exist in Palestine. The white paper policy, and the violent resistance to it, continued.

On June 16 the Hebrew Resistance Movement blew up fourteen bridges linking Palestine to its neighboring countries. Two weeks later the British carried out an operation that the Yishuv dubbed "Black Saturday": 17,000 troops swooped down on Jewish towns and villages across the country and arrested thousands of people suspected of involvement with the resistance movement. Hundreds were incarcerated in a detention camp in Latrun, among them Moshe Sharett and other members of the Jewish Agency Executive.

Ben-Gurion himself was in Paris, in contact with the few leaders who had escaped arrest; he ordered reprisal action. But Weizmann, who was in Palestine but had not been harassed by the British, countermanded those orders and ordered all operations stopped. Moshe Sneh, head of the Haganah's national command, resigned and managed to slip out of the country, joining Ben-Gurion in Paris. Weizmann pursued his contacts with the Mandatory authorities with a view, as it seemed to Ben-Gurion from afar, of creating a new, more moderate leadership for the Yishuv. Ben-Gurion fulminated about the despicability of a "Petain" regime. But his own standing and authority were gravely weakened in July when the Etzel—still part of the Hebrew Resistance Movement—blew up a wing of the King David Hotel in Jerusalem, killing ninety British, Arabs, and Jews. The wing had housed the Mandatory offices. The bombers had telephoned a warning, but somehow it had not been heeded.

In the chanceries of the world, meanwhile, the concept of the partition of Palestine into two states, raised and dropped by Britain before the war, was gaining traction once more. Ben-Gurion had reason to believe, or at least to hope, that Truman would support it. Later he wrote that he was confident that Stalin too would back Jewish independence. He himself had met with the French foreign minister, Georges Bidault, immediately after the war and had enlisted the support of his government.

At a session of the Zionist Executive in Paris in August 1946, Ben-Gurion made it clear that he favored partition. Nahum Goldmann, an important leader of the American Zionists, suggested the wording "a viable Jewish state in a sufficient portion of the Land of Israel." This was the position that Ben-Gurion put forth at the opening of the Twenty-second Zionist Congress in Basel in

December 1946, the congress that I attended as a young man, where Ben-Gurion almost stormed out to "create a new Zionist movement." Great speeches were made there, and powerful positions staked out.

The Jewish people, Ben-Gurion stressed, had the right to the whole of Eretz Yisrael. But "we are prepared to discuss a compromise arrangement if, in exchange for the reduction of territory, our rights are immediately granted and we are given national independence." He condemned terrorism but praised

> resistance . . . The resistance movement is a new event in the annals of Israel. There are Jews in the Diaspora for whom immigration to Palestine is a matter of life and death. For them the Land of Israel is not Zionism, or ideology . . . but a vital need, a condition for survival. The fate of those Jews is life in the Land of Israel or death. That, too, is power.

Weizmann for his part urged caution. "What will happen to the Jewish people, what will happen to Palestine if we upset the basis on which we have built this thing by our efforts and by our blood and toil?" He attacked American delegates who backed Ben-Gurion's activism while sitting comfortably in New York. "Demagogue!" a heckler shouted. Weizmann's reply brought the congress to its feet in a prolonged and emotional standing ovation. "Calling me a demagogue . . . I have gone through all the agonies of Zionist toil . . . In every farm and in every stable in Nahalal, in every building in Tel Aviv or Haifa down to the tiniest workshop, there is a drop of my life's blood." He went on to warn against "short cuts . . . false prophets . . . I do not believe in violence . . . 'Zion will be redeemed through righteousness'* and not by any other means."

It was heady stuff. I listened agog. These two enormously impressive men laid out with dignity and force their different political approaches. Weizmann, the gradualist, said the time would

---

* Isaiah 1:27.

come when everyone would become a Zionist. Tall and pale, he spoke in Yiddish and peppered his remarks with his folksy shtetl humor, which now had such a bitter nostalgia to it. To illustrate his point, he told a story about Motol, the shtetl where he had been born. Motol, he said, had two doctors. The elder one took a lot of money from patients and refused to speak Yiddish. Only Russian. Then a younger doctor came, took less money, and spoke Yiddish. People flocked to him. And they told the elder one why. "Wait," he replied. "He'll soon start speaking Hebrew."

B en-Gurion was not prepared to wait. He was determined this time to remove Weizmann from his position of influence, and he prevailed on his party to use its votes to do it. A predominantly activist Zionist Organization executive was elected. Weizmann was offered an honorary presidency, but he proudly dismissed the demeaning offer. "I have enough honor," he remarked bitterly. Ironically, the congress then voted in favor of the immediate policy that Weizmann was advocating: agreeing to take part in a new British-Arab-Jewish conference in London that the British government wanted to convene in January 1947. Ben-Gurion reluctantly went along with it.

Ben-Gurion was reelected chairman of the Zionist Executive, but he also asked the congress to appoint him to the nonexistent defense portfolio. "Only in the political committee of the Congress, whose proceedings were not made public, could I dwell on security matters which I felt would determine the fate of the Yishuv," Ben-Gurion recorded later. He explained to the delegates, as he had explained more than a year earlier at the home of his friend Rudolf Sonneborn in New York, that the mortal danger stemmed not from the Palestinian Arabs but from the neighboring states: "We must prepare immediately . . . This is the most important task facing Zionism today."

True to his word, Ben-Gurion began devoting more and more of his own time to studying the art of war, meeting with Haganah commanders, poring over military manuals and history books, and paying discreet visits to Haganah units and training facilities. Some of the veteran commanders laughed at the idea of the "Old Man," as he was already known, proposing to run an army. But as time passed, the smiles left their faces; all acknowledged that Ben-Gurion meant business.

The balance of forces, which he meticulously recorded in his diaries, was hopelessly skewed against the Yishuv. The Haganah, for all its vaunted exploits, was in truth a modest territorial force that mustered barely 40,000 troops, of whom only 2,000 were full-time soldiers serving in the Palmach strike units. As of April 1947, the date of Ben-Gurion's comprehensive inventory, it deployed no heavy weapons whatsoever and precious few light ones: 10,000 rifles, 2,000 submachine guns, 600 light and medium machine guns, 800-odd mortars. A more serious arsenal was being purchased, in many places and in all manner of discreet and devious ways, but nothing obtrusive could be brought into the country so long as the British ruled, for fear of it being impounded. Ben-Gurion knew that when the Union Jack was eventually pulled down and the Arab armies attacked—as they surely would—his overriding aim would be to hold on until the newly acquired guns, tanks, and warplanes could be brought into play.

The Arab armies, to the best of the Haganah's fledgling intelligence service's knowledge, could field some 150,000 men all told. Egypt, with armored units, an air force, and even a navy, was the best equipped. Transjordan, with the British general John Glubb in command of its Arab Legion, was the best trained and posed the greatest threat. Other Arab countries pledged to enter the battle at the Palestinian Arabs' side were Iraq, Syria, Lebanon, and Saudi Arabia. There had been a number of secret meetings between emissaries of the Yishuv and the Emir Abdullah of Transjordan, and an understanding seemed to be evolving whereby when the British left, he would step in and annex the West Bank to his kingdom, with the tacit assent of the Arab world and of the British. But there was no certainty that this would happen peaceably, and the Jewish state-in-the-making had to arm against Transjordan too.

As was inevitable, the London Conference ended in failure, and the British, in a sudden change of policy, now dumped the Palestine problem in the lap of the newly formed United Nations. It set up a Special Committee on Palestine (UNSCOP) to investigate the entire issue and propose a solution. The committee's visit to Palestine in July 1947 fortuitously coincided with the Royal Navy's heavy-handed interception of the crowded refugee ship *Exodus*. Two passengers and one crew member were killed when it was forcibly boarded twenty miles from shore. Then it was hauled to Haifa, and its 4,515 passengers were unceremoniously transferred to three British prison ships and sent back to Europe. The world, including the UNSCOP members, looked on, appalled.

In his testimony before UNSCOP, Ben-Gurion tried to head off the committee's known inclination to exclude all of Jerusalem—even the new, western part of the city that had been built by the Jews over the last fifty years—from the Jewish (or the Palestinian) state. "To partition," he said, "according to the Oxford dictionary, means to divide a thing into two parts. Palestine is [to be] divided into three parts, and only in a small part are the Jews allowed to live. We are against that."

UNSCOP's eleven members were unconvinced. Their majority recommendation was for the partition of Palestine into Jewish and Arab states, with Jerusalem a *corpus separatum* under international control.

A period of intensive diplomacy followed, with the Jews lobbying the chanceries of the world in favor of partition and the Arabs fulminating against it. Eventually, on November 29, 1947, the UN General Assembly voted by the required two-thirds majority to adopt the UNSCOP report. The UN map was not as restrictive to the Jews as the British 1937 partition proposal had been, but it was hardly generous toward Zionist aspirations. The Jewish state was to incorporate the eastern Galilee, the coastal plain, and most of the Negev: in all, 56 percent of Mandatory Palestine (not including Transjordan, which had been lopped off in 1922), but most of it in the barren south of the country. The three Jewish areas were to be linked by "kissing points." The British Mandate would end on May 15, 1948.

Thirty-three member states voted in favor (among them the United States and the USSR), thirteen voted against (most of them Muslim states or states with Muslim minorities), and another ten abstained (including Great Britain). The entire Yishuv followed the vote glued to their radio sets. Ben-Gurion watched the crowds dancing in the streets at the conclusion of the vote, but his own heart was heavy. "I knew that we faced war," he wrote in his diary, "and that in it we would lose the finest of our youth."

The decision by Ben-Gurion himself, by the majority of the Yishuv, and by the majority of the Zionist movement to accept partition represents, for me, a historic act of political wisdom whose logic is as cogent today as it was then. It also represented the acme of leadership. Ben-Gurion's fortitude and certitude in facing opposition from both the left and the right were all the more impressive because, obviously, he too would have liked to see the Jewish state set up in all of Eretz Yisrael. He was no less profoundly attached to the hills and wadis of the homeland than any of his traducers. But courageous decision making means the ability to take a less-than-perfect decision and stick with it.

A nd now I turn again to David Landau, to argue the meaning of partition and its place in Ben-Gurion's thinking. It is connected to our earlier exchange about Israel's responsibility during the Holocaust, but it also speaks to issues at the burning heart of Israel's political life today.

DAVID LANDAU: Let's look more closely at Ben-Gurion's commitment to accepting a partition he disliked. Ben-Gurion deliberately didn't put the partition borders into the Declaration of Independence. Apparently he hoped—

SHIMON PERES: It's not important what he hoped. What's important is what he agreed to. It's easy to hope. What he agreed to was the most disadvantageous partition plan imaginable. The pressures that brought him to agree to it were threefold: (a) the plight of the Holocaust refugees in the displaced-persons camps; (b) his sense that the British were preparing to leave, whatever happened; and (c) his conviction that the Arab states would attack us as soon as the British did leave, and that without a sovereign state of our own, we could have no regular army and would not be able to purchase arms and bring them in to defend ourselves. Ben-Gurion hoped all along that our right to the entire Land of Israel would be preserved somehow. But now the moment of decision was at hand, and he decided! He saw it as a tragic decision, but as an indispensable decision. He thought it was a tragedy, but he had to decide between two tragedies. And he did not shrink from deciding.

DAVID LANDAU: *That's* what he was saying to you in the taxi about Lenin? He was making that analogy?

SHIMON PERES: Yes. The analogy was between the Treaty of Brest-Litovsk in 1918 and the partition of Palestine. Why did he say what he said to me? Because Lenin faced the choice of peace at a painful price for Russia, or more war with attendant dangers. And he made his decision.

DAVID LANDAU: Still, what was the meaning of the word *accept*? Ben-Gurion shed so much Jewish blood to keep Jewish Jerusalem—the battles for the road to Jerusalem were among the most costly of the war—even though under the partition plan, which he had "accepted," Jerusalem was to be a *corpus separatum*.

SHIMON PERES: Because there was a war. The moment the Arabs rejected the partition plan and went to war, partition ceased to exist. There was only war. And in the war, Jerusalem was certainly a central objective. The central objective of accepting partition was establishing an independent state, even on a small part of Eretz Yisrael. Once war broke out, at the center of the war stood the fate of Jerusalem—because partition was no longer valid. You could hardly fight a war and at the same time say you were preserving partition, which the Arabs were rejecting.

DAVID LANDAU: At the time, did you think or fear that we were shedding so much blood to open the road to Jerusalem, to save and protect Jerusalem, and yet in the end we might lose Jerusalem and it would revert to being a *corpus separatum*?

SHIMON PERES: I did not think that way. I thought the war had changed the rules of the game—regarding everything.

DAVID LANDAU: That's why I'm asking what the meaning was, in real time, of the word *accept*.

SHIMON PERES: "Accept," because if it had gone through peaceably, we would have had the partition borders. Here I come back to the matter of the Shoah, because Ben-Gurion's key consideration in striving to set up a Jewish state *le'altar* was to take in the refugees. Therefore territory was not the only consideration for him. Shelter was important. Maybe had it not been for this, he would not have accepted partition. But the moment this option ended—it ended. There was a new ballgame. Even then, though, Ben-Gurion didn't want the army to go to El Arish*; he ordered Yigal Allon back from there. He didn't want to cross the original borders of Palestine.

DAVID LANDAU: When you would sit with him in the period before May 15 and he would explain that there was going to be a war with the Arab armies, was your working assumption that the partition borders would be extended?

SHIMON PERES: Yes, because the moment the borders that are supposed to be the fruit of agreement and peace don't exist— there are no borders! We knew we'd have to fight for new borders. What they'd be, we didn't know. And hence in the Declaration of Independence there is no reference to borders. Borders would be written in by reality. If not by agreement,

---

*In December 1948 IDF units reached the northern Sinai town of El Arish.

then by reality, which was also the reality of war. Certainly it was Ben-Gurion's desire that there would be no *corpus separatum* and no kissing points, and that we'd have a contiguous state. That was his desire. Definitely. But did he think the Arabs would accept partition? He certainly thought they might. The map was all in their favor. He took into account when he accepted partition that the other side would accept it too. And if they had accepted, there would not have been a war.

DAVID LANDAU: May I just ask you from another angle: Since Oslo in 1993 you have basically favored returning the territories taken in 1967 in return for peace. Why didn't the same logic apply in 1948? In other words, we'll fight the war, and then return to the partition border for peace?

SHIMON PERES: The 1948 war wasn't over borders. It was over our existence. It was over the existence of the State of Israel. The focus of the war was that they wanted to destroy us. In regard to the priorities that each side set for itself once the war was under way, history played a greater role than borders. Ben-Gurion and Abdullah both fought for Jerusalem as their highest priority. Because for them history took precedence over strategy. The Egyptians, by contrast, wanted to attack Tel Aviv by coming up the coast. Their goal was Tel Aviv, and that made strategic sense. But the Jordanians' priority was Jerusalem, and Israel's priority was Jerusalem. Ben-Gurion wanted Eilat very much too. I had headed a field mission mapping the route to Eilat three years earlier. Ben-Gurion predicted that we would get it without a battle, which was pretty incredible and turned out to be totally accurate. The whole southern Negev was empty. The Gulf of Eilat was important strategically. It was to be our outlet to Asia and Africa. But it was priority number two. Number one for Ben-Gurion was Jerusalem.

That was his argument with Yigael Yadin,[*] who wanted to

---

[*]Yadin (1917–84) was the IDF chief of operations during the War of Independence.

fight in Ashkelon because the Egyptians had reached Ashkelon. And Ben-Gurion said no; Jerusalem first. It was the same on the Jordanian front: John Glubb, the commander of the Arab Legion, said we'll cross from Beisan to Haifa and bisect the Jewish state, and Emir Abdullah said no; first Jerusalem. Interesting, that parallel.

DAVID LANDAU: Even though Ben-Gurion was careful to avoid putting the partition borders into the Declaration of Independence, was there to your knowledge or in your assessment a point in time in 1947–48 when Ben-Gurion actually believed there would be a Palestinian state alongside Israel and that the two would live with each other in peace?

SHIMON PERES: He believed then that the Palestinian issue could be wrapped into the Jordanian issue. That there was a "Jordanian option."

DAVID LANDAU: That's why he sent Golda to meet with Abdullah?

SHIMON PERES: Abdullah thought he could be king of the Palestinians too. The Jordanian option existed all the time. Bear in mind, the UN Partition Resolution speaks of an Arab state, not a Palestinian state. Two states, a Jewish state and an Arab state. Ben-Gurion thought that the common denominator was Arab, with the Palestinian identity finding expression within it. The Palestinian issue as such came to the fore only after the London Agreement.* Ben-Gurion didn't reject separate Palestinian na-

---

*In April 1987 Peres, then vice prime minister and foreign minister in a Likud-Labor unity government, negotiated secretly in London with King Hussein of Jordan and reached written agreement on "modalities" for concluding peace between Israel and Jordan. Under that agreement, which was designed to pave the way for a peace conference, "the Palestinian issue will be dealt with in the committee of the Jordanian-Palestinian and Israeli delegations," and "the Palestinians' representatives will be included in the Jordanian-Palestinian delegation." The agreement effectively presupposed Israeli withdrawal from most if not all of the West Bank, though this was not stated explicitly. It was rejected by then-prime minister Yitzhak Shamir, the

tionalism; he rejected Palestinian terrorism. Some Arab theorists embraced Communism, some nationalism. Ben-Gurion felt we must fight neither the one nor the other but terrorism. Abdullah and his successor, King Hussein, were against a separate Palestinian state. They thought it would endanger their Hashemite kingdom.

DAVID LANDAU: And you cooperated with them?

SHIMON PERES: What would you have us do? Cooperate with Arafat, who was a terrorist . . . ?

DAVID LANDAU: That's what you did in the end.

SHIMON PERES: Yes, after the Jordanian option was destroyed by our side by the repudiation of the London Agreement, and after Arafat renounced terror.

DAVID LANDAU: Yes, the repudiation of the London Agreement was a historic disaster. But we've jumped ahead forty years. In 1948 Ben-Gurion sent Golda to Abdullah, effectively to empty the Partition Resolution of its original import—a separate (Palestinian) Arab state. Yes?

SHIMON PERES: No, the way it looked to him at the time was that either Transjordan would take over the Palestinians or the Palestinians would take over Transjordan. Which they tried to do twenty-two years later during Black September.*

DAVID LANDAU: But the British wouldn't have allowed it. Glubb was there till the mid-1950s.

SHIMON PERES: Yes, but the Palestinians were subverting all the time. They murdered Abdullah. In the battle between them, we were on the side of the Jordanians.

Likud leader. He informed the U.S. secretary of state, George Shultz, that it had been negotiated without his consent.

*In September 1970 the Palestine Liberation Organization (PLO) in Jordan fought pitched battles against Jordanian government forces. Syria intervened on the Palestinians' side, invading Jordan from the north. Israel, at the urging of the United States, mobilized its forces to deter Syria from advancing. In the event, King Hussein's army smashed the PLO forces and drove them and their political leadership out of the country, mainly into Lebanon.

DAVID LANDAU: To what extent, in your view, did that influence Ben-Gurion in his standoff with Ahdut HaAvoda and the Palmach, who wanted him to try to conquer the West Bank?

SHIMON PERES: Ben-Gurion did not want to rule the West Bank. He wanted the Jordanians to rule there. It wasn't clear then that the Palestinians themselves wanted to set up a state there. They wanted to conquer Transjordan too. We had no other option; the Palestinians didn't want to talk to us.

For Ben-Gurion, the main thing was not to rule over another nation. That was his principle. To him, it was against morality and against political wisdom to rule over another nation. So that meant reaching an agreement, and the only figure available for that was Abdullah. The mufti didn't want an agreement. Ben-Gurion hoped and even expected that he could get a peace treaty with Abdullah. There was the Feisal-Weizmann agreement of 1918 as a precedent.* There was already dialogue back then.

---

*Drafted by T. E. Lawrence ("Lawrence of Arabia"), Emir Feisal's close aide and military commander, that agreement expressed Feisal's encouragement of the Zionist enterprise in the interest of both nations. Feisal, Abdullah's elder brother, became king of Iraq after World War I.

7

Birth Pangs

I spent that night with a rifle in my hand in Ben-Gurion's office, in case the headquarters compound was stormed by demonstrators.

The war with the Palestinian Arabs didn't wait for the British to evacuate or the Jewish state to be declared. The day after the vote at the United Nations, a spate of Arab attacks left seven Jews dead and scores more wounded. By February 1, 1948, according to a British report to the UN Security Council, there were 869 killed and 1,909 wounded: British—46 killed, 135 wounded; Arabs—427 killed, 1,035 wounded; Jews—381 killed, 725 wounded; others—15 killed, 15 wounded. The report said that without "the efforts of the [British] security forces over the past month, the two communities would by now have been fully engaged in internecine slaughter." To many members of the two communities, it seemed like they already were.

Irgun bombings in East Jerusalem killed scores of Arabs. Big bomb blasts in downtown West Jerusalem killed scores of Jews and sapped the Yishuv's morale. In Haifa an Irgun bombing triggered Arab attacks on Jewish refinery workers, leaving nearly forty of them dead. On March 11 a car bomb exploded in the forecourt of the Jewish Agency building in Jerusalem, killing thirteen. In the north, the famous Iraqi fighter Fawzi al-Kaukji slipped into the country at the head of the Arab Liberation Army, a legion of volunteers who reinforced local Palestinian armed bands.

As the countrywide guerrilla warfare intensified, especially around Jerusalem, Ben-Gurion grew frustrated with what he felt was the inability of the Haganah commanders to plan ahead for the much bigger military challenges that he saw as inevitable once independence was declared. "I was surprised to find a lack of understanding on the part of several Haganah commanders as to the need for heavy armament," he confided to his diary. "There's going to be a war," he declared to the Haganah commanders. "The Arab countries will unite and . . . there will be battle-fronts. This will no longer be a war of platoons. It is essential to set up a modern army." The response on some parts was smug incredulity. He tried to bring in men who had learned their soldiering in the British Army and the Jewish Brigade but ran into resistance from the "Haganah party," who jealously guarded their egalitarian tradition and despised the rigid formalism of the "army party."

Ben-Gurion's basic strategy, in the face of the Palestinian gangs and the gathering Arab armies, was that no Jewish settlement was to be abandoned, even those outside the boundaries of the Jewish state under the Partition Plan. As he explained in his diary, on the eve of the partition vote: "If the UN decision is favorable in terms of territory, we will defend every settlement and control the entire area of the state that is allotted to us. If we don't get a favorable resolution, we will defend every settlement, we will repel every attack, and we will not determine in advance territorial boundaries."

He dispatched top aides like Ehud Avriel, Teddy Kollek, and Munia Mardor to scour Europe and America for arms. Avriel concluded a contract with Czechoslovakia, presumably with Soviet consent, for guns and planes. There was no money to pay for it all, so Ben-Gurion prepared to fly to the United States with Eliezer Kaplan, the Jewish Agency treasurer, to raise funds from the Jews there. Golda Meir intervened. "What you're doing here I can't do," she reasoned. "But I can do what you want to do there." Their party colleagues sided with her, and off she went. All told, she was able to raise more than $50 million, double the target that Ben-Gurion had hoped for. "When history comes to be written," he told her, "it shall be said that there was a Jewish woman who found the money which enabled the establishment of the state." April was a month of extreme crisis. On the diplomatic front, the Jewish Agency representatives in Washington reported ominous backsliding by the American government. The State Department was now advocating a "provisional trusteeship" for Palestine under UN auspices, rather than immediate partition. This was supposed to give the protagonists more time to reach a settlement. Ben-Gurion called it "a capitulation to the terrorism of Arab bands armed by the British Foreign Office and allowed into the country under its protection."

In a public statement he reassured the Yishuv that while the UN Partition Resolution had been "of great political and moral value," the creation of the Jewish state would not depend on the resolution. "It depends on our ability to emerge victorious. If we have the will and the time to mobilize all our resources, the State will still be established. We will not consent to any trusteeship, neither provisional nor permanent, not even for the briefest period. We will no longer accept the yoke of foreign rule, whatever happens." To drive his point home, Ben-Gurion announced the appointment of a thirteen-member provisional government, to be known as the People's Executive. All the main political parties were represented, except the Revisionists and the Communists.

On the military front, the situation worsened fast. The Etzion bloc of settlements south of Jerusalem was under constant attack. In January a unit of thirty-five fighters sent to reinforce it was ambushed and massacred. Jerusalem itself was effectively cut off from the rest of the country. On March 29 a convoy of trucks trying to get from Tel Aviv to Jerusalem was attacked and had to turn back. The Haganah assembled a five-hundred-man force to bolster the beleaguered city. Ben-Gurion dismissed that plan as altogether inadequate. "The battle for the road to Jerusalem is the one burning question right now," he told Yadin and his officers. "The fall of Jewish Jerusalem would be a death blow to the Yishuv." He demanded a much larger force, which would attack the Arab strongholds in the villages overlooking the winding road up to the city. Reluctantly, Yadin stripped soldiers from other fronts and was eventually able to amass fifteen hundred fighting men for what was code-named Operation Nachshon. A shipload of rifles and machine guns, hidden under onions, somehow made it through the British blockade and was unloaded at Tel Aviv port. The weapons were rushed up to the Jerusalem foothills where the troops were preparing to attack.

In a series of brutal engagements, a number of the villages were taken and the Jerusalem road opened. On April 5 a first convoy got through. It was followed by others. On April 13 a convoy of 235 trucks reached the city, bringing provisions that were to prove vital in the later fighting. On April 20 Ben-Gurion himself drove up to Jerusalem and held meetings there in a demonstrative act of solidarity with the hard-pressed Jerusalemites.

This somewhat brighter picture was darkened, however, by an outrage perpetrated by Etzel and Lehi men at the village of Deir Yassin, on the outskirts of Jerusalem. The village was attacked by Etzel and Lehi on April 9, in coordination with the Haganah. They claimed later that the civilian inhabitants had been urged to flee but had refused to do so. After heavy fighting the village fell to the Jewish forces. But then a deliberate killing of civilians took place. It left more than one hundred dead, including women, children, and the elderly. It triggered a countrywide wave of fear and panic among the Arabs, which certainly contributed to the mass flight of hundreds of thousands of them across the borders. The question of why they left—whether they were forced out by the Haganah and, later, the IDF, or whether their own leaders urged them to leave while the nascent Jewish state was overrun by Arab armies—has been the stuff of much historical research and debate, as well as political polemics, for the last sixty years. The Palestine refugee problem continues to dog peacemaking efforts in the region to the present day.

I was at Ben-Gurion's side for much of that time, and I never heard him speak in favor of expelling Arabs from Israel. On the contrary, during the war I heard him speak in condemnation of this practice. Everyone has his own story about this. For instance, some claim that when Yitzhak Rabin, then a senior commander in the Palmach, told him of the expulsion of Arabs from the town of Lydda, Ben-Gurion made a gesture with his hand that implied approval. In Haifa, which was a mixed Jewish-Arab city, I personally heard him tell Abba Houshi, the city's Jewish mayor—I think this was during the first truce, which began on June 11—that we must stop the flight of the Arabs from the town.

Ben-Gurion constantly thought on two planes, the immediate and the historical. He would not have expressed himself in such a way that history would judge him as guilty of reprehensible acts. Never in the World Zionist Organization or the Labor Zionist movement was a plan to expel Arabs on the agenda. There was a time when an exchange of populations was discussed, and the British Labor Party supported this idea at one point. But never expulsion. That would would have been against our fundamental ideology, and I don't think Ben-Gurion would have countenanced any ideological compromise in this matter. It is true that during the truce Ben-Gurion referred to Lydda and Ramle as two "thorns." But he never ordered the expulsion of Arabs from either of those cities. He was, however, opposed to the return of Arab refugees to Israeli territory both during the war and after the war ended. They had by then become the enemy. It's one thing not to expel members of a resident population, but quite another not to permit an enemy's return.

We did agree to permit the return of Arab refugees to enable families to be reunited. I would estimate that we have taken in close to 200,000 Arabs over the years under our policy of family reunion. That is not a negligible number. Moreover, the mufti's policy—and after him, Ahmed Shukeiri and Yasser Arafat[*]—was

---

[*] Ahmed Shukeiri (1908–80) founded the PLO in 1964 and was its first chairman. Yasser Arafat (1929–2004) became chairman of the PLO in 1967 and headed the organization for thirty-seven years, until his death.

not to dismantle the refugee camps but to keep them in existence as a permanent irritant. The Palestinians' demand for return was in the context of a mass return following Israel's presumed defeat. Most did not want to return individually. Many had believed the tales they were told: that the Arabs would defeat Israel by force of arms and that they would then be able to return to their homes. The long-term strategy later adopted in countries such as Lebanon and Jordan was deliberately to leave the Palestinians living in refugee camps. The refugee issue was destined to turn into a permanent disaster for Israel—politically, militarily, and diplomatically. But Ben-Gurion had no real options.

In this context, I would point too to the more than 700,000 Jews who, beginning in the 1940s and continuing through 1967, had to leave the Arab countries—Egypt, Syria, Libya, Iraq, and Yemen among them—where their families had been living for centuries. In some of these countries, they experienced discrimination and persecution. Some countries refused to permit them to leave, and we had to spirit them out in clandestine ways. Almost all of them were forced to leave their property behind and arrived in the new State of Israel destitute. They were all absorbed here. We thought, perhaps naïvely, that this would be an example for the other side.

The first mixed Jewish-Arab town to be taken by the Haganah was Tiberias, on the Sea of Galilee, inside the partition borders. "On April 18," Ben-Gurion writes in his diary, "all the Arabs of Tiberias were evacuated by the British Army, even though the Haganah commanders announced that they would safeguard the lives and property of members of all communities."

Of Haifa, also inside the partition borders and taken on April 22, he wrote, "The local Arabs of Haifa accepted the Haganah demands [to hand over their weapons], but the Mufti, who was in Egypt, ordered the Arabs of Haifa to reject the demands and leave the city." They would be able to return, he said, with victorious Arab forces. Safad, Beisan, and Jaffa, all mixed cities that were to have remained within the Jewish state under partition, were also taken by the Haganah before statehood, and most of their Arab inhabitants fled.

B en-Gurion's wrangles with the army brass continued right through the war and repeatedly led to either him or some army officer threatening to resign, as though they were oblivious of the mortal perils that hung over the newborn state. But Ben-Gurion felt that there were times when he had to dig in his heels.

Apart from the tensions between the old-time partisans and the ex–British Army professionals, political allegiances were involved too. On April 26, 1948, Ben-Gurion announced that he was abolishing the position of head of the national command of the Haganah because it complicated the command structure between himself and the army-in-waiting. The position had originally been held by two civilians, one appointed by the Histadrut and the other by the Citizens' Union, a body run by the General Zionists. The present incumbent was one man, whom Ben-Gurion himself had appointed the year before.

The trouble was that this man, the wise and widely respected Yisrael Galili, was a prominent member of the breakaway party Ahdut HaAvoda (formerly Siah Bet), and Ben-Gurion was suspected of ulterior motives. *Al Hamishmar*, the newspaper of the Mapam party, wrote of "a personal dictatorship" by Ben-Gurion. Ten days before the state was to be declared, with the country submerged in a welter of bloody guerrilla warfare, the Haganah's senior commanders threatened to quit. Ben-Gurion climbed a little way down, agreeing that Galili could return to the general staff of the Haganah, but not in his previous post, which was abolished.

No sooner was this issue settled—though not permanently resolved—than Ben-Gurion was faced with a wave of hesitation on the part of the politicians over whether to actually go ahead with the declaration. On May 11 Golda Meir returned from Amman with the worrisome news that Emir Abdullah seemed to be caving in to pan-Arab pressure to fight. The next day the Jordanian Arab Legion, with its artillery and armored vehicles, joined the ongoing Palestinian attacks on the Etzion bloc of villages, whose situation quickly turned desperate.*

Yigael Yadin and Yisrael Galili briefed the Provisional Government on behalf of the Haganah; neither of them was prepared to predict the outcome of the inevitable war. Moshe Sharett met with the U.S. secretary of state, George Marshall, a strong opponent of American recognition of the future Jewish state, and came away deeply troubled by the eminent soldier-statesman's warning that the Yishuv might not survive the anticipated Arab attack. Sharett returned to Tel Aviv and reported privately to Ben-Gurion. Ben-Gurion told him to make the exact same presentation to the party leadership the next day. Sharett presented his report and then lined up firmly on the side of Ben-Gurion in favor of declaring the state on May 14 as planned.

Ben-Gurion tried to instill confidence in his colleagues. It's true, he said, that based on the present balance of forces

> our situation will be very perilous. But . . . it will improve if we manage to bring into the country not even everything we have but, let us say, 15,000 rifles and a few million cartridges, and the cannon and the bazookas, and the warplanes fitted with machine-guns and bombs . . . We would be able to land a powerful blow on the Arabs at the outset of their invasion and undermine their morale.

He put the issue to the vote: Declare the state in two days' time as planned, or wait? By a vote of six to four the ministers of the Provisional Government decided to go ahead. They then turned

---

*They were ordered to surrender the next day. In all, 151 defenders were killed, some of them massacred after the fighting ended and before the International Red Cross could step in to arrange the surrender terms. Under those terms, 320 defenders were taken into captivity in Jordan and returned to Israel after the war. The Etzion bloc, as part of the West Bank, remained under Jordanian control until the Six-Day War in 1967.

their attention to a draft of the declaration that had been prepared. It referred to the borders "as laid down in the United Nations resolution." The future justice minister, Pinhas Rosen, said there could be no declaration of statehood without defining the borders of the state. But Ben-Gurion demurred. "The American Declaration of Independence contains no mention of territorial boundaries," he observed.

Nothing obligates us to mention them . . . We should say nothing about them because we don't know what they will be. They are preparing to make war on us. If we defeat them and capture western Galilee or territory on both sides of the road to Jerusalem, those areas will become part of the State. Why should we obligate ourselves to accept boundaries that the Arabs don't accept in any case?

On the afternoon of Friday, May 14, 1948, before the onset of the Sabbath, a festive session of the People's Assembly (the Yishuv's parliament) convened at the Tel Aviv Museum on Rothschild Boulevard, formerly the home of the city's longtime mayor, Meir Dizengoff. The delegates and hundreds of other invited dignitaries sat with bated breath as Ben-Gurion read out the proclamation. "The Land of Israel was the birthplace of the Jewish people," he began in his familiar, raspy voice and clipped, undramatic delivery. All over the war-torn country, people strained to listen to radio receivers. Tears flowed freely.

Here their spiritual, religious, and national identity was formed. Here they achieved independence and created a culture of national and universal significance. Here they wrote and gave the Bible to the world. Exiled from their land, the Jewish people remained faithful to it in all the countries of their dispersion, never ceasing to pray and hope for their return and for the restoration of their national freedom.

The declaration went on to survey the preceding decades of settlement in Palestine, Zionist diplomacy, the Balfour Declaration, the Mandate, and the Holocaust, which "proved anew the urgency of the re-establishment of the Jewish state, which would open the gates of the homeland wide to every Jew and confer upon the Jewish people the status of a fully privileged member of the family of nations."

It referred to "the recognition by the United Nations of the right of the Jewish people to establish their independent State" and affirmed that it was "the natural right of the Jewish people to control their own destiny, like all other nations, in their own sovereign State."

After this stirring preamble came the formal, political act.

ACCORDINGLY, WE, the members of the People's Council, representatives of the Jewish community of the Land of Israel and of the Zionist Movement, are here assembled on the day of the termination of the British Mandate over the Land of Israel and, by virtue of our natural and historic right and on the strength of the Resolution of the General Assembly of the United Nations, HEREBY DECLARE the establishment of a Jewish State in the Land of Israel, to be known as THE STATE OF ISRAEL . . .

THE STATE OF ISRAEL will be open to the immigration of Jews and for the ingathering of the exiles from all countries of their dispersion; will promote the development of the country for the benefit of all its inhabitants; will be based on the precepts of liberty, justice, and peace as envisioned by the prophets of Israel; will uphold the full social and political equality of all its citizens without distinction of race, creed, or sex; will guarantee full freedom of conscience, worship, education, and culture; will safeguard the sanctity and inviolability of the shrines and holy places of all religions; and will dedicate itself to the principles of the Charter of the United Nations.

THE STATE OF ISRAEL will be ready to cooperate with the agencies and representatives of the United Nations

in the implementation of the Resolution of the General Assembly of November 29, 1947, and will take steps to bring
about the economic union of the whole of the Land of
Israel . . .

   We extend our hand of peace and neighborliness to all the
neighboring states and their peoples, and invite them to establish bonds of cooperation and mutual help with the
soverign Jewish people settled in its own land. The State of
Israel is prepared to do its share in a common effort for the
advancement of the entire Middle East . . .

   Placing our trust in the rock of Israel, we affix our signa-
tures to this Declaration at this session of the Provisional
State Council, on the soil of the homeland, in the city of Tel
Aviv, on this Sabbath eve, the fifth day of Iyar, 5708, the four-
teenth day of May, 1948.

This last reference to "the rock of Israel," perhaps referring to the
Deity or perhaps to some less divine national destiny, was the upshot of last-minute wrangling between religious and agnostic
members of the Provisional Government over whether God should
be invoked at all, and if so how.

   Ben-Gurion then said, "Let us rise to indicate our support for
the Declaration of Independence." All rose. "Please be seated," he
said. "There is one more announcement to be made, but before I
make it I would like to call upon Rabbi Yehudah Leib Fishman."
The white bearded leader of the religious Mizrachi Party recited
the traditional *Shehecheyanu* blessing celebrating a new or festive
experience. Ben-Gurion then read out a decision by the provisional government "in accordance with the Declaration of Independence." The regulations emanating from the white paper "are
hereby declared null and void . . . The Land Transfer Regulations, 1940, are abolished retroactively." ("Stormy applause," he
later recorded in his diary.) Thirty-seven minutes after entering
the hall, the new prime minister of the new state rapped his gavel
and announced, "The State of Israel has arisen. This meeting is

now adjourned." In his diary he wrote, "Throughout the country there is profound joy and jubilation and once again, as on November 29, I feel like the bereaved among the rejoicers."

Now the war that Ben-Gurion had predicted with such certainty began in earnest. Armed forces from five Arab states—Egypt, Transjordan, Iraq, Syria, and Lebanon—invaded Israel from all sides. The new state's survival would depend on its ability to hold them off until the weaponry that could defeat them arrived and was deployed.

Eleven minutes after Ben-Gurion's proclamation, the U.S. government announced that it would recognize the new state. President Harry Truman's announcement read, "This Government has been informed that a Jewish state has been proclaimed in Palestine, and recognition has been requested by the provisional government thereof. The United States recognizes the provisional government as the de facto authority of the State of Israel." It was Truman's personal decision, overruling the professionals at the State Department.

Before dawn Ben-Gurion was awakened with a request from Israel's diplomats in the United States that he broadcast live to the American people over the radio. He was driven to the Haganah's radio station in north Tel Aviv. As he spoke, Egyptian bombs fell on the Sde Dov airfield nearby. Unruffled, he wove an explanation of the explosions in the background into his broadcast. He drove back in an open jeep. "From all the houses, people in pajamas were gazing out," he wrote in his diary. "But there were no signs of panic. I felt that these people would stand their ground."

They would need to. The first days of the war were unrelievedly dark. In the north, Syrian armor pressed down on the Sea of Galilee, smashing through the Haganah's inadequate defenses at Tzemach. In the south, the Egyptians hurled their forces against Kibbutz Yad Mordechai. The fighting there went on for five days; if the Egyptians had broken through, the road to Tel Aviv would have been open before them. In Jerusalem, Transjordan's Arab Legion attacked at multiple points and threatened the west of the city. In Tel Aviv, forty-two people died in a single bombing raid by Egypt on the central bus terminal.

Old farmers from the Jordan Valley settlements, Ben Gurion's friends from years back, came to beg for reinforcements. The army had just received four antiquated 65-milimeter mountain-guns, which Yadin wanted to send up to Lake Galilee to try to stop the Syrian tanks. Ben-Gurion refused: The guns were for Jerusalem, he insisted. They argued; Yadin slammed down his first and broke the glass on Ben-Gurion's desk. Outside, the farmers from the north cried bitter tears. In the end, Ben-Gurion agreed to send the guns for twenty-four hours. They were duly deployed and did indeed make the requisite impact on the Syrians, who pulled back their forces.

The most difficult day was May 22. Kibbutz Ramat Rahel, on the southern perimeter of Jerusalem, changed hands repeatedly in bloody fighting. An IDF force trying to break through the Zion Gate and reinforce the beleaguered Jewish Quarter of the Old City was repulsed. Large sections of the western city were under incessant shelling. In the south an Egyptian column entered Beersheba. "There was nothing left to fight with," a Mapai party colleague later recalled. "Ben-Gurion stalked about like a wounded lion." But the defenders on most of the myriad front lines somehow held on.

By the next night Ben-Gurion could see the first glimmers of hope. Messerschmitt warplanes bought in Czechoslovakia began to arrive; five Czech technicians worked feverishly on assembling them and getting them airborne. A first ship carrying light arms and artillery was approaching Haifa. "That will be the beginning of the turning point," Ben-Gurion wrote. He focused his attention on Jerusalem. "We have to hold on in the Negev," he told the army general staff. "The battle for Jerusalem is the most important, both politically and to a large extent militarily, too." Yadin strongly demurred. Ben-Gurion was exaggerating the precariousness of the situation there, he recalled later. "I thought the Egyptians were the most dangerous enemy and I gave priority to the south."

Ben-Gurion thought otherwise, and he now asserted his full authority to bend the general staff to his will. Two food convoys had reached Jerusalem on May 16 and 17, but then the Arab Legion cut off the road again. The linchpin was the British-built Tegart fort* at Latrun, in the Jerusalem foothills, which commanded the road up to Jerusalem and the surrounding lower-lying areas. The legion held it, and Ben-Gurion was determined to oust them from it. He ordered the army to concentrate men and equipment for a massed attack on the stronghold. The men included young immigrants literally just off the boats and barely aware of how to fire a rifle. The equipment was no match for the defenders' field guns, machine guns, and mortars. Three times over the next weeks Israeli forces tried to storm Latrun, and three times they were repulsed with heavy losses. In the meantime the Jewish Quarter of the Old City of Jerusalem fell to the legion; the remaining handful of able-bodied defenders were taken into captivity in Transjordan, and the wounded and noncombatants were sent across the lines to West Jerusalem.

The siege of West Jerusalem was eased by the discovery, at the beginning of June, of an alternative route through the hills. Hundreds of civilians from Tel Aviv were mobilized to carry matériel up the stony slope, assisted by mules and jeeps, while work went on feverishly to clear the path and pave it. This "Burma Road," as it was called, was functioning by June 8.

On other fronts, the Iraqis advanced westward from Tulkarm toward Netanya, threatening to cut the country in half. They were stopped and turned back at Kfar Yona on May 25–28. Other Israeli units pushed Fawzi al-Kaukji's Arab Liberation Army forces back from the southern Galilee toward Jenin. At Kibbutz Negba,

---

*A series of concrete fortresses, built at strategic points all around Palestine, were named for Sir Charles Tegart, a British police officer and engineer.

near Gaza, approximately one hundred defenders equipped with one Piat gun and small arms managed to hold out against an Egyptian armored force numbering one thousand men. Yad Mordechai, however, finally fell on May 24, and the Egyptians moved on northward toward Isdood (present-day Ashdod). The Egyptian advance up the coast was slowed on May 29 by the first appearance of Israeli air power: Four Messerschmitts strafed the advancing column. Their success was limited (two crashed), but their psychological impact, on both sides, was important.

Summing up that period, Ben-Gurion wrote later, "The month of battles from the Arabs' invasion of the country until the first truce was the most difficult and dangerous period of the War of Independence. For the most part, the Arabs enjoyed the initiative. Operations that we initiated were not always successful. The weapons purchased overseas trickled in slowly. Heavy weapons, in which the Arabs had the greatest advantage, took longest to arrive because of transport difficulties."

The United Nations sent a peace emissary, the Swedish Count Folke Bernadotte, together with its own senior diplomat, the American Ralph Bunche, to try to end the fighting. They first called on Ben-Gurion on May 31. The next day his office in Ramat Gan, near Tel Aviv, was bombed and strafed from the air. "Apparently," he wrote in his diary, "a spy in Bernadotte's party had informed the Arabs of the location of my office. Perhaps it was hit in retaliation for our bombing of Amman." Israel had sent three planes, the bulk of its then–air force, on two bombing runs over the Transjordanian capital the previous day. "Three-quarters of a ton of bombs were dropped," Ben-Gurion meticulously recorded. "Fires were started." Ben-Gurion himself refused to take shelter during the air raid. I remember him sitting impassively at his desk, writing. When a guard outside was hit by shrapnel, Nehemia Argov, his military aide, and I ran out with a stretcher. Ben-Gurion got up, but only to lend us a hand carrying the wounded man to an ambulance. Then he returned to his writing.

For Israel, sorely pressed on every front, a four-week truce arranged by the UN Security Council, which finally went into effect on June 11, was a godsend. "I asked the members of the General Staff whether a truce would be to our advantage," Ben-Gurion wrote in his diary on May 26. "All of them agreed that it would." The period of quiet was spent rearming and training. It was a re-invigorated IDF that took to the field when battle was rejoined on July 8. This was the case in more than just the logistical sense. For while the Arab guns had been silent, Ben-Gurion faced his sternest test—from within his own side.

The Provisional Government had issued an ordinance on May 26 establishing the Israel Defense Forces (IDF) and prohibiting "the establishment or maintenance of any other armed force." On June 1, Menachem Begin, the Etzel leader, signed an agreement with the government whereby Etzel units would join the IDF in battalion formations and take an oath of loyalty. The Etzel's separate command structure would be disbanded within a month, and the organization would cease buying arms abroad.

Nevertheless, on June 11, the *Altalena*, a ship that the Etzel had purchased, set sail from southern France with a large quantity of arms and explosives on board as well as some 850 immigrants. As it approached the shores of Israel, Begin informed the government that 20 percent of the arms would be sent to Etzel units in Jerusalem. Since Jerusalem was not yet formally under Israel's jurisdiction, Yisrael Galili, negotiating for the IDF, agreed. Begin then proposed that the remaining weaponry go first to equip Etzel units within the IDF. Whatever was left could then be allocated to other units. Galili balked. He reported to Ben-Gurion on June 19 that the danger of a "private army" was evolving. Ben-Gurion convened the cabinet. "There are not going to be two states," he declared, "and there are not going to be two armies. And Mr. Begin will not do what he feels like . . . If he does not give in we shall open fire!" The cabinet resolved unanimously to "authorize the defense minister to take action in accordance with the law of the land."

Ben-Gurion feared that Begin might use the arms aboard the

Altalena to equip Etzel units outside the sovereign jurisdiction of the state—thus ostensibly not violating his commitment—in order to extend the war with the Arabs into the West Bank (Judea and Samaria), thereby defying government policy.

The *Altalena* anchored off Kfar Vitkin, a moshav between Tel Aviv and Haifa, and hopefully far from the prying eyes of UN observers, and began off-loading the weapons with the help of hundreds of supporters who had gathered at the site. Galili and Yadin deployed troops to surround the beach and ordered Begin to surrender. Some of the troops with Etzel sympathies crossed the lines and joined the *Altalena* crew and its enthusiastic sympathizers. The ship, with Begin and other Revisionist leaders now on board, weighed anchor and put out to sea, chased by IDF craft. It sailed south toward Tel Aviv and eventually ran aground close to the shore. At army headquarters in Ramat Gan, I spent that night with a rifle in my hand in Ben-Gurion's office, in case the headquarters compound was stormed by demonstrators.

Off the Tel Aviv boardwalk, a traumatic scenario unfolded the next day. Etzel soldiers and civilian sympathizers streamed to the site. Some waded into the sea and swam out to the ship. At military headquarters, Ben-Gurion paced back and forth, fuming. Eventually he issued written orders to Yadin to concentrate "troops, fire-power, flame-throwers, and all the other means at our disposal in order to secure the ship's unconditional surrender." Yadin was then to await the government's instructions.

Ben-Gurion then convened the cabinet again. Some colleagues suggested possible compromises, but he was of no mind for any such weakness. "This is an attempt to destroy the army," he thundered. "This is an attempt to murder the state. In these two matters there cannot be any compromise." The cabinet backed him. Small-arms fire broke out between shore and ship. The government evacuated homes and shops in the line of fire. The Palmach commander Yigal Allon, now a senior IDF general, was put in charge of the operation. He ordered a cannon deployed. Yitzhak Rabin was in command of it. The first shell fell wide, but the second struck the vessel. Fire broke out in the hold. Those on board began to abandon ship. (It stood barely one hundred yards from the beach.) But before they could all do so, an explosion tore through the ship, destroying it. Sixteen Etzel men and three IDF soldiers died in the episode; dozens more were wounded.

Begin delivered a two-hour broadcast live on Etzel radio that night, roundly cursing Ben-Gurion who, he claimed, had been out to kill him. He for his part, Begin said, would continue to restrain his men and thus prevent the outbreak of civil war: "We will not open fire. There will be no fraternal strife when the enemy is at the gate." Ben-Gurion spoke at the People's Assembly, the transitional parliament. He said that since the arms had not been destined for the IDF, he was glad they had been destroyed. He added a line praising "the blessed cannon" that had fired at the *Altalena*—a phrase that Revisionist stalwarts never forgot nor forgave.

Less than a week later Ben-Gurion was again facing down what he angrily termed "a political mutiny in the army," this time from the left. He was determined to bring more ex–British Army/Jewish Brigade officers into key posts. And he was determined too to reduce the influence of Mapam (since January, an amalgam of the Hashomer Hatzair and Ahdut HaAvoda parties) in the army, which was exercised primarily through the Palmach commanders, most of them Ahdut HaAvoda adherents. The two aims dovetailed and succeeded in raising the ire of Yigael Yadin, the (nonpolitical) chief of operations (Chief of Staff Yaakov Dori was ill for most of the war), and of the Mapam-affiliated generals, who now tendered their collective resignation. Ben-Gurion accused Yadin of mutiny. Yadin said he was prepared to serve as a simple soldier but not to take responsibility for decisions that he found unjustifiable. At a cabinet meeting, Ben-Gurion threatened to resign. And he again demanded Galili's dismissal as the sine qua non for any new arrangement.

A five-man ministerial committee was set up to investigate the charges and countercharges. Yadin testified before it, excoriating Ben-Gurion's incessant interference in operational matters. He restated his profound disagreements with the prime minister and defense minister over the battle for Jerusalem. Galili testified too, also criticizing Ben-Gurion's performance of his duties as defense minister. The ministers recommended the creation of a formal war cabinet. They recommended too that Galili be restored to his old role as head of the national command—effectively interposing him between Defense Minister Ben-Gurion and the general staff. Ben-Gurion promptly resigned, just days before the truce was due to end. With the prime minister demonstratively at home, and the generals no longer at their posts either, the entire political and military establishment went into a paroxysm of negotiations to find some saving formula.

Here one sees graphically how even Ben-Gurion's opponents, who blithely accused him of autocratic ways, were desperate not to lose him. Galili altruistically offered his own head. In the end, Yadin went around to Ben-Gurion's home, braved Paula, and put before the Old Man a compromise scheme designed to get on with the war (once the truce ended) without making an immediate string of controversial appointments. Yigal Allon, the Palmachnik accepted by all, was given command of the key Jerusalem front.

The confrontation subsided, but for Ben-Gurion it was just a tactical retreat. The sequel came in October, on the eve of a third round of hostilities against the Egyptians in the Negev. Ben-Gurion issued orders to dismantle the Palmach's separate command structure, explaining that it was anomalous in an integrated army. Mapam appealed the decision before the executive of the Histadrut, and there the arguments raged for two days. Ben-Gurion accused Mapam of endangering "the integrity of the state." A Mapam leader warned that the right was plotting to seize power undemocratically, and that by eliminating the Palmach, Ben-Gurion was heightening the risk that this might succeed. This time Ben-Gurion enjoyed his own party's solid support, and the Mapam appeal was voted down. After the war Ben-Gurion achieved his goal of a fully integrated army by disbanding the separate Palmach brigades.

For Ben-Gurion, these two dangerous brushes with rebellion, the one from the right, the other from the left, required him to impose, without compromise and without delay, his hallowed principle of *mamlachtiyut* (state before party) upon the fledgling nation. He was shocked to discover that the principal fighting force of the army, the Palmach, was party-oriented, to the point where, in the first round of tensions over Galili's role, Yitzhak Ben-Aharon,* a key Ahdut HaAvoda figure, seriously proposed that the Palmach be subordinate to the Histadrut, the socialist-run trade union organization. Ben-Gurion was appalled to hear that from one of the most intelligent people in politics. It showed that the fundamentals of national sovereignty had not yet permeated the political echelon.

If Ben-Gurion had not faced down Etzel and disbanded the Palmach, we would have had a seriously compromised state right from the start. Over the years there were still occasionally army officers who felt—or at any rate claimed they felt—that they were discriminated against because they weren't affiliated with the Mapai Party. Ezer Weizman† was one particularly high-profile example. His affiliations were with the right, and he in fact joined Menachem Begin's Herut Party after retiring from the IDF. But he was wrong to think his military career was slowed or stymied (he wasn't appointed chief of staff) because of it. Yigael Yadin was a chief of staff, and he wasn't a Mapai Party man. Neither was Mordechai Makleff, Yadin's successor. Tzvi Tzur,‡ who succeeded Haim Laskov as chief of staff, didn't come in as a party man. They were all strictly army men.

---

*Ben-Aharon (1906–2006) was later a cabinet minister and secretary-general of the Histadrut.

†Chaim Weizmann's nephew, Weizman (1924–2005) was a commander of the Israeli Air Force; a cabinet minister under Eshkol, Begin, and Peres; and, from 1993 to 2000, president of the state.

‡Tzur was IDF chief of staff, 1961–63.

In fact, contrary to the legends, it was often Ben-Gurion who had to fight over military appointments against the serried ranks of his opponents, both in the general staff and in the Mapai. He had no clique of his own. During the War of Independence the generals ganged up time and again and threatened to quit en bloc. And in 1953 the party bridled at his appointment of Moshe Dayan as chief of staff. Levi Eshkol referred to Dayan as Abu Jilda.* Golda opposed him too, as did Sharett. Ben-Gurion ignored the party because he thought Dayan's appointment was in the national interest.

Mamlachtiyut was a strict and uncompromising code. Yadin helped Ben-Gurion to inculcate it in the army. At one point in time the director-general of the treasury ministry was scheduled for reserve duty on the eve of the presentation of the national budget, and Yadin refused to release him from his obligation to serve. The director-general stayed in his office, anyway, to prepare the budget. And so Yadin sent him to jail!

---

*Abu Jilda was a famous Arab brigand.

8

Settling In

He sent me on many assignments. For some reason he
thought I could do things, let's say, unconventionally.

On July 7, 1948, the day before the truce was officially to end,
the Egyptians went into action in the south, and soon battles were raging again on all fronts. The IDF was now bigger—
there were 63,800 men (and women) under arms, compared with
under 40,000 in May—and much better equipped than before. It
scored some successes, extending the areas under its control in the
Jerusalem corridor and the Galilee. Ramle, Lydda, and Lydda Airport* were taken. Israeli planes bombed Cairo and Damascus as
well as the Egyptian airfield at El Arish in the Sinai. But Israel
failed during the ten days of this second round of fighting to dis-
lodge the Egyptians from the northern Negev, the Jordanians from
East Jerusalem and the Old City, and the Syrians from the northeastern Galilee. The IDF was not fully in control even of the areas
allocated to the Jewish state in the 1947 Partition Plan, especially
in the south. The Negev settlements were largely cut off by the
Egyptian advance and had to be supplied from the air. A second,
UN-ordered indefinite truce went into effect on July 18.

Despite the still-inconclusive outcome of the fighting, and despite the relatively heavy casualties, the overall atmosphere was
much improved. The state's permanence and confidence steadily
strengthened in the minds of its citizens, whose numbers were al-

*Now Ben-Gurion International Airport.

ready being augmented by the first arrival of new immigrants from the displaced-persons camps in Europe. Ben-Gurion ordered a military parade in Tel Aviv, which was held on July 27. The UN envoy, Count Folke Bernadotte, reported to the secretary-general that "a feeling of greater confidence and independence had grown out of Jewish military efforts during the interval between the two truces. Less reliance was placed in the United Nations and there was a growing tendency to criticize its shortcomings with regard to Palestine."

Influenced apparently by the British, Bernadotte now produced a peace plan that proposed lopping off the Negev from Israel and annexing it to Transjordan. Israel would retain the western Galilee areas that it had conquered but would emerge much truncated (the Negev was 60 percent of its territory) and would have to take back the Palestinian refugees who had fled the country, numbered by Bernadotte at more than 300,000. In an early version of his plan, in June, Jerusalem was to have been part of Transjordan; in the second version, in September, it was to be internationalized. Both Israel and the Arabs rejected Bernadotte's proposals.

On September 17 Bernadotte was ambushed in his car and shot dead in West Jerusalem, apparently by the Lehi. The organization had ostensibly disbanded, but a hard-core group of activists still held together. Ben-Gurion, shocked and embarrassed, had hundreds of known Lehi and Etzel members around the country arrested. Natan Yellin-Mor and Matti Shmuelevitch, two prominent Lehi leaders, were charged with the murder and sentenced to long jail terms. (They were released under a general amnesty, after the war finally ended in 1949.)

The assassination intensified international diplomatic efforts to produce a settlement in Palestine. In December the UN General Assembly, angered by the envoy's murder and stirred by the plight of the still-growing number of Palestinian refugees, passed Resolution 194, which called for a cessation of hostilities and the return of refugees who wished to live in peace.

Ben-Gurion meanwhile decided on a bold military operation to take the entire southern portion of the West Bank (Judea) and link it up with the northern Negev. In late September he ordered the army to prepare the troops and took his plan to the cabinet. There, however, he was firmly resisted by the majority of ministers. He termed their position a *bechiya ledorot* (literally, a "cause for sobbing for generations"),* but his colleagues remained adamant, and he was forced to order the army to make do with a more modest, though also not unambitious, plan to attack the Egyptians in the northern Negev and attempt to drive them out of the country. The campaign, code-named Operation Yoav, developed into the largest and bloodiest battle of the entire war.

The Egyptians provided the required pretext by attacking a food convoy in violation of the terms of the truce. The IDF, under Allon, attacked on several fronts, with air support. In the end, Israel managed to capture Beersheba and open a secure corridor into the Negev. The invading Egyptian Army was cut into four separate and isolated brigades, pinned down by IDF forces. On October 28 the Egyptians evacuated Isdood, and on November 6 they retreated from Majdal (Ashkelon). Most of the Arab inhabitants in those areas left with the retreating Egyptian forces. They were to remain as Palestinian refugees living under Egyptian rule in the Gaza Strip until the Six-Day War in 1967.

In December further IDF initiatives in the south drove the Egyptians from more of the Negev. At year's end Israeli troops were in control of northeastern Sinai. Forward units reached Bir Hasanah, deep inland and some fifty miles from the border of Palestine. Other units closed on El Arish, the seaport lying on the Mediterranean coast. A dogfight with British RAF planes led to several of them being shot down and dramatically heightened international tensions. Ben-Gurion quickly pulled the troops back. The future Egyptian leader, Gamal Abdel Nasser, was among the

---

*Asked, however, after the war, "Why didn't you liberate the whole country," Ben-Gurion cited the demographic consideration as well as international pressures. "There was a danger of getting saddled with a hostile Arab majority," he explained.

officers of a four-thousand-man force surrounded at Faluja, near present-day Kiryat Gat. (That force was eventually released and repatriated under the terms of the armistice agreement signed between Israel and Egypt in February 1949 on the island of Rhodes.) In the north, the IDF mounted a large and successful operation against Fawzi al-Kaukji's Arab Liberation Army at the end of October, driving them and Lebanese forces out of the Galilee and pushing the Syrians eastward. IDF units swept into southern Lebanon as far as the Litani River.

In March a Palmach unit in the south reached Umm al-Rashrash on the Red Sea coast and, famously, ran up an improvised flag drawn on a sheet with ink. Then they sang "Hatikva," which has gone down in Israeli history as marking the end of the War of Independence. Armistice agreements, brokered by a UN-appointed conciliation commission, were eventually signed with Egypt, with Lebanon in March, with Transjordan (which now became the Hashemite Kingdom of Jordan) in April, and with Syria in July. Six thousand Israelis had died in the war—1 percent of the population. Four thousand of them were soldiers and the rest civilians. Israel ended up with some 50 percent more territory than was originally allotted to it by the Partition Plan; its borders under the armistice agreements covered 78 percent of pre-state Palestine. The war created some 600,000 Palestinian refugees. Gaza fell under the jurisdiction of Egypt. Judea and Samaria, the area along the west bank of the Jordan River, was occupied by Jordan and later officially annexed, an act recognized only by Britain and Pakistan.

A t the first meeting of the Provisional Government after independence was declared in May 1948, Ben-Gurion proposed that Chaim Weizmann be elected president of the state. "I doubt whether the presidency is necessary to Dr. Weizmann," he said, "but the presidency of Dr. Weizmann is a moral necessity for the State of Israel." This was duly done, and Weizmann, who had gone to the United States to lobby President Truman on behalf of the soon-to-be-born state, was then formally feted at the White House as a fellow head of state. On February 16, 1949, Weizmann was officially sworn in as president at a special session of the newly elected Knesset.

No sooner was the fighting more or less over than Ben-Gurion led the country to elections, on January 25, 1949. Despite the objective difficulties—tens of thousands of people were still under arms—a whopping 86.9 percent of the eligible electorate (499,095 out of 506,567) exercised their democratic right to vote, a turnout that has never been bettered since. Ben-Gurion's Mapai Party won a plurality of 46 seats in the 120-seat Knesset. That meant a coalition government, in which no single party had a majority. This was to be the pattern of political life in Israel going forward, with all the inherent instability that it entails. The next-largest party was Mapam, with 19 seats. But Mapam refused to join a coalition with Mapai, and Ben-Gurion was forced to make do with the Religious Front (16 seats), the Progressives (5 seats), and two tiny parties, an inherently unstable alliance that indeed proved to be intermittently shaky and fell apart within two years.

On April 4, 1949, the new Knesset, meeting in the old San Remo Hotel on the Tel Aviv beachfront, held its first great political debate. The day before, on the island of Rhodes, representatives of Israel and Jordan had signed an armistice agreement, formally ending the fighting and formally enshrining Jordan's annexation of the West Bank. All the old opponents of partition, from all their various positions on the Zionist spectrum, hurled upon Ben-Gurion a final chorus of criticism. He rebutted them with words of timeless relevance:

> A Jewish state, or *shleimut haaretz* [the integrity of the biblical Greater Israel]? Well, a Jewish state . . . over the entire country can only be a dictatorship of the minority. A Jewish state, even just in western Palestine [i.e., not including Transjordan], cannot possibly be a democratic state because the number of Arabs in western Palestine is larger than the number of Jews.

To have held out for Greater Israel, he continued, would have meant the imposition of a United Nations–sponsored international mandate over the entire country.

We want a Jewish state, even if not in the whole country. Who is "we"? The Zionist Movement, a large majority of the Yishuv, and a large majority of the pioneers and the fighters and the soldiers and those who died fighting for it . . . And so, when the question before us was Greater Israel without a Jewish state or a Jewish state without Greater Israel—we chose a Jewish state without Greater Israel . . . We did [initially] demand a Jewish state over the whole country. And it would have been possible had the Mandatory Power [Great Britain] fulfilled its duty and enabled the immigration of a million Jews over two years . . . But now, we do not want to launch further war against the Arabs. I want one thing to be clear. We believe that the creation of the state, albeit on less than Greater Israel, was the greatest act in Jewish history since ancient times . . . The criterion by which to judge these armistice agreements is whether they are better than no agreements, not whether they are better than a miracle. If a miracle happens and the Messiah comes, there will be peace in the world and all will be good. But it is our task to save the Jewish people by natural means, until the supernatural miracle happens. And judged by natural means, these armistice agreements have advanced our prospects. They have strengthened our international standing. They have enhanced our ability to bring in immigrants. They have enhanced the possibility of eventual peace and friendship with the Arabs.

The armistice agreement with Jordan was approved by a large majority. Mapam voted against it. Apart from the scarring from the internal battles over the Palmach, Mapam was ideologically at odds with Ben-Gurion at that time, still believing in "the world of tomorrow"—that is, the Soviet Union. Throughout the 1940s and 1950s, Mapam and Ahdut HaAvoda pinned their hopes on support from the Soviet bloc for Israel as a progressive and anticolonialist state. The Ahdut HaAvoda leaders Yisrael Galili and Yitzhak Tabenkin, despite their Greater Israel views, believed there would be some sort of reconciliation between Zionism and Soviet Russia, though at the same time they did not want to forgo the friendship of the United States or the support of American Jewry.

Another prominent Ahdut HaAvoda leader, Lyova Levite of Kibbutz Ein Harod, boasted that he read no paper but *Pravda*. And Ahdut HaAvoda leader Nahum Nir (formerly Refalkes) was voted Knesset speaker in 1959 by the opposition parties against Ben-Gurion's wishes. "In your room there's a picture of Stalin on the wall!" Ben-Gurion would scream at him. And there was. It's hard to recall, and even harder to explain, the atmosphere of those times. Many members of the Soviet Politburo were Jewish. In the end Stalin killed most of them, but until then some of our people deluded themselves into thinking that this "Jewish connection" in the Soviet Union could somehow work in our favor. The Russians were in constant contact with the French intelligentsia; many of them were Jewish too.

Meir Ya'ari, the Mapam–Hashomer Hatzair leader, sat in his kibbutz, Merhavia, and spoke of the dictatorship of the proletariat. He insisted on "ideological collectivism." He had a rabbinical air about him, and his followers were like disciples. He quoted from Lenin but still managed to sound like a rabbi! Moshe Sneh thought that if we supported Russia, Russia would support us. During his Mapam period, he was in close contact with Soviet diplomats. Mordechai Oren,* another senior Mapam figure, was also much too close to the Soviet Union. Even farther to the left were the Israeli Communists, who claimed that they could bring peace to the Middle East because they were class warriors and not nationalist warriors. They were ideologically anti-Zionist, though

---

* Oren (1906–85) was convicted and imprisoned in Czechoslovakia in 1953 on trumped-up charges of spying for Israel *against* the Soviet bloc. He was released in 1956.

Shmuel Mikunis of Maki, Israel's Arab-Jewish Communist Party, always claimed that he was responsible for the Czech arms deal with Israel in 1948.

It was inevitable that Zionism and Communism would frequently come into conflict over ideological issues. The Yevsektsia* was set up in the Soviet Union to fight Zionism by pitting a form of Jewish communism against Jewish nationalism. But some of our people wanted to be both Zionists and Communists. They were a minority, but vocal and passionate. Ben-Gurion fought them with all his strength.

Among the European socialist parties too, there were social revolutionaries who espoused Marxism. The British Labor Party, on the other hand, was staunchly social democratic; it had no truck with Communism. On the world stage, nonaligned meant nonaligned with America and, more often than not, aligned with the Soviet Union. The Indian prime minister Jawaharlal Nehru, one of the original apostles of nonalignment, was Soviet oriented. He upbraided us over the Sinai War in 1956, writing to Ben-Gurion, in effect, If you've got a regional dispute, take it to the UN. Don't collude with others and launch a war. Later, in 1962, when India and China became embroiled in a conflict over Ladakh, Nehru asked world leaders for military and diplomatic support. And Ben-Gurion wrote back to him, telling him to take it to the UN.

The formation of the government in the aftermath of the war in 1948—when Ben-Gurion moved, in effect, from supreme commander of army and country to democratically elected leader— still stirs up passionate debate about Ben-Gurion, Israel, and the nature of governance itself, especially in the fledgling days of a

---

*Yevsektsia was an agency established after the Russian Revolution to draw Jews to Communist ideology. In line with official Soviet doctrine, the Yevsektsia was deeply opposed to both Bundism and Zionism, labeling them forms of "bourgeois nationalism." Many Yevsektsia activists were subsequently executed in the Stalinist purges.

newly established democracy. In America's formative experience, George Washington famously stepped down after two terms as president, but his successor, John Adams, wound up with a vice president, Thomas Jefferson, from a different party, which created a bitter rivalry that tugged at the country as it found its footing. Ben-Gurion's insistence on excluding Menachem Begin's Herut Party; his decision to elevate—in effect, isolate—Chaim Weizmann in the office of the presidency; even Israel's place in the larger geopolitical environment of the Cold War world was a perennial subject of argument. To some degree it still is and offers another occasion for authorial dialogue.

DAVID LANDAU: Very early on, Ben-Gurion made a conscious, strategic decision to align Israel with the West. Some asked at the time, why be an American satellite?

SHIMON PERES: Ben-Gurion said the Cold War was not between two blocs, but between a bloc and a civilization. The West wasn't a bloc. It wasn't organized and disciplined like the Comintern was. He said of the Cold War that this was the first confrontation in history that was not over natural resources or territory but over the soul of man. Nikita Khrushchev taunted Western leaders with the prediction that "your grandchildren will be Communists." And the Americans predicted the opposite. Each side invested enormous resources to win hearts and minds. The Soviets were fortunate in that they had no Senate to investigate their huge foreign-aid ventures: to Indonesia, for instance, to build a vast stadium just because Sukarno wanted it; to Egypt, for arms and for the Aswan Dam. Did either effort succeed in winning over those societies to Communism? No; the Communist Party was outlawed in both countries!

The West, being free, was not a regimented "bloc" or "camp," which is itself a totalitarian concept. So Ben-Gurion didn't have formally to decide that we weren't part of the totalitarian camp. We just weren't. Israel's government was democratic. Anyway, the totalitarian camp didn't want to conquer our hearts. It made a mathematical calculation: how many people were there on our side, how many on the Arab side.

DAVID LANDAU: Could this question of Israel's orientation have ended up differently? Nahum Goldmann* thought so.

SHIMON PERES: Goldmann was too much of a man-of-the-world to be a national leader. And he didn't live in Israel. How could you be a leader if you didn't live here? Ben-Gurion was an ascetic. He had lived and worked on the land. He walked around in khaki fatigues!

DAVID LANDAU: Did Ben-Gurion want Goldmann to settle here and become leader of the opposition? How was it that Ben-Gurion was totally committed to setting up a parliamentary democracy and yet at the same time had such unveiled contempt for Begin, the leader of the opposition? How does that square?

SHIMON PERES: Israel's political culture was determined before the state came into being. It was transplanted en bloc from the Zionist movement to the Knesset and became the new state's democratic process. Ben-Gurion couldn't change it. He wanted to change the electoral system. He tried from the very beginning, but he couldn't. He never had a majority in the Knesset to change the system of proportional representation.

He understood that you can't solve all your problems at once. His method therefore was to take one issue at a time. The main problem was to set up the state. So even things that deeply worried and angered him, like the electoral system, had to be put off. He never stopped talking about electoral reform and trying to move it forward. But he didn't succeed. All the parties joined to foil him. It was convenient for them to continue with the old

*A prominent Diaspora Zionist leader, Goldmann (1895–1982) was born in Germany, lived in the United States for many years, and later moved to Switzerland. He was president of the World Jewish Congress (1948–77) and president of the World Zionist Organization (1956–68); a political "dove," he advocated Israeli neutrality under international guarantees.

system, which had been inherited from the Zionist Organization and the pre-state Yishuv.

DAVID LANDAU: But he did set up a parliamentary democracy, which is normally based on government versus opposition, even though he had contempt for the opposition.

SHIMON PERES: It wasn't "*the* opposition." When there are two parties, one is an opposition. When there are fourteen parties, there's chaos, there's scrambled eggs. Each time he had to confront a coalition-of-the-opposition, which kept changing like a kaleidoscope. But he wasn't one to be deterred. That was the game—so he played the game. He was a tactician with the best of them. One time he stitched together a governing coalition like this, another time like that.

DAVID LANDAU: But they accused him of autocracy. In real time—

SHIMON PERES: In real time they didn't see the reality. Only now the reality is clear to all. Now he stands taller than he did then. Now there's a consensus around his greatness. Then he was controversial. Why? Because he fought! You're controversial when you don't agree with everyone. And who says controversy's a bad thing! Once I was the most controversial man in Israel. Now I'm the most popular. And I don't know which is better! If you ask me, I miss times of controversy! What is popularity? It's not when people follow you; it's when you seek to please them! What is controversy? It's when you march ahead even though they're not following you. So people said things about him, so what? Did he ever put anyone in prison for saying things? The concept of leadership that we learned from him was not to be on top, but to be ahead.

DAVID LANDAU: You yourself behaved very differently from Ben-Gurion as prime minister and as leader of the opposition. As prime minister you would invite the leader of the opposition for regular briefings. As leader of the opposition, you were invited by them. And when governments were being formed, you at least talked to each other about serving together, and sometimes the talks led to agreements. Those were the democratic, parliamentary procedures in your time.

SHIMON PERES: Ben-Gurion ruled out Herut because he saw them as mere wordmongers.

DAVID LANDAU: What kind of disqualification is that?

SHIMON PERES: He didn't disqualify them. But if he could oppose them, what's wrong with that? He wasn't the pope. He didn't give orders. He fought them. He ridiculed them. Everyone else was afraid to fight, to clash, to confront. He wasn't afraid.

DAVID LANDAU: He admired the British system. But at least in this respect, he didn't apply it.

SHIMON PERES: Because there weren't only two or three parties in Israel, as there were in Britain. If there had been, he would have. If there were fourteen parties in Britain, it wouldn't be a parliamentary democracy at all! And if there were fourteen parties in America, it wouldn't be a democracy with a president as head of state. *That* was the essence of the problem.

Ben-Gurion saw the Communists as upholding loyalty to a foreign entity, and he slashed at them, ridiculed them. Made them a laughingstock. Fought them with irony.

DAVID LANDAU: Fought them with the Shin Bet*?

SHIMON PERES: No. I think the Shin Bet simply warned him on rare occasions when there were serious suspicions of foreign espionage. There was some serious Soviet espionage here in Israel, in the top political echelons. People were caught. There was real danger. But who didn't watch their own backyard at that time? The United States didn't do it? England didn't do it? The whole world seethed with conspiracies.

DAVID LANDAU: Sitting here in this room, in your current job, do you sometimes think critically about Ben-Gurion's relations with Weizmann, especially during those last years of Weizmann's life? I'm especially thinking about Weizmann's immor-

---

*The Shin Bet is Israel's internal security service.

tal but poignant comment that the only place he was permitted to stick his nose was into his handkerchief.

SHIMON PERES: As I've said, Ben-Gurion respected and admired Weizmann, despite their differences over the years. Those differences were very real. Remember, a significant part of the Mapai leadership leaned at times toward Weizmann rather than toward Ben-Gurion. People like Sprinzak, Kaplan, and Sharett.*

DAVID LANDAU: Why didn't he have the generosity of spirit to change his attitude toward Weizmann after all their old arguments had become history?

SHIMON PERES: He gave him respect. He accompanied him to his inauguration as president.

DAVID LANDAU: So why did Weizmann have the feeling that apart from honor they gave him nothing? They made no use of his political wisdom.

If you'll permit me, without making comparisons: We are having this conversation in 2010, when there is a politically "contrary" configuration between president and prime minister. You and Benjamin Netanyahu were political rivals. Yet the two of you appear to have achieved a good constitutional relationship, in which you speak to each other frequently and project a sense of mutual regard. Which seems to mean it's possible, if you try.

SHIMON PERES: When he became president, Weizmann was elderly, and he was already ill. Weizmann may have viewed the presidency on the American model, but Ben-Gurion saw it more as a symbolic role. This was something of a disappointment for Weizmann. After Weizmann's death in November 1952, Ben-Gurion offered the presidency to Albert Einstein. He wanted a scientist in the position. Like Socrates, he thought a savant should stand at the head of the nation. Einstein declined, and Ben-Gurion's old friend Yitzhak Ben-Zvi was elected president

---

*Yosef Sprinzak (1885–1959) was the first speaker of the Knesset (1949–59); Eliezer Kaplan (1891–1952) was Ben-Gurion's first minister of finance.

and graced the position as a modest and much-loved figure for two five-year terms.

DAVID LANDAU: Did you ever hear an expression of regret from Ben-Gurion regarding the course of his relations with Weizmann?

SHIMON PERES: Ben-Gurion was not a gossip.

9

Jewish People, Jewish Policy

Ben-Gurion didn't cry tears, but in his heart he was weeping.

Even before the War of Independence ended, Ben-Gurion was directing a good deal of his energies to the challenge of immigration. He swept aside all doubts and hesitations—some from within his own party—over the wisdom of encouraging an unfettered mass immigration of Jews into Israel, without regard to the "absorptive capacity" (that hated Mandatory term!) of the new state's economy. The figures are indeed phenomenal. More than 100,000 immigrants arrived during the war itself—from May to December 1948. In 1949 the number was 239,576; in 1950, 170,249; and in 1951, 175,095. In all, 686,748 immigrants arrived in four years—more than the original Jewish population of the newborn state.

The newcomers were housed at first in empty British Army camps and abandoned houses. When these were filled to overflowing, the government supplied tents and tin shacks. Toward the end of 1949, with the physical conditions in some of the immigrants' camps really wretched, Levi Eshkol, then treasurer of the Jewish Agency, initiated the idea of *maabarot*, or transit camps, for immigrants, in the suburbs of major cities or in outlying areas of the country where the government was interested, for strategic reasons, in dispersing the population. The idea was that the newcomers could live in these facilities for longer periods than they could in the very rudimentary immigrants' camps, and that they would be encouraged to go out to work—often in public works projects initiated by the government—rather than sinking into a lifestyle of unemployment and reliance on state handouts.

On April 4, 1950, Ben-Gurion and Eliezer Kaplan took part in a meeting of the Jewish Agency Executive at which this new approach to immigrant absorption was endorsed, and in May the first *maabara* was built, in the Jerusalem hills. Over the next two years, an additional 120 *maabarot* were put up around the country; in their heyday they were home to more than a quarter of a million new Israelis. Most came from neighboring countries in the Middle East and North Africa; some came from Romania, the only Eastern European country then permitting aliyah. The project was administered jointly by the agency and by the ministry of labor, under Golda Meir.

Conditions in the hastily built *maabarot* were not much better than in the earlier immigrant camps. Roofs leaked in the winter and provided no insulation from the torrid summer sun. Medical facilities were inadequate, sanitary conditions poor, education for the children patchy. Ben-Gurion sent the army to work in the immigrant camps and later in the *maabarot*. His view was that the IDF was not solely a fighting force but also an important social instrument for assisting the absorption of its own immigrant-soldiers and for helping absorb others. I remember visiting one camp with Ben-Gurion. It was winter, and it was freezing cold in the huts, pouring rain outside. There were children swarming about us, some clearly sick. No one had jobs. They cried, and we cried. Ben-Gurion didn't cry tears, but in his heart he was weeping.

At first, the soldiers taught Hebrew and life skills to the newcomers. But when the ravages of a hard winter took their toll on the *maabarot* in 1950–51, the IDF began taking a much more central role in the physical maintenance of the buildings and in the social, educational, and medical welfare of the immigrants. The same thing happened the following winter. But the soldiers' work encountered opposition from religious circles, who claimed that their goal was to woo the immigrants away from their religious lifestyles and turn them into Mapai voters, which was as untrue as it was cynical.

Some of the North African immigrants came with messianic ideas, but Ben-Gurion never exploited their simple faith or tried to pass himself off as the messiah (as his critics accused him of doing). He said the country welcomed immigration for reasons of both "salvation" and "redemption"; that is, for people who needed to get away from where they were living, and for people who came out of choice, to enrich their lives as Jews. He didn't distinguish between them. Some officials wanted a policy of "selective aliyah," with priority given to younger and more productive people. I don't think it was ever a serious proposition. Ben-Gurion, at any rate, was moved and excited as soon as the aliyah from Yemen and North Africa got under way. He would not hear of any reservations or any selectivity.

I n the early 1950s Ben-Gurion instituted a prize of 100 *lirot* (more than $100, not an insignificant sum then) for mothers who gave birth to ten children. The letter accompanying the check was signed by the prime minister himself. "It is a token of admiration and encouragement for a Mother in Israel who has delivered and raised ten children," the letter read. "Rejoice that you have been blessed to raise them to Torah [i.e., to study], to work, and to do good deeds for the benefit of the homeland and the nation. May your hands be strengthened."

"Mother in Israel" was a traditional Jewish phrase, although the prize money was also made available to Arab mothers who fulfilled the required complement of offspring. This in no way deterred Ben-Gurion, although his intention was obviously to boost the Jewish population of Israel. Somewhere in the back of his mind there was always a vague, inchoate thought that some Arab Israelis might one day become Jewish Israelis by some process of voluntary conversion. And anyway, as he wrote to a doctor who protested that his prize spurred the birth of poor, weak, and sickly children, "I don't think a woman has ten children in order to win the prize, just as I don't think a scientist or author—if I may resort to such analogy—does his creative work in order to win prizes." He pointed out to the protesting doctor that the prize was sent "to a mother who has ten living children, not to a mother who gave birth to a total of ten children, even if some of them have died meanwhile."

And alongside all of this absorption and acculturation of Jewish immigrants into the new Israel, there was the question, sometimes addressed overtly and sometimes implicitly, of what Israeli Judaism would consist of. What role would religion play in the life of the state?

Ben-Gurion's 1949 coalition with the Religious Front, an alliance of the Zionist-Orthodox Mizrachi Party and the non-Zionist, ultra-Orthodox Agudat Yisrael, flowed from a concordat that he had reached almost two years earlier with Agudat Yisrael on matters of state and religion in the still-to-be-created Jewish state. In a letter signed by himself, Rabbi Yehudah Leib Maimon, and Yitzhak Gruenbaum,* Ben-Gurion noted that the anticipated state must provide and protect freedom of conscience for all its citizens and must not be a theocracy. It would thus win the endorsement of the United Nations, which it needed in order to come into existence. It would have within its borders, moreover, Christians and Muslims as well as Jews, and "obviously must undertake in advance full equality for all its citizens and no coercion or discrimination in matters of religion." Furthermore, the constitution of

---

*Rabbi Yehuda Leib Maimon (born Yehuda Leib Fishman; 1875–1962) was a leader of the Mizrachi Party and a member of the board of the Jewish Agency; he later served in the Knesset and as minister of religions and war victims. Yitzhak Gruenbaum (1879–1970) was a member of the Jewish Agency Executive and the Provisional Government; he was also the first minister of the interior.

the new state would be determined by its citizens and could not be laid down in advance. Having said that, however, the Jewish Agency Executive was prepared to pledge to Agudat Yisrael that its own position on the key issues of state and religion was as follows:

1. Shabbat. Clearly, the legal day of rest in the Jewish state will be the Sabbath day, with obvious exceptions for Christians and others to rest on their religious day of rest.

2. Kashrut. All the necessary measures will be taken to ensure that in every state eating facility . . . there will be kosher food.

3. Personal status. All the members of the Executive understand the seriousness of the problem and the great difficulties it entails, and all the component-parts of the Agency will do whatever is possible to facilitate the deep need of believing Jews to prevent, Heaven forfend, a split within the House of Israel. [That meant, in practice, that marriage and divorce would be administered exclusively by the Orthodox chief rabbinate for Jews, and by other statutory religious authorities for Muslims and Christians.]

4. Education. Each educational stream will have its autonomy ensured, as is the case in the Yishuv now, and there will be no infringement on the freedom of religion of any group. The state, of course, will determine the required minimum of compulsory studies in Hebrew language, history, sciences, etc., and will supervise the fulfillment of this minimum requirement.

This letter became the core of what is known as the "status quo," an uneasy arrangement governing issues of state and religion that has been the subject of incessant political strife to the present day. In addition, and even more controversially, Ben-Gurion had agreed in 1948 to exempt full-time yeshiva students from military service. There were only a few hundred of them at the time. Nevertheless, this was not an easy decision. The war was raging throughout the country, and all able-bodied men had been mobilized. The yeshiva deans threatened to move their institutions abroad if the concession was not granted. I was instrumental later in negotiating on Ben-Gurion's behalf with the ultra-Orthodox Council of Yeshivot and in formalizing the exemption. Over the years, and with the changing demography, it has grown to embrace tens of thousands of men of military age who would otherwise be serving in the regular army or the reserves. It is a perennial focus of political and judicial battles. And it offers an opportunity to assess not only Ben-Gurion's leadership but also the complex twinning of religion and nationhood that had not been an option since the destruction of the Temple, but that the creation of the state made possible once again. This historical context is very important.

Ben-Gurion was a master tactician, and his confrontation with the Orthodox was a prime example of that. If he had made it a fight against faith, he would have lost, because the number of people in Israel who defined themselves as people of faith was huge.

Ben-Gurion's approach to the Rabbinate was in some sense deeply personal, at times almost conversational. He was pitting his self-assured Jewishness against theirs, but he also saw the state itself as a place of natural overlap and organic resolution for religious differences within a larger context of Jewish nationalism. And in that spirit, we break once more into conversation ourselves.

DAVID LANDAU: Did Ben-Gurion think the number of traditionally observant Jews would decline?

SHIMON PERES: That's not important, because his fight was never against the individual Orthodox Jew but against the Orthodox political establishment. If an Orthodox Jew or an Orthodox Jewish community made aliyah, he was automatically and wholeheartedly supportive.

But beyond that, yes, he saw changes developing in the Jewish state. We believed that the Diasporic version of Judaism was transient. We didn't think we Israelis would stop being Jews! You can't be Zionist without being Jewish. But we saw two historic perversions in this Diasporic version of Judaism: the Diasporic condition itself—statelessness, homelessness—and the aping of non-Jewish values. Ben-Gurion's objection was not to the religion but to the organized "church." He maintained that pristine Judaism had no hierarchy, no God's deputy, no bishops. Judaism is a faith, he held. Everyone is connected directly to God.

DAVID LANDAU: And therefore?

SHIMON PERES: Therefore the Rabbinate should not run our lives. Therefore *halacha* [Jewish religious law] should not be the law of the land.

DAVID LANDAU: But the opposite happened.

SHIMON PERES: No, it didn't. Israel is a secular state. The Orthodox have bargaining power, so everything had to be done by compromise. But Israel is not under religious control: It's not a *halachic* country, it's not a theocracy. Ben-Gurion opposed religious coercion and opposed antireligious coercion.

DAVID LANDAU: Ideally, would Ben-Gurion have preferred an American-style constitution with separation of church and state, rather than a European-style nation-state with religious antecedents?

SHIMON PERES: No, he thought it would be possible to provide another interpretation of Jewish law, one that holds that Judaism consists of variations. What you're asking is complicated: Judaism is both *leom*, nationality, and *dat*, religion. Therefore, it is impossible to separate the two. To say "I am a Jew" is like saying "I am a white horse." "White horse" is not two things, white and horse. It's a white horse. When you say you are a Jew, you are stating your nationality and your religion at one and the same time. They are inseparable. What is separable are the institutions. Ben-Gurion wanted to separate the institutions of faith and state. In the Bible there were kings, prophets, judges, and priests. The prophets reflected and articulated dissatisfaction; morally at least, they were more exalted than the kings.

In Poland (then part of the Russian Empire) with members of the Plonsk branch of the socialist-Zionist organization Poalei Zion, sometime in the early 1900s. Ben-Gurion, still known as David Gruen, is in the bottom row, center. "David and his comrades drafted their response to the Uganda Plan, which had been submitted to the 1903 Sixth Zionist Congress in Basel. 'We have reached the conclusion that the way to fight Ugandism is to make *aliyah*.' They were not yet adults, but their thinking at that time would inform and shape their entire adult lives." (*Government Press Office, State of Israel*)

With Yitzhak Ben-Zvi (*right*) as law students in Turkey in 1912. "At that time, Ben-Gurion believed that the Yishuv's basic political interest lay in nurturing its loyalty to Turkey." (*Government Press Office, State of Israel*)

As a member of the Jewish Legion of the British Army during World War I. "Ben-Gurian's unit of the Jewish Legion eventually marched into Palestine from Egypt in December 1918, after the war was officially over. Unable to distinguish himself in military prowess, Ben-Gurion, by now a corporal, plunged straight back into his foremost field of distinction— Zionist affairs." (*Government Press Office, State of Israel*)

Paula and David Ben-Gurion in New York in 1918, shortly after their wedding. "Russian-born and Yiddish-speaking like himself, she was by some accounts a member of Poalei Zion, but by her own account was not a particularly ardent Zionist." (*Government Press Office, State of Israel*)

The family at home in Tel Aviv in 1929. *From left to right:* David, Renana (on his lap), Paula, Geula, Avigdor Gruen (his father), and Amos. "Ben-Gurion tried, but the fact is he did not give much time to family life. He spent long periods traveling abroad, alone. And even at home he was busy around the clock with his work." (*Government Press Office, State of Israel*)

With Chaim Weizmann, who would become Israel's first president, in Switzerland in 1945. "There was never much love lost between them, even though Ben-Gurion wrote to Weizmann in 1937, 'All my life I have loved you . . . I have loved you with all my heart and soul.' Weizmann was to mention Ben-Gurion precisely twice in his six-hundred-page autobiography." (*Government Press Office, State of Israel*)

May 14, 1948. Reading Israel's Declaration of Independence at the Tel Aviv Museum to the People's Assembly and to the world. "Throughout the country," he wrote in his diary, "there is profound joy and jubilation . . . I feel like the bereaved among the rejoicers." (*Zoltan Kluger/Government Press Office, State of Israel*)

June 22, 1948. The *Altalena* on fire off the coast of Tel Aviv. "'This is an attempt to destroy the army,' Ben-Gurion thundered. 'This is an attempt to murder the state. In these two matters there cannot be any compromise.' The cabinet backed him . . . The Palmach commander Yigal Allon, now a senior IDF general, was put in charge of the operation." (*Hans Pinn/Government Press Office, State of Israel*)

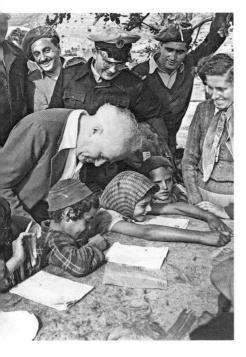

With new immigrants at a school in Farradiya, a transit camp in northern Israel, in 1950. "More than 700,000 Jews, beginning in the 1940s and continuing through 1967, had to leave the Arab countries where their families had been living for centuries. They were all absorbed here. We thought, perhaps naïvely, that this would be an example for the other side." (*David Eldan/Government Press Office, State of Israel*)

As prime minister and defense minister in 1953, with the Israel Defense Forces senior staff and Shimon Peres, who was director-general of the defense ministry at the time. Peres is seated at Ben-Gurion's left, Moshe Dayan at his right, and Yitzhak Rabin is standing between Ben-Gurion and Peres. "Ben-Gurion wanted to join the paratroopers [so that he could] do the required series of jumps from airplanes. Dayan said, 'You want to be a paratrooper? So, I'm your commander. I command you to be something else: be prime minister!'" (*Government Press Office, State of Israel*)

With Paula and a newborn goat at Kibbutz Sdeh Boker in 1954. "I feel here like I felt the first time I set foot in Eretz Yisrael," he wrote. (*Fritz Cohen/Government Press Office, State of Israel*)

Ben-Gurion standing on his head, on the beach at the Sharon Hotel in Herzliya in 1957. A devoted student of Moshe Feldenkrais, Ben-Gurion claimed that the Israeli physicist's exercise methods cured his lumbago. (*Paul Goldman/Eretz Israel Museum, Tel Aviv*)

At the White House with President Harry Truman and Ambassador Abba Eban in January 1951. "Eleven minutes after Ben-Gurion's proclamation of independence, the American government announced that the United States would recognize the new state. It was Truman's personal decision, over-ruling the professionals at the State Department." (*Fritz Cohen/Government Press Office, State of Israel*)

With Eleanor Roosevelt, at home in Tel Aviv, in 1952. "It seems to me," Mrs. Roosevelt wrote to President Truman in January 1948, "that if the UN does not pull through and enforce the partition and protection of people in general in Palestine, we are now facing a very serious situation in which its position for the future is at stake." (*Fritz Cohen/Government Press Office, State of Israel*)

Finally meeting Sir Winston Churchill, in London in 1960. "Ben-Gurion was in awe of Churchill's 'magnetic leadership, powerful eloquence, contagious courage . . . deep sense of history, and an unshakeable faith in the destiny of his people . . . History would have been quite different if there had been no Churchill.' He would never have written or said that of himself, of course. But I say it without reservation: I truly believe that without Ben-Gurion the State of Israel would not have come into being." (© *From the Jewish Chronicle Archive/Heritage Images/Imagestate*)

With West German chancellor Konrad Adenauer in New York in May 1960. At this meeting Ben-Gurion obtained from Adenauer an agreement for a half-billion-dollar loan, beyond the original $700 million in goods and services West Germany had agreed to provide as reparation payments. (*Gamma-Keystone via Getty Images*)

With French president Charles de Gaulle, at the Palais de l'Élysée in Paris, in June 1960. "Ben-Gurion was skeptical at first about the French connection, though he let me pursue it without hindrance. I saw we were not going to get weapons from the Americans or from the British, and definitely not from the Russians. I visited de Gaulle in his office. He knew what we were doing, and he supported it." (*Fritz Cohen/ Government Press Office, State of Israel*)

With President John F. Kennedy in New York in May 1961. "As Kennedy walked Ben-Gurion alone to the elevator, he said, 'I know that I owe my election to your people.' How could he repay the Israeli leader for this support? he asked. 'You can repay us by being a great president of the United States,' Ben-Gurion replied." (*New York Daily News via Getty Images*)

With Frank Sinatra in Jerusalem in May 1962. Sinatra had just come from Nazareth, where he presided at the groundbreaking ceremonies for the Frank Sinatra International Youth Center for Arab and Jewish children. (© *David Rubinger / Courtesy of the family of Frank Sinatra*)

From left to right: Ben-Gurion, Ezer Weizman, and Menachem Begin at the King David Hotel in Jerusalem, in November 1967. "When Ben-Gurion attacked someone, it was over his position, not his characteristics. He didn't hate Begin personally. Personal hatred was not a factor at all." (*Ilan Bruner / Government Press Office, State of Israel*)

With Southern Command General Ariel Sharon at an Israeli army installation near the Suez Canal in January 1971. "'As for the Sinai Peninsula,' Ben-Gurion said after the Six-Day War, 'we should demand direct negotiations with Nasser, and if he agrees to peace with us and to free navigation in the Straits of Tiran and in the Suez Canal, then we should evacuate Sinai.' This is in fact what happened, in stages, after the Yom Kippur War." *(Getty Images)*

With Prime Minister Golda Meir in January 1972, at the Twenty-eighth Zionist Congress in Jerusalem. "When history comes to be written," Ben-Gurion told her in 1948, "it shall be said that there was a Jewish woman who found the money which enabled the establishment of the state." *(Hulton Archive / Getty Images)*

With Shimon Peres and Moshe Dayan in 1972. "Ben-Gurion deeply respected Dayan. Dayan and I were like two colts galloping in the field." (*Photo by David Harris/© Rivka Harris*)

October 24, 1984. Shimon Peres at Ben-Gurion's graveside at Sdeh Boker, during his first visit to the Negev as prime minister. "Ben-Gurion seems to me now to be an emblem not only of the energy that created the State of Israel but also of the sort of leadership that the country so desperately needs today if it is to find its way to peace and security." (*Chanania Herman/Government Press Office, State of Israel*)

The priests had a function to fulfill. But they weren't a decision-making institution; they were, rather, service providers. Ben-Gurion didn't want a priestly establishment; he didn't want any religious establishment. But Ben-Gurion decided not to fight this ideological battle. His leadership was based on prioritization—both because he believed this was the way to lead, and because the objective circumstances of coalition life dictated that you couldn't deal with even two things at once. You had to choose one issue and gather a coalition around it. He couldn't have held a coalition together had he pushed, say, four separate issues at once, because that would have created a common denominator for all the rejectionists on all four issues to unite against *him*. For instance, the dispute between socialism and social revolution did not interest the Orthodox. But if he'd fought on all fronts simultaneously and with the same passion—socialism versus communism, secularism versus religion, a free-market economy versus a centrally directed economy—he'd have united all of them against him and remained in the minority. So he took up one issue with total passion: setting up the state.

In his battles with the Orthodox, he exploited the fact that many of them tended to focus on the Talmud and neglected the Bible. He put the Bible at the center of his philosophy and of the national ethos as he sought to fashion it, because the basis of the Bible was in Eretz Yisrael, whereas the Talmud, the "Oral Law," was a product of the Diaspora. The Orthodox weren't ready for that. They didn't know how to handle it. If he'd have come out against everything relating to Jewish religious practices, they'd have said he wasn't an authentic Jew, that he was an assimilationist. But he advocated the restoration of the Jewish people to the Bible and of the Bible to the Jewish people. As he famously declared in his testimony to the Peel Commission, "The Bible is our Mandate." He initiated a Bible-study circle at his home, and the annual Bible Quiz, which became a popular national event, was his idea. Religious Zionist leaders like Rabbi Yehuda Leib Maimon and Dr. Yosef Burg* were captivated by his enthusiasm. He liked Maimon, partly because Maimon understood what he meant by *mamlachtiyut*. Maimon was a serious intellectual but was a very practical politician at the same time. Ben-Gurion, for his part, thought he would be able to understand the Orthodox viewpoint better through conversations with Maimon than with anyone else. They seemed to enjoy each other. Ben-Gurion told me that Maimon once asked him, "What's the one thing God can't do?" Ben-Gurion, taking on the proffered role, insisted that God can do everything. To which Maimon replied, "No, even God can't change the past."

DAVID LANDAU: He seems to have had a fairly good relationship too with the leader of the ultra-Orthodox Agudat Yisrael, Rabbi Yitzhak-Meir Levin, who was a brother-in-law of the Hasidic Rebbe of Gur. I heard this story from Levin's son-in-law and aide, Moshe Sheinfeld. One night during the War of Independence, Ben-Gurion arrived unannounced at Levin's home on Ben-Yehuda Street in Tel Aviv. They closeted themselves away for two hours. Sheinfeld presumed they were discussing urgent matters of state; Levin was a minister in the government. But Levin reported later that Ben-Gurion had asked about the Orthodox view of the famous eighteenth- century dispute between two leading scholars of that age, Rabbi Jonathan Eybeschutz and Rabbi Jacob Emden. He explained that he'd been reading all the Haskalah literature [writings on Jewish subjects by secular Jews] on the subject but wanted to hear the Orthodox viewpoint.

SHIMON PERES: That sounds authentic, and I'm sure it was sincere on Ben-Gurion's part. He was unboundedly curious. Though at the same time, of course, this sort of intimate, schol-

---

*Burg (1909–99) was a longtime leader of the Mizrachi Party and held many ministerial positions over the course of his career.

arly conversation was intended to create confidence on their part in his leadership and his good faith.

DAVID LANDAU: You were his emissary in the matter of exempting yeshiva students from army service. Would you say that his subtext in this mission of yours was that with time this problem would simply disappear, or at least would not grow? History has of course shown that that was not the case, and the yeshivot have grown exponentially.

SHIMON PERES: His purpose was to remove every obstacle on the path to the creation of the state, which for him was an ongoing process, not a one-time event that took place in 1948. He wasn't thinking about what was going to happen later. He sent me on many assignments. For some reason he thought I could do things, let's say, unconventionally. So for all sorts of unconventional things, he'd send me. He once asked me, for instance, to set up a national soccer team that would beat the world.

DAVID LANDAU: And why weren't you successful?

SHIMON PERES: Because it was impossible. There's a limit to what you can do.

DAVID LANDAU: You didn't think of buying foreign players?

SHIMON PERES: No, it never occurred to me. The team was going to be purely Israeli.

DAVID LANDAU: So this was one of your failures?

SHIMON PERES: Yes, you can put that on the list. Anyway, to be completely frank, in negotiating with the venerable rabbis, I felt like I was sitting with my grandfather.

DAVID LANDAU: Who was murdered by the Nazis.

SHIMON PERES: Yes, who was burned to death in his synagogue as the head of his community. And who influenced my life, in a positive way, more than anyone else. Personally, I had *yirat kavod* [reverence] toward these people. I didn't sit with them to haggle. At the same time, I knew that Ben-Gurion's approach was *mamlachti*, and that was the basis of my mission. First, I asked myself: Imagine there were Buddhists in Israel and they'd asked for 150 of their people to be monks. I would have approved. So for Jews not? Second, they claimed very cogently that throughout the Diaspora period even the czars and other rulers had facilitated the existence of yeshivot. Did I want all the yeshivot to be abroad? I thought this was a powerful argument. I reported everything to Ben-Gurion—except the bit about feeling like I was sitting in front of my grandfather.

DAVID LANDAU: That's what I wanted to ask: Could you have said to Ben-Gurion that you felt reverence for these people?

SHIMON PERES: Yes, I had no difficulty with that. But strange though it may sound, I'm shy. I'm an introvert. So I didn't mention it. But not because I was worried about how he would have reacted. I had no fear of Ben-Gurion in that way.

10

A Nation Among Nations

*For him the Zionist tenet that Israel was the state of all
the Jewish people was a meaningful and practical precept.*

The first major international challenge that Ben-Gurion faced
after the war was a move by the international community in
late 1949 to revert to the internationalization of Jerusalem, as pre-
scribed in the original Partition Plan. A counterproposal by
Ben-Gurion to leave the city divided between the two neighboring states, Israel and Jordan, but to internationalize the Holy
Places received no support. The UN General Assembly passed an
internationalization resolution on December 9, 1949. The next day
Ben-Gurion proposed to the cabinet that Israel declare Jerusalem
its capital and move the seat of government there without further
delay. Until then the Knesset and the ministries had functioned,
temporarily, in Tel Aviv. Sharett cabled his resignation from New
York, but Ben-Gurion rejected it and neglected to inform the
other ministers of it. The ministries, apart from the defense ministry and the foreign ministry, loaded their files and desks on
trucks and made their way up the hills of Jerusalem to the capital.

The move triggered an uproar in foreign chanceries, but
Ben-Gurion ignored it, confident that he was effectively repre-
senting both claimants to the divided city. Secret negotiations
were proceeding at this time between his emissaries and King
Abdullah, with a view to concluding a full peace treaty with Jordan. Sadly, though, that was not to be: The king was assassinated
on the steps of the al-Aqsa Mosque in East Jerusalem on July 20,

1951. A pro-peace Lebanese statesman, Riad Sulh, was also assassinated at around this time. With Syria endemically unstable and the Egyptian monarchy weakening (it was to fall within a year), peace prospects faded.

Ben-Gurion, searching for a patron among the Great Powers with whom to ally, conducted a brief and unsuccessful flirtation with the British, with a view to Israel possibly joining the British Commonwealth. Overtures to President Dwight Eisenhower's new Republican administration were cold-shouldered too. Secretary of State John Foster Dulles made it clear that his sights were set primarily on strengthening America's ties with the Arab world.

On the financial front, where a crisis loomed even more imminently, Ben-Gurion scored a notable triumph in launching Israel Bonds at a mass rally in New York, at Madison Square Garden, in May 1951. In addition to the traditional forms of philanthropy, Jews throughout the Diaspora would be able to support the Jewish state by investing in its sovereign debt. But the amounts raised were nowhere near enough to cover the costs of defense and immigrant absorption. Nor were the austerity measures that the government implemented sufficient to raise income and save hard currency. Ben-Gurion now began a discreet dialogue with the government of the newly established Federal Republic of Germany, with a view to obtaining massive cash restitution for the economic devastation visited on the Jewish people by the Nazis. The State of Israel, he held, could legitimately claim to be the heir of the murdered millions. "The reason lay in the final injunction of the inarticulate six million, the victims of Nazism, whose very murder was a ringing cry for Israel to arise, to be strong and prosperous, to safeguard her peace and security, and to prevent such a disaster from ever again overwhelming the Jewish people."

Whatever the cogency of this logic, many Israelis could not bear the thought of taking the tainted "blood money." The negotiation with West Germany triggered sustained and sometimes violent political protests. They were led by Begin and the right, but they expressed the anguish and bitter opposition felt by some of the survivors and their families across the entire political spectrum. At the end of 1951 Nahum Goldmann procured from the West German chancellor, Konrad Adenauer, a commitment to accept an Israeli claim for $1 billion as the basis for the negotiation. On January 7, 1952, Ben-Gurion addressed the Knesset. "A crime of such enormity can have no material compensation," he declared.

Any compensation, of whatever size, is no compensation for the loss of human life or expiation for the sufferings and agonies of men, women, and children, old people and infants. However . . . the government of Israel considers itself bound to demand of the German people restitution for the stolen Jewish property. Let not the murderers of our people also be the beneficiaries of its property.

As Ben-Gurion spoke in the Knesset, Begin addressed a rally in a city square nearby: "When you fired at us with a cannon, I gave the order: No! Today I shall give the order, Yes! This will be a battle of life and death." Begin insisted that "every German is a Nazi," and that the proposed restitution was a moral abomination. He led a raucous crowd toward the Knesset building, where they clashed with police and threw stones through the windows. He mounted the rostrum in the chamber, but pandemonium erupted, and the Speaker tried to silence him. "If I do not speak, none shall speak," the leader of the opposition vowed.

The next day Ben-Gurion broadcast to the nation. He said he took Begin's threat of civil war seriously but assured the public that "the State possesses sufficient forces and means to protect Israel's sovereignty and freedom and to prevent thugs and political assassins from taking control."

In the Knesset the debate raged for two full days. In the end the government won the vote by a majority of nine. One month later the reparations agreement with Germany was signed, providing Israel with more than $700 million worth of goods and services over a twelve-year period. And the German government paid an additional $100 million to Jewish organizations.*

Coupled with what might be called his policy of single-minded pragmatism focused unswervingly on the State of Israel's needs, Ben-Gurion conducted a foreign policy that was consciously and consistently Jewish and designed to save or assist Jews wherever in the world they were. For him the Zionist tenet that Israel was the state of all the Jewish people was a meaningful and practical precept. It required, he believed, that the foreign policy of the State of Israel be a Jewish foreign policy.

For instance, he feared for Soviet Jews, who were in danger of spiritual destruction. To assist them, he founded Netiv, also known as Lishkat Hakesher, a discreet agency under his trusted aide Shaul Avigur that forged links with Soviet Jews suffering under Stalin's persecutions. Its purpose was to save every Jew from the claws of Communism, and to try to maintain Jewish education and Jewish culture within the Soviet Union through myriad underground contacts. Compounding the challenge was the fact that the NKVD, the Soviet Union's secret police organization, was full of Jews. Some were still believing Communists, right up to the end. They were ready to turn in their own parents and their friends. The same was true at the top. What kind of a Jew was Stalin's close Politburo colleague Lazar Kaganovitch? He was a Jew against Jews. It is said that Vyacheslav Molotov's Jewish wife, in prison for "treason," wept at the news of the death of Stalin. It's incredible. These people were drugged.

In the spring of 1953 Ben-Gurion was driving through the Negev on his way back from Eilat when he chanced on a group of young people working in the sun. They explained to him that they had served in the area during the war and had decided they wanted to

---

*This was in addition to personal reparations paid out to survivors of the Holocaust.

set up a kibbutz there. It was to be called Sdeh Boker. Ben-Gurion did not, as far as is known, ask on the spot whether he could join.

But very soon afterward he informed his wife, his colleagues, and his future kibbutz comrades that he had decided to quit his job and make his home at Sdeh Boker, working alongside these pioneers on what he believed needed to be the next great challenge for Israel: making the desert bloom in the most literal sense. In November 1953 he submitted his formal resignation to President Ben-Zvi, and one month later he and Paula set out on their new life in the far south. Soon the local and world press published photographs of him shearing sheep and earnestly engaging in other agricultural toil.

"I feel here like I felt the first time I set foot in Eretz Yisrael," he wrote from Sdeh Boker to the girl who was his first love and who now, forty-seven years later, saluted his latter-day act of pioneering. "You can't imagine how happy I was to receive your letter," he wrote to Rachel Nelkin, now Rachel Beit-Halachmi. "It took me back to years even earlier [than our aliyah], to the years of our youth in Plonsk." The two of them stayed in touch after that. In 1959, with Ben-Gurion back in office, she asked him for "half an hour" to show him a memorial book on Plonsk that she was preparing. He replied that he would gladly grant her much more than half an hour and would arrange a meeting in his Tel Aviv office so that she needn't trouble to come up to Jerusalem. When he finally stepped down in 1963, engulfed in controversy, she wrote to console him, and he replied reassuring her, "I'm not overwhelmed when I hear praise and adulation, and I'm not stricken when I read attacks and calumnies."

"I admire you and have always admired you, and feel close to your family," she wrote to him in 1968. "The whole world knows that David brought us our state, our independence."

"I don't have to tell you what your letter means to me," he replied, inviting her to Sdeh Boker. He visited her and her two daughters at her home in Givatayim, near Tel Aviv. They talked over old times and evidently both enjoyed it; later on she went to visit him "at your oasis in the desert."

11

Defense of the Realm

Ben-Gurion was so brave that he didn't fear being afraid.
You need courage to fear. He didn't hide it. I often heard
expressions of very deep anxiety but also of faith that
we'd overcome.

Before leaving the prime minister's office for Sdeh Boker in December 1954, Ben-Gurion sought to ensure that things would function adequately in his absence. He blundered by announcing that Levi Eshkol was his preferred candidate for prime minister, apparently without ascertaining whether Eshkol was interested in the position. As it turned out, he was categorically not interested, and the party's choice was Moshe Sharett, whom Ben-Gurion accepted without good grace. Sharett continued to hold the foreign ministry, while the key post of minister of defense was to be held by Pinhas Lavon who, as minister without portfolio, had filled in for Ben-Gurion several times in the past, including during a three-month vacation prior to his official departure.

Relations between these two senior ministers, Sharett and Lavon, were bad from the start, and they steadily worsened as Lavon adopted an extremely activist policy in response to Arab border infiltrations, in open and demeaning disregard of Sharett's policy of moderation. The new IDF chief of staff, Moshe Dayan, whom Ben-Gurion had put in place before his departure, was himself an activist by outlook and temperament. But relations between him and the vain and suspicious Lavon soon deteriorated too. I was director-general of the defense ministry, and I soon fell out of Lavon's good graces as well.

A precursor of things to come had already occurred while Ben-Gurion was on his pre-departure vacation. Infiltrators from across the Jordanian border murdered a woman and her two children on the night of October 12, 1954. This was the latest and one of the most heinous in a long series of attacks by Palestinian infiltrators from across the Jordanian border in the east and the Gazan border in the southwest, which were taking a serious toll in life and limb on farmers and villagers in the border areas. Nineteen Israeli civilians were killed by infiltrators in 1950, forty-eight in 1951, forty-two in 1952, and forty-four in 1953.

In response to this latest attack, the army's crack Unit 101, under Major Ariel Sharon, attacked the Palestinian village of Qibya, in the West Bank. They briefly engaged Jordanian troops, who retreated, and then blew up dozens of houses in the village. Sharon and his men later swore they had believed the homes were empty. But in the light of dawn, seventy bodies were uncovered in the rubble, many of them women and children. Israel faced a wave of outrage from around the world. Ben-Gurion, back from his vacation, adopted the version that had been put out by Lavon, that the atrocity had been perpetrated by enraged Israeli border villagers and not by IDF troops, and he broadcast this on national radio. Sharett, who had been acting premier at the time but had not been told in advance of the planned reprisal, bridled at this ploy, even though it had been suggested by an official of his own ministry as a means of mitigating the international condemnation.

The episode that then took place, which was to poison Israeli politics for many years to come and to blight Ben-Gurion's last years in office, grew out of the insalubrious relationships that now surrounded Lavon. A group of Egyptian Jews who had been formed into a spy network by agents of the IDF's military intelligence were ordered in July 1954 to carry out firebombings of Western cultural centers in Cairo and Alexandria. The thinking behind this scheme was that the attacks would show that the government of the new prime minister, Gamal Abdel Nasser, was weak, and they would prompt the British government to rethink its recent decision, at Nasser's behest, to withdraw its forces from the Suez Canal. The plot failed, and many of the spies were caught. Two were eventually hanged, and others were sentenced to long jail terms. Meir Max Bineth, an Israeli intelligence agent based in Egypt and linked to the network, was arrested too; he committed suicide in prison. Israelis were shocked and humiliated by the public trials in Cairo and the obvious foul-up that they exposed. But behind the scenes, sheltered by the military censor from the public gaze, a conflagration began to burn.

Who had given the order to set the bungled and hopelessly amateurish chain of provocations into motion? Binyamin Gibli, the head of military intelligence, claimed that he had been instructed to do so by Lavon. Lavon flatly denied it. (Dayan had been out of the country when the order was given.) Accusations of slander, forgery, and suborning of witnesses flew thick and fast between the two men and the camps that began to form around them, especially after Sharett, at Lavon's demand, set up an ad hoc commission of inquiry to discover the truth.

The commission consisted of Yitzhak Olshan, a justice of the Supreme Court, and Yaakov Dori, the former IDF chief of staff. It heard evidence from all those involved, including, as was later claimed,* false, suborned, and doctored evidence. It failed to reach an unequivocal conclusion. "We find it impossible to say more than we are not convinced beyond all reasonable doubt that [Gibli] did not receive orders from the defense minister. At the same time, we are not convinced that the defense minister did give the orders attributed to him." Lavon, in a paroxysm of fury, demanded justice and refused the suggestion of some of his Mapai colleagues that he quietly step down. Ben-Gurion was consulted, and he too voiced the view that Lavon would have to resign.

*See pages 184–185.

Lavon duly resigned, but planted a time bomb in his letter of resignation. "I reserve the right," he wrote, "to bring the reasons for my resignation to the knowledge of the Party and of the Foreign Affairs and Defense Committee of the Knesset." The party duly rejected his resignation, whereupon he in turn demanded Gibli's resignation—and mine too, for good measure. Now Dayan balked. If Lavon stayed, he told Sharett, everyone else would stay too. Lavon did finally resign. Ben-Gurion, importuned by party colleagues, agreed to return as minister of defense, serving under Prime Minister Sharett. "Defense and the army come before everything," he wrote in his diary. Sharett cabled him at his kibbutz: "Admire your step as a model of noble citizenship and testimony to profound comradeship between us." But the comradeship, it soon became clear, was not so profound. Nor was the Lavon Affair by any means over.

Ben-Gurion and Sharett quickly began to clash over the reprisals policy, as the raids into Israel intensified from both the West Bank and from the Gaza Strip. An Israeli raid against the Egyptian Army in Gaza in February 1955, again under Arik Sharon, resulted in thirty-eight Egyptians dead and dozens more wounded. Sharett had been assured in advance there would be low casualties on the other side. He professed himself "horrified." There was no such reservation from Ben-Gurion. After another terror raid from Gaza in March, Ben-Gurion proposed that the IDF be ordered to conquer the Gaza Strip and drive the Egyptian Army out. He was voted down in a cabinet meeting, which further soured relations between him and the prime minister. Elections in the summer brought Ben-Gurion back as prime minister. Despite their deepening differences, and despite another showdown over another large-scale retaliation in Gaza, he insisted that Sharett serve as his foreign minister once again.

Both the domestic and diplomatic equations changed dramatically, however, in the fall of 1955, when Nasser announced a massive arms deal with Czechoslovakia. It was clear that this meant a wholesale shift of Egypt's strategic orientation, toward the Soviet bloc. The Czechs were to supply Soviet-made jet fighters, bombers, tanks, armored personnel carriers, self-propelled guns, torpedo boats, and even six submarines. The deal would put the Egyptian military on an entirely different footing, far outclassing the IDF, unless Ben-Gurion could somehow find a source of modern military hardware for Israel too.

Egged on by Dayan, and before Egypt could acquire and absorb her new armaments, Ben-Gurion proposed a sweeping attack on the Egyptians in the Sinai, culminating in the capture of the Straits of Tiran, which Nasser had blocked to Israeli shipping. There was scant support among the ministers. President Eisenhower sent a close friend, Robert Anderson, as his personal peace envoy to the region, in the hope of brokering an Israel-Egypt deal and thus heading off Egypt's defection to the Soviet camp. Ben-Gurion urged Anderson to bring about a direct meeting with Nasser. He would make offers, he promised, "that he hasn't even thought of." But the Egyptian leader declined. He did not want to end up like Abdullah, he told Anderson with candor.

Months of desultory diplomacy now followed between Washington and Jerusalem, conducted by Sharett and Ambassador Abba Eban, in an ultimately unsuccessful effort to produce a defense agreement that Ben-Gurion could regard as an effective deterrent. As the months elapsed, his resolve hardened: If there were no diplomatic solution, there would have to be a military one.

I spent these months flying back and forth from Tel Aviv to Paris, assiduously building a relationship that was to supply us both with the arms that we so desperately needed and with the alliance that Ben-Gurion believed was vital. The French socialists under Guy Mollet, strong supporters of Israel, came to power in January 1956 at the head of a new coalition. Mollet became the prime minister. The minister of defense, Maurice Bourgès-Maunoury, a member of France's Radical Party, favored cooperation with Israel in the context of France's struggle with the FLN in Algeria, which was armed and financed by Nasser. Arms agreements signed during the spring and summer provided us with Mystère warplanes that were even better—in the hands of our pilots—than the Soviet MiGs. We also received French AMX tanks that were a match for the Soviet T-55s, as well as howitzers, mortars, and ammunition.

Ben-Gurion was skeptical at first about the French connection, though he let me pursue it without hindrance. The dalliance with France was contrary to the pronounced Anglo-Saxon orientation of virtually the entire top political echelon in Israel at that time. Golda, who grew up in the United States; Sharett, who studied in Britain; Dov Yosef, who was Canadian-born; Reuven Shiloah,* who maintained close professional contacts with senior American intelligence people—all of them were Anglo-Saxon by background and outlook. Sharett was totally Anglophile, with all the mannerisms of an English gentleman. Abba Eban, born in South Africa and educated in England, had a special status: He was considered a genius. They all had a deep contempt for Charles de Gaulle, which they had inherited from the British and the Americans. Both Roosevelt and Churchill disdained de Gaulle. Churchill famously quipped that "of all the crosses I have had to bear during this war, the heaviest has been the Cross of Lorraine [de Gaulle's symbol of Free France]."

It was into this settled and fairly homogeneous policy-making group that a *tsutsik* (young imp) like me came along and announced that only France would save Israel! There was not another Francophile in the entire Israeli establishment. I had no preconceptions and no prejudices. I saw we were not going to get weapons from the Americans or from the British, and definitely not from the Russians. The Czech arms deal with Israel in 1948 had been a short-lived exception. I visited de Gaulle in his office, which he

*Shiloah (1909–59) was the first director of the Mossad, the Israeli intelligence agency, from 1949 to 1952. He was then assigned to the Israeli embassy in Washington, D.C.

maintained in Paris along with his home in Colombey-les-Deux-Églises when he was out of power. He knew what we were doing, and he supported it.

Ben-Gurion still disdained him. When de Gaulle published his three-volume war memoirs, I tried to persuade Ben-Gurion to write a preface to the Hebrew edition, but he refused. I told him the memoirs were brilliant, as good as or better than Churchill's. De Gaulle wrote it alone, without help. I dearly wanted this book to be translated into Hebrew, but the potential publishers said they would translate and publish it in Hebrew only if Ben-Gurion wrote a preface. Otherwise no one would read it. In the end, I wrote the preface to the first edition, and Ben-Gurion wrote a preface to the second—after he'd read it.

It took Ben-Gurion years to wean himself of this prejudice against France. Whenever I brought a French guest to meet him, Ben-Gurion would ask, "Why did you lose the war?" It was really embarrassing. Quite frankly, it irritated me a bit, and I finally said to him, "I've asked them and the answer is: The enemy did not cooperate!"

B en-Gurion shifted the domestic political equation by shifting Sharett from the foreign ministry to the secretary-generalship of the Mapai Party. Golda Meir, who did not shrink from the idea of preemptive war, took over at the foreign ministry. In July 1956 Nasser announced that he was nationalizing the Suez Canal, prompting the French and the British to think seriously about using military force to remove him.

At a meeting that month with Bourgès-Maunoury and his generals, I was asked how long it would take the IDF to conquer all of Sinai. "Five to seven days," I replied at once. They were taken aback; they seemed to assume we would need much longer. The follow-up question was even more dramatic: Would Israel be prepared to invade the Sinai in concert with a French-British attack on Egypt? Again without hesitating, I replied in the affirmative—subject, of course, to the confirmation of Ben-Gurion and the cabinet. As we walked out, Yosef Nahmias, the Israeli defense ministry envoy in Paris, whispered, "You deserve to be hanged." He rightly said that I had no power or authority to offer either of those replies. I replied that I'd rather risk my neck than lose an opportunity like this. If I had responded otherwise, I argued, our entire relationship with France might have been compromised.

In September, Ben-Gurion sent Golda to head up a ministerial mission to Paris to discuss Israel's defense needs. She was accompanied by transport minister Moshe Carmel, a general in the 1948 war and now leader of the Ahdut HaAvoda Party* (and a fluent French speaker), Dayan, and me.

As luck would have it, Mollet was tied up when we arrived and sent word that he would not be able to attend our talks. For Golda, who had been sour and skeptical all along, this proved that there was no deal in the offing, just my dreams and fantasies designed to captivate Ben-Gurion. I begged Mollet's office to have him show up, at least for some of the meeting. Eventually he received Golda, which helped a little.

Christian Pineau, the foreign minister, who attended with Bourgès-Maunoury, delivered the most dour and somber picture of the situation. He spoke bleakly of the likely negative American reaction to an attack on Egypt and the even more negative—and possibly dangerous—Soviet reaction. He was a deeply sad man who, paradoxically, wrote children's books in his spare time. He'd written a book about a bear with green feet that was different from all the other bears. People said it was an allegory for the Jewish people. His sadness was ammunition for Golda when she returned home. She reported that Mollet hadn't shown up, Pineau was opposed, and we couldn't rely just on Bourgès-Maunoury. She warned Ben-Gurion—behind my back—that I was misleading him. To her, everything I did was wrong. Luckily for me, Carmel

---

*Ahdut HaAvoda had by this time split from Mapam and was a separate party.

and Dayan had been there too. Their more upbeat reports saved my credibility. But what really saved my credibility? The arms started arriving!

Now the idea of an Israeli attack serving as pretext for an Anglo-French action began to gain traction. Ben-Gurion did not like it at first, but gradually, as the talks with France intensified and the relationship burgeoned, he began to soften. The negotiations climaxed with an invitation, which I engineered, to Ben-Gurion to attend a secret summit conference in Sèvres, outside Paris, in October 1956.

We flew out from a military airfield, Ben-Gurion with a hat pulled low over his head and Dayan in dark glasses to conceal his famous eye patch. In the car and again at the foot of the gangway up to the plane, Ben-Gurion turned to me and said angrily, "Have you *told* them I'm not committed to anything? Are you *sure* they know I'm not committed?" He was determined that Israel not be taken for granted. He was determined too that his own eventual decision not be taken for granted, even by Dayan and me. He preferred, in the interests of the negotiation, that we not know what his position was.

On the first evening at Sèvres, the three French statesmen, Mollet, Pineau, and Bourgès-Maunoury, together with the French army chief of staff and other generals, gathered for an opening session with Ben-Gurion. They were plainly eager to get to know their prospective ally. "Monsieur le Premier Ministre," said Mollet, "you're the guest of honor, you open the discussion." Ben-Gurion took his time. He thought deeply, and then looked up. "Mr. Prime Minister," he said, "I would like you to explain to me when you in France stopped teaching Latin and went over to French." An argument over French linguistics developed from there, and it went on the whole evening.

Mollet, with whom I'd grown quite close, couldn't contain himself. "What's this?" he whispered to me. "You don't know the man," I replied. "He's leaving the negotiations to us. He's not a merchant. You asked him to open the discussion, so he opened it on a subject that he feels is of extreme importance—and the whole evening went to hell!"

Ben-Gurion had no inferiority complex. He was a short man, but he looked tall. He was mostly bald, but he looked like he had a wavy shock of hair. When he walked into a room, there was no doubt at all that someone special had entered. In this particular instance, he didn't want to open the negotiation. He wanted to be sure that he hadn't invited himself to this party, but that he had been invited to it by the hosts. Even aboard the French plane to Sèvres, he kept saying, "Shimon, are you sure they've invited us? If you're not sure, I'm not going." That's why he didn't want to open the negotiations. *You invited me, you open them.*

"Better an open Suez Canal and a closed conflict than a closed Suez Canal and an open conflict," Dayan famously proclaimed in the early 1970s.* This was the essence of Dayan's thinking at Sèvres too, in the negotiations with both the French and the British. He said that Israeli forces would not go all the way to the canal. Dayan's strategy was for our troops to parachute down at the Mitla Pass on the western side of Sinai but some thirty miles east of the canal. This dovetailed with Ben-Gurion's broader political idea of separate wars "coordinated in time, not in mission." Ben-Gurion was concerned that we not look like mercenaries for the French and British.

Our own war, the Sinai Campaign (in Hebrew, Mivtza Kadesh, or Operation Kadesh) had three trajectories:

1. To Sharm el-Sheikh, at the southern tip of the Sinai Peninsula, because Ben-Gurion held that Egypt's closure of the Straits of Tiran to Israeli ships was itself a casus belli.
2. To Gaza, because the fedayeen, the armed bands of Palestinians who infiltrated Israel, were centered there with Nasser's funding and support.

*As defense minister under Golda Meir in the early 1970s, Dayan proposed an interim agreement with Egypt, under which the IDF would withdraw from the Suez Canal Zone and Egypt would reopen the waterway, shut since the 1967 war. His proposal was not taken up.

3. To the Mitla Pass, to trigger a battle with Egypt in the Sinai so as to destroy the Soviet weaponry in the hands of the Egyptian Army.

The negotiations between France and Israel would have proceeded with the utmost smoothness and amity but for the fact that France was tied to Britain in its response to Nasser's provocation in nationalizing the Suez Canal. The British could barely conceal their distaste at the prospect of colluding with Israel. They sent over their foreign secretary, Selwyn Lloyd, to take part in the conference, and he and Ben-Gurion fairly bristled at each other.

Lloyd's first proposal was that Israel invade the Sinai and reach the Suez Canal; then Britain and France would issue an ultimatum to both sides to pull back. Egypt would refuse, and the two powers would attack her. Ben-Gurion rejected that out of hand. A major concern for him was the possibility of Israeli cities being bombed. He also feared Russia flying in "volunteers," or even parachuting them down onto the battlefields to help the Egyptians. He wanted Britain and France to bomb the Egyptian military airfields within one day of the outbreak of war.

At this point Dayan weighed in with his Mitla Pass proposal. One advantage of it was that the force initially involved would not be too large, and the Egyptians might regard it as a major retaliation raid rather than the first stage of a full-fledged war. It was sufficient, on the other hand, to trigger the proposed Anglo-French ultimatum. Lloyd was dubious; he wanted "a real act of war." The next day, not relying on Lloyd, Pineau took Dayan's detailed proposal to Prime Minister Anthony Eden in London. Eden accepted it.

The following morning Dayan and I drove out to Sèvres, where Ben-Gurion had been staying throughout the conference, to see whether he would now give the final green light. He was sitting in the garden, outwardly calm. But we assumed that he had been wrestling with himself all night. He began asking us specific questions, from which we inferred that he was inclined to approve the plan.

Being a genius is a matter of character no less than of intellect.

Of being unafraid to ask questions, to take new positions, to ignore conventions. And of being unafraid of fear. Ben-Gurion was so brave that he didn't fear being afraid. You need courage to fear. He didn't hide it. I often heard expressions of very deep anxiety, but also of faith that we'd overcome whatever obstacles were in our way.

Returning home, he convened the cabinet and received its approval. (Only the Mapam ministers voted against the war.) He didn't lay out the detailed operational plans; he just said what the three goals were. And he explained the coordination with France and Britain. Until last night we didn't have an agreement, he said. Now we've got an agreement, so you decide, yes or no. Prior to that moment, he had not felt it necessary to involve the whole cabinet. His proposal the year before, for the IDF to invade Sinai, capture Sharm el-Sheikh, and open the Straits of Tiran, was to have been a purely Israeli initiative and therefore required a cabinet decision at the planning stage. Now there was a war being planned by others that we could simply join. Ben-Gurion went to Sèvres with clean hands, because he hadn't yet decided himself whether Israel should join in this war. He didn't need the cabinet's formal approval to go to Sèvres to discuss their war plans with France and Britain. After hearing what they had to say, when he returned to Israel he submitted the plan to the full cabinet for their approval.

Ben-Gurion had written in his diary on the last morning of the Sèvres conference, "I have weighed the situation, and if effective air measures are taken to protect us during the first day or two until the French and British bomb the Egyptian airfields, I think the operation is essential. The two powers . . . will try to eliminate Nasser [and] we will not face him alone."

That is not quite the way things worked out. While the Israeli military action, which began on October 29, 1956, was a success on all counts—the Egyptian Army in the Sinai was smashed, the guns commanding the Straits of Tiran were spiked, and Gaza and all of Sinai were occupied by the IDF—the Anglo-French landings in the Canal Zone were slow and ran into resistance. Soviet threats and American pressure brought them to a peremptory and premature halt with their aims unachieved. The canal did not revert to Western control, and Nasser, instead of being deposed, emerged a hero from his confrontation with the two waning Great Powers. His military defeat at the hands of Israel was somewhat eclipsed.

Soviet threats against Israel were even more brutal than they were against France and Britain. "The Israeli government is criminally and irresponsibly playing with the fate of the world and with the fate of its own people," Marshal Nikolai Bulganin, the Soviet premier and minister of defense, wrote to Ben-Gurion on November 5, 1956. "It is sowing hatred that places in question the very existence of Israel as a state . . . The Soviet government is at this moment taking steps to put an end to the war and restrain the aggressors." The message was not immediately published. Two days later, in the Knesset, a euphoric Ben-Gurion congratulated the army for "the greatest and most splendid military operation in the chronicles of our people." He pronounced the 1949 Armistice Agreement with Egypt dead and buried. In his message to a military victory ceremony at Sharm el-Sheikh, he wrote of the "Third Kingdom of Israel," which extended to two little islands off the tip of Sinai.

Ben-Gurion did not seriously intend to remain in the Sinai, and he told the cabinet as much immediately after the fighting. Asked sometime later at a meeting in Kibbutz Negba why he had spoken publicly in such sweepingly euphoric terms, he explained that his motives were tactical, with an eye on the negotiations that were soon to begin over the terms and timetable of Israel's withdrawal.

The euphoria, in any event, was swept away the next day by a UN General Assembly resolution demanding Israel's withdrawal, and even more by a blunt message from President Eisenhower, who had just been reelected for a second term. Israel's failure to withdraw, he wrote, would "impair the friendly collaboration between our two countries." The United States threatened a cutoff of all funding to Israel, including Jewish philanthropy, possible eviction of Israel from the UN, and, most ominous in Ben-Gurion's mind, nonintervention in the event of an attack by Soviet "volunteers." The volunteers were more virtual than real, but they cast a shadow of fear over the world and brought about Ben-Gurion's quick retreat. In his broadcast to the nation, he read from Bulganin's and Eisenhower's letters and from his replies. He assured the army that "there is no power in the world that can reverse your great victory . . . Israel after the Sinai Campaign will never be the same again."

While Israel was forced out of Sinai, and later out of Gaza too, in return for the deployment of a UN force along the border and less-than-ironclad assurances from the international community of free passage in the Straits of Tiran, Ben-Gurion's bitter boast to the soldiers turned out to be true. Israel after 1956 was not the same country, neither in the eyes of its enemies nor in its own eyes. The military victory ushered in a decade of consolidation and development. The country enjoyed quiet along its borders and remarkable economic growth and political success, especially among the emerging nations of Africa and Asia, many of which forged strong ties with the Jewish state.

A n informal conversation at the Sèvres conference that did not include the British focused on our attempts over the previous several years to build up a nuclear capacity and our earnest desire that France, a nuclear power, help us do so. It's awkward for me to say so, but although I was and remain a faithful follower of Ben-Gurion, in certain things he listened to me. One example was our nuclear program. As with the outreach to the French, he was equivocal at first, but then he let me run with it. He always gave me every encouragement to strike out on bold and unconventional paths.

Israel's nuclear aspirations first surfaced back in 1949, when someone approached Ben-Gurion with a vague idea of developing atomic energy. At that stage Ben-Gurion and Professor Ernst David Bergmann, his scientific adviser, wanted to create nuclear energy for peaceful purposes, to desalinate water. It started from that. Various exotic ideas were raised before I came on the scene. Some people claimed, for instance, that the Tiberias hot springs were radioactive water. Some said that there was uranium in the potash extracted at the Dead Sea. Some said that in Norway they were cutting down trees using nuclear energy. All that sort of thing excited people, and Bergmann's approach was that everything was possible. When I entered the picture, I said, Sorry, I don't know much about these various ideas, but we need to be more realistic.

By then, the first enterprise I had set up, working initially from the United States, was Israel Aircraft Industries Ltd., formally incorporated in 1953. In that, too, Ben-Gurion gave me a free hand. To this day I don't understand how he let me just forge ahead. If I have any criticism of him, it's over the authority he vested in me! In his place I wouldn't have done it.

The complicated relationship between Weizmann and Ben-Gurion impinged on the nuclear debate that now raged within the Israeli political and scientific elite. The Weizmann Institute of Science at Rehovot, which was very much Dr. Weizmann's brainchild and was under his strong influence, was intended to give Israel a leading role in the scientific world. Weizmann himself, of course, was an eminent scientist whose work for the British government in both world wars is well known. Ben-Gurion believed Israel needed to harness science to secure its existence. Weizmann did not disagree; he was no pacifist. But the Weizmann Institute didn't want that to be the character or main focus of its work.

There was a silent battle that centered on the person of Ernst David Bergmann. When he set up the institute in the 1930s, Weizmann asked Albert Einstein to recommend a brilliant chemist, and Einstein recommended Bergmann, who was without a doubt a genius. At a certain point Bergmann transferred from the institute to the defense ministry, where he became chief scientific adviser and a close aide to Ben-Gurion. He was the first and almost the only top-grade scientist to make that move. It wasn't I who brought him over; nor was his move directly connected to the atomic program. He was attracted by Ben-Gurion. Later, he helped to set up Israel's Atomic Energy Authoritiy; Rafael, the weapons research company; and many other vital components of the defense complex. He became an enthusiastic *bitchonist* (defense advocate).

The Weizmann Institute, on the other hand, wasn't terribly enthusiastic about defense. In fact, the institute became a center of opposition to Dimona.* This didn't come from Israel Dostrovsky,† the institute's top chemist, but from Meyer Weisgal, Weizmann's longtime aide and amanuensis, who effectively maintained the institute. He was the strongman there, and he came out against Dimona and the whole nuclear effort, against all our experiments and attempts to make progress. Amos de Shalit, a nuclear physicist and the director of the institute, felt the same way. They were very cold toward us, and they didn't help at all. But when it all succeeded and we had set up the reactor in Dimona, Amos convened a meeting of scientists and said they needed to ask my forgiveness, because they'd said nothing would come of it, that it was all my fantastic dreams.

But in fact I'd had the support I needed, and that came from Ben-Gurion himself. I could enter his office freely when I had something to ask him, tell him, or discuss with him. As director-general of the defense ministry, I was in Tel Aviv most of the time, dealing with defense business. I would go up to Jerusalem midweek, when I needed to see him. He sat with me more than with

---

*A city in the Negev, Dimona is the site of Israel's major nuclear reactor and the metonym for the entire nuclear program.

†Dostrovsky succeeded Bergmann as head of the Israel Atomic Energy Authority in 1965.

the older party people of his own generation, which of course added to their dislike of me. His conversation with them was more formal. With us younger fellows he was completely free.

But I also felt the tension when I was in a room with him. And alongside that tension there was a sort of festive atmosphere, a feeling that I had entered a historic space. Ben-Gurion's presence, wherever he was, created that atmosphere.

It wasn't just I who was conscious of it. Everyone was, except perhaps Teddy Kollek, but that was Teddy's personality.* And he wasn't totally captivated by Ben-Gurion like the rest of us. He also flirted with Sharett and the doves. He was one of a kind.

B en-Gurion didn't really open up to us, his close aides. I never knew until after his death how hard he fought for me, how many people kept demanding that he fire me. He never said a word to me, apart from once or twice saying, "Try to be nicer to Golda." In the matter of Dimona, they drove him mad! They said I was irresponsible. That it was a bluff and not to be taken seriously. That I was a fantasizer. He didn't talk about this to my face, but behind my back he was defending me.

When I started working for him, I was a young man of twenty-four. When I became director-general of the defense ministry, in 1952, I was twenty-nine. At that time Yigael Yadin said to Ben-Gurion, right in front of me, "How could you appoint him to such a job?!" Of course, Yigael himself had been only thirty-two when Ben-Gurion named him chief of staff of the IDF in 1949. But I suppose that at that age, every year makes a difference. And apart from that, he *was* already a general!

Yigael wasn't actually aware of the controversy that arose over his own appointment. He had no real field experience. He had

---

*Teddy Kollek (1911–2007) was a Viennese-born kibbutznik and aide to Ben-Gurion who later became mayor of Jerusalem, a post he held for close to a quarter of a century.

never commanded in combat. But Ben-Gurion had stood up for him, just as he later stood up for me. Ben-Gurion appointed him first and foremost because he was a brilliant man. In addition to that, he was an archaeologist and knew the Bible. And he spoke beautifully. Seriously, though, he had one overridingly positive attribute: he was not part of any party or faction—not the Jewish Brigade, not Siah Bet. Also, he never voiced one word of criticism of Ben-Gurion behind his back. To his face, at cabinet and staff meetings, he would attack him furiously. This was exactly the opposite of other people, who would extol him to his face and whisper disloyalties behind his back.

Why did Ben-Gurion take to me? Probably because he found in me, more than in others, a certain quality of daring. Even in the matter of Dimona, he never gave me an explicit order. He knew what I was doing, and he let me get on with it. It was the same regarding negotiating with France. I didn't know French. I didn't know France. I wasn't a military man. But he let me go anyway, against the advice of all his old friends and his own gut feelings. Why? Because he saw that my early forays had produced results.

When I returned from trips, I would sit with Ben-Gurion for an hour, and he would eagerly drink in my impressions. People didn't know what we were talking about, and some thought I was bewitching him, telling him whom to favor and whom to reject. It was all baseless. He wasn't like that; he wasn't that kind of person.

If I hadn't brought results, my various detractors would have had my head! But I managed to win the French over and to break the embargo on the weapons we so desperately needed. A youngster like me comes along, the entire establishment says that what I want to do is a waste of time and that I'm talking rubbish, and he lets me do it anyway! I'm saying this to Ben-Gurion's credit, not mine. It wasn't because I was a genius, but because I was the most daring of the people around him.

I knew that if I erred through daring, he would forgive me. But if I erred because I lied, I'd be out on the spot. That was his immutable rule. If you lie once, you're out. If you err once while trying to do the right thing, it's okay to keep trying, and to keep erring.

The same thing happened again later, not with France this time but with Germany, when, in the late 1950s, I was engaged in negotiations over a secret deal in which Germany would supply Israel with arms, gratis. Ben-Gurion had already made the fateful decision, in the early part of the decade, to accept reparations from Germany. And so in 1957, with Ben-Gurion's approval, I went to the German defense minister, Franz-Josef Strauss, to negotiate an arms deal that was a form of reparations.

I said to Strauss as I said to Ben-Gurion: The Americans give us money and the French sell us arms; Germany must give us arms without money. That seemed natural to me. But it was hard for me, going to Germany. I felt physically ill the first time I went there. Everything brought to mind the war years, the police uniforms in particular. But I was there to assist in the defense of Israel. Ben-Gurion once said that if you put all other values on one side of the scale and defense on the other, defense wins. If you are killed, your human rights die with you. The first priority, therefore, is to defend and protect life.

When I came back home, there was a storm of protest and debate that echoed the controversy over reparations earlier in the decade. How were we to relate to the new Federal Republic of Germany, the sucesssor to the Third Reich? Ben-Gurion had a powerful moral argument on his side: Was the embargo that the nations of the world were imposing on us moral? With Germany's help, Israel was overcoming that embargo. Much later, when Strauss came to Israel, Ben-Gurion was totally supportive of me. There were demonstrations outside my home: *"Peres und Strauss, heraus!"* (Peres and Strauss, out!) The left and the right both opposed the agreement with Germany. But Ben-Gurion purposefully announced that he would like to meet with Strauss. And when he next visited Paris, I asked Strauss to come to France and meet with him.

Because the deal with Germany, like the deal with France for arms and nuclear assistance, involved my working intimately with

Ben-Gurion—and often pitted me against others in his cabinet—
it seems fitting to conclude this chapter with a personal exchange
that addresses my own relationship with Ben-Gurion, as well as
his style of leadership.

DAVID LANDAU: Did Ben-Gurion give Dayan the same freedom
that he gave you? And as a consequence, did the reprisal raids
extend beyond what he intended?

SHIMON PERES: He stopped Dayan many times. He said no
many times. The idea behind the reprisals was to hit the Jordanians and the Egyptians so that they in turn would rein in the
fedayeen based in their territory: the West Bank and the Gaza
Strip. During a reprisal raid on Kalkilya, on October 10, 1956,
the Jordanian Army surrounded some sixty of our soldiers. We
sent in tanks. That same morning at dawn, the British chargé
d'affaires knocked on Ben-Gurion's door and said, I want to re-
mind you of our defense treaty with Jordan. If you attack Jordan, we will intervene. There were rumors at the time that we
intended a large-scale attack on Jordan. But in fact, our moves
were camouflage for the preparations for our imminent attack
on Egypt, in concert with France and Britain. We had no intention of mounting a large-scale attack on Jordan.

In general, Ben-Gurion deeply respected Dayan. Dayan and
I were like two colts galloping in the field.

DAVID LANDAU: Despite your enormous admiration of him,
did you ever find yourself, in private, critical of Ben-Gurion's
policies?

SHIMON PERES: No!

DAVID LANDAU: That's almost impossible. You're a critical person by nature. You couldn't have abnegated your entire personality. Looking back, can you not recall anything that you had
reservations about, but kept silent about?

SHIMON PERES: In minor matters, maybe yes. But not in the
major issues. I became a Ben-Gurionist before I met him. I knew
him from reading his speeches. I said to myself, Here's a man

who speaks the truth. I wasn't impressed by Communism, or by Siah Bet, or by *shleimut haaretz* [the integrity of the biblical Greater Israel]. I felt that the people affiliated with these movements didn't have the ability or the courage to see the truth.

DAVID LANDAU: Did Ben-Gurion demand total obedience? Or would he accept criticism? And from a youngster like you?

SHIMON PERES: Of course he could accept criticism. There were many moments of lighthearted banter between us. I would joke at his expense; he wouldn't care.

DAVID LANDAU: That's different from criticism.

SHIMON PERES: It's true that he lacked a sense of humor. He had no time for such luxuries. One longtime Labor activist, Akiva Govrin, used to tell jokes all the time. Once he said to Ben-Gurion, People say you don't like jokes, you don't understand them.

> BEN-GURION: Why would they say that?
>
> GOVRIN: Let me tell you a joke.
>
> BEN-GURION: Please do.
>
> GOVRIN: You and Begin were traveling together from Tel Aviv to Haifa—
>
> BEN-GURION: When?
>
> GOVRIN: I told you, it's a joke.
>
> BEN-GURION: Okay. So what happened?
>
> GOVRIN: You were driving, and Begin was sitting next to you. And you said to Begin: *Ich vel fyiren und du vest fyfen.* [I'll drive and you whistle.]
>
> BEN-GURION: Lies and falsehoods!! There was never such a thing! They've made it up! It's baseless!

DAVID LANDAU: Did you ever hear him express regret over anything?

SHIMON PERES: I don't think so. His was an intellect that could not live with doubt. Five minutes after reading something— he's got an opinion about it! But he didn't demand the discipline of obedience. When he didn't like something, he ignored you. If you were in his bad graces and he met you in the corridor, he would say, "What are you doing here?"

I was usually the victim, and usually completely innocent, of his perceived favoritism. Once Golda decided to attend a meeting of the International Labor Organization. The cabinet gave its formal approval, as required. A few days later she came by to take her leave of the prime minister.

BEN-GURION (looking up from his writing): Yes, you're traveling. To where?

(She was insulted that he'd forgotten. She reminded him.)

BEN-GURION: How are you flying?

GOLDA: El Al to Paris.

BEN-GURION: When?

GOLDA: Tomorrow morning.

BEN-GURION: What time?

GOLDA: Ten.

BEN-GURION: Shimon will be on that plane too.

Golda was extremely insulted. Not only had he forgotten her cabinet-approved trip, but he remembered all the details of my trip. The point was, of course, that for him defense was more important than anything else. That's why he knew all the details of my trip. It wasn't that Shimon was more important to him than Golda.

12

Soured Fruits

"You can repay us by being a great president of the United States," he said. It's . . . shortsighted strategy to suggest that Israel can somehow benefit from a confrontational or adversarial relationship with the president of the United States.

Average wasn't his goal. He wanted us to be above average morally. He thought lying is a terrible erosion of strength and he would not tolerate it.

The years following the Sinai Campaign were the most serene and in many ways the most gratifying of Ben-Gurion's premiership. Working mainly through the Mossad, he spun a web of mutual interest with three important non-Arab states on the periphery of the region: Turkey, Iran, and Ethiopia. "Our object," he wrote to President Eisenhower, "is the creation of a group of countries, not necessarily a formal and public alliance, that will be able to stand up steadfastly against Soviet expansion through Nasser."

Interestingly, that wasn't the original motivation. Rather, Ben-Gurion saw these overtures in an ideological context more than a strategic one. He believed that Israel's future depended to an important degree on our ability to develop relations with Asia and Africa. He wanted ties with China and India but failed to achieve them. He sent Sharett on missions to Asia, but somehow Sharett's heart wasn't in them. Ben-Gurion sent his close aide Ehud Avriel to be ambassador to Ghana, one of the leading new African states.

I too was mobilized as part of this effort. We set up soldier-farmer units, on the pattern of our own Nahal, in a number of African countries. Together with Yitzhak Rabin, then the IDF head of operations, and Nahman Karni, a defense ministry official, I toured Kenya, Ethiopia, and Zambia. We helped set up the Ethiopian Air Force and trained their troops in Israel. One time in Addis Ababa we saw the most beautiful, regal-looking woman. "What a looker," Karni blurted out in Hebrew. She cooled his ardor in fluent Yiddish! It turned out she was a member of Emperor Haile Selassie's family and had been with him during the time he had spent in exile in Jerusalem. Now she was married to an Ethiopian prince and served as head of the government information service.

Ben-Gurion's outreach to Turkey was also not purely a strategic calculation. We're not Prussia! Things here are not nearly so regimented or so militaristic. Ben-Gurion was deeply drawn to Turkey's effort to build a modern society. There were close links too between Mapai and the Turkish socialist party. This all fit in with Ben-Gurion's overall weltanschauung, and one thing led to another. Later the intelligence community came aboard, and they naturally wanted to invest these relationships with the "countries of the periphery" with a structured strategic content.

Separately, Ben-Gurion extended our relationship with West Germany to provide significant arms supplies to Israel. I was put in charge of that project, which included obtaining defensive equipment like transport planes and antiaircraft guns, and which was eventually expanded to include combat planes, helicopters, air-to-air missiles, and submarines. The terms we obtained from the Germans were hugely advantageous. In some cases they demanded no payment at all; in others, the weapons were "lent" to Israel. Additionally, Ben-Gurion met with Konrad Adenauer in New York in 1960 and obtained from him a half-billion-dollar loan (beyond the original reparations), repayable on easy terms over ten years, for civilian development.

The German connection continued to draw criticism at home, from the right and the left. This was muted, though, by the capture in 1960 and trial in 1961 of Adolf Eichmann. The Knesset spontaneously stood and applauded when Ben-Gurion delivered to them, on May 23, 1960, the sensational news that the man who had personally supervised the implementation of the Nazis' "Final Solution" was in Israel's hands. Isser Harel's Mossad agents had stalked him for weeks in Buenos Aires. They swiftly overpowered him one evening on a lonely street a few yards from his home and nine days later deftly sneaked him onto an El Al plane that brought him to Israel via Senegal.

Ben-Gurion had given the green light for the abduction, knowing it could damage relations with Argentina and deciding to go ahead nonetheless. The Argentinian government had some advance knowledge of what Israel was up to, and indeed, Argentinian police agents observed the abduction. Argentina's formal protests to Israel and to the UN Security Council were satisfied by Golda's parenthetical apology for the kidnapping in a speech she gave at the UN that pointed out that Eichmann's captors could have lynched him "on the nearest tree" instead of turning him over to authorities to be tried in a court of law.

Ben-Gurion made sure that the trial, presided over by a three-judge panel in Jerusalem, was as much a seminar on the history of the Holocaust for the entire nation—and for the world at large—as a forensic process. He believed this was a unique opportunity to explain what the millions who died and the hundreds of thousands who managed to survive had actually experienced.

While Ben-Gurion was determined that the Eichmann trial help the nation grapple with the tragedy of the recent Jewish past, he was equally determined that Israel shore up its ultimate anti-Holocaust protection for the future. The reactor being built in Dimona was a source of tension and concern as demands mounted for it to be placed under international inspection. But at the end of the day, both the French, who were actively helping us build it, and the Americans, who were following it closely, accepted the formula that I proposed: Israel will not be the first to introduce nuclear weapons into the Middle East. That has remained the core of our policy in this sensitive area to the present day.

A meeting between Ben-Gurion and the newly elected President John Kennedy in New York in May 1961 ended without rancor regarding this sensitive issue. Israel had permitted two American scientists to visit the reactor, and Kennedy, whatever he might have thought, chose to inform Ben-Gurion that he was satisfied that it was intended for peaceful purposes.

As the president walked the prime minister alone to the elevator, he said, "I know that I owe my election to your people." How could he repay the Israeli leader for this support? he asked. Ben-Gurion was extremely uncomfortable and declined to be drawn into that line of wink-and-nod politics. "You can repay us by being a great president of the United States," he said.

There was more in that statement than merely a reluctance to horse-trade on American Jewish sympathies. There was a profound and lastingly relevant articulation of Israel's core interest. Israel, by virtue of her abiding strategic, political, and democratic quintessence, needs the president of the United States to be strong and successful. It's poor politics and the most shortsighted strategy to suggest that Israel can somehow benefit from a confrontational or adversarial relationship with the president of the United States.

Granted, the American attitude was not always supportive, as I myself learned early on, the hard way. At our time of most dire need in 1948, Washington would not sell us even rifles to defend our lives, let alone heavier weapons. The embargo was ostensibly on both sides, but the Arabs had no problem procuring arms. I remember Ben-Gurion's anxiety. "We can't exist forever on contraband," he kept repeating during those crisis days, as our people scoured the world for arms. Years later, when I accompanied Eshkol on his first visit to the United States as prime minister, Averell Harriman, who had served American presidents from Franklin Delano Roosevelt to Lyndon Johnson in a wide variety of diplomatic and cabinet-level positions, asked me to lunch for a freewheeling give-and-take on relations between our two countries. "Why didn't you let us have even rifles?" I asked him straight out. "My dear friend," he replied, "I don't have an answer."

Ben-Gurion's great wisdom was never to ask for American soldiers to defend us, even in the most trying situations. The nations of Western Europe had no such compunction, but he didn't want American mothers to feel that their sons were endangering their lives for the Jewish state. Overcoming ideological opponents within the Israeli government, he made pro-American sentiment the Israeli consensus. Permit me the irony of saying that today, even though we're America's friend, we're still pro-American, unlike so many other countries. On the strategic level, we were the only American friend that successively fought against and destroyed two generations of Soviet weaponry during the Cold War. That is a factor of major historical significance that needs to be given its due in any reckoning. Subsequently, cooperation on weapons research and production has worked to the advantage of both sides. Pilotless planes, for example, an increasingly important component of modern-day warfare, were originally an Israeli invention.

In the November 1959 election, despite tensions within Mapai between the old guard—Sharett, Golda, Pinhas Sapir, Zalman Aranne, Pinhas Lavon—and the younger men like Dayan, Abba Eban, and myself, whom Ben-Gurion wanted to promote, the party had won its biggest-ever plurality: forty-seven seats. This idyllic period, however, was not to last. The Lavon Affair, like a bad dream, returned to haunt Ben-Gurion and all his colleagues. It would eventually drive him from office, angry and embittered.

The trigger was a closed-door trial, in the summer of 1960, of Avry Elad, an Israeli intelligence agent who had been dubbed "the third man" in the heavily censored press coverage of the original "mishap" in Egypt. He revealed during interrogation that he had been suborned to commit perjury by emissaries of Binyamin Gibli, the head of intelligence whom Lavon had accused of giving the ill-starred order. Elad also attested to forgeries carried out by a certain individual in Gibli's interest. Ben-Gurion, as defense minister, ordered a new inquiry to investigate these disclosures. Lavon, upon hearing of this, demanded a full, formal, and unequivocal exoneration.

Ben-Gurion refused. For him the issue was not who was right but how right and wrong were to be established. He saw this question as going to the very heart of democratic governance. He said he was "neither judge nor investigator." He had not condemned Lavon when the affair first surfaced, and he was not authorized to exonerate him now, because that would entail, by implication, condemning Gibli. Only a judicial process could do that.

As he had previously threatened to do, Lavon now took his case to the Knesset Foreign Affairs and Defense Committee. From there, in sensational daily headlines, his bitter catalog of accusations made its way into all the newspapers. He saw Dayan and me as part of a cabal arrayed against him, and we too were sucked into the storm. For the most part, the press and public failed to distinguish between Ben-Gurion's principled position and the increasing antipathy between him and Lavon. In October 1960, in a last-ditch effort to contain the volcanic eruption that was threatening to bury the government, the cabinet voted to set up a committee of seven ministers to examine all the material pertaining to the affair and decide on a procedure to resolve it. Ben-Gurion, chairing the session, did not object to this decision.

Led by Eshkol and Justice Minister Pinhas Rosen, the seven sorted through the written evidence but did not summon witnesses to appear before them. On December 20, 1960, they rendered their verdict, which, it turned out, went much further than merely recommending a procedure. "We find," they wrote, "that Lavon did not give the order cited by 'the senior officer' [Gibli] and that 'the mishap' was carried out without his knowledge . . . Investigation of 'the affair' should be regarded as concluded and completed." Ben-Gurion resigned.

He insisted that "there is a certain procedure by exclusive means of which the truth can be revealed. Witnesses are cross-examined and confronted with one another; both sides have lawyers; the lawyers examine the evidence. What is this fear of yours of a judicial commission of inquiry?" The Mapai leadership recoiled in horror at the effects of their own action. Eshkol and the others now forced Lavon to resign his post as secretary-general of the Histadrut in order, they hoped, to woo Ben-Gurion back. The Mapai secretariat backed Lavon's dismissal by majority vote. "This was the end of Lavon," writes Ben-Gurion's biographer, Michael Bar-Zohar. "But Ben-Gurion's young disciples, who toiled with great enthusiasm to canvass votes against Lavon, did not comprehend that it was also the end of the Old Man."*

For Ben-Gurion, however, there could be no end to the battle for truth, the supreme value in his order of priorities and the chief bulwark, as he saw it, of a strong and moral state. In wartime, one could dissemble and even lie. The Bible itself advised, "With cunning deceit make thee war" (Proverbs 24:6). But cover-up is a legitimate instrument only when employed in the defense of the realm, Ben-Gurion held. There's a huge difference between lying to yourself and lying in the face of the enemy. In peacetime situations, truth was above all else, truth as elicited by due judicial process in a court of law or quasi-judicial inquiry. His mantra was "Ministers can't be judges." He was warning against a license to lie, to play fast and loose with judicial process, which is a civilized society's only legitimate way to get at the truth. He feared that the Diaspora had imprinted on us a certain tendency to prevaricate, and he wanted to uproot it.

Ben-Gurion's war over the Lavon Affair was, in this deeper sense, a continuation of his war against *galutiyut*. He believed that the difficulties inherent in Diaspora life over the centuries had forced Jews to become accustomed to telling untruths to survive. Of course there were all kinds of Jews, just as there are all kinds of

---

*Michael Bar-Zohar, *Ben-Gurion* (New York: Adama Books, 1977).

Gentiles. But Ben-Gurion wanted us to be a different nation. Average wasn't his goal. He wanted us to be above average morally. He thought lying is a terrible erosion of strength, and he would not tolerate it. If he found someone lying—that was the end of him. And he believed his Mapai colleagues in the cabinet wanted to whitewash or cover up lies. They wanted to shut the mouths of Lavon's accusers.

Ben-Gurion's most powerful argument was that to be moral is to be wise too. I think Ben-Gurion was wiser than Eshkol. I liked Eshkol, but setting up a committee of cabinet ministers to judge an army officer—that was wrong. All are equal before the law, and ministers can't be judges. I think Ben-Gurion was right. I accepted his basic position. I am against lying in public life as much as in private. I don't think politics achieves perfection, but politics should *aspire* to perfection. One has to recognize this distinction. There is a legitimate need for compromise in public life. Ben-Gurion didn't pretend there wasn't. What Ben-Gurion rejected was falsehood and covering it up once it had been discovered. That a group of ministers got together to defend one of their own against people who didn't have that ability, in this case military people, was intolerable. He expressed no opinion regarding the guilt or innocence of Binyamin Gibli. He just said that cabinet ministers couldn't act as judges. He demanded a comprehensive inquiry, with all the powers and the safeguards of a quasi-judicial process, so that the army would not lie to itself in the future.

One time, while I was traveling with Eshkol from Jerusalem to Tel Aviv, he turned to me and said, in the Yiddish of which he was fond, "*Yungerman, vos vil ehr fun mein leben?*" (Young man, what does he want from my life?)

"Eshkol," I replied, "he just wants one thing. He wants you to tell the truth."

"*Nu,*" Eshkol said, "and you, do you tell Sonia [my wife] all the truth?"

Eshkol was essentially a man of compromise. He once said that everyone is in love with his own compromise. Ben-Gurion rejected any compromise in the Lavon Affair. That doesn't mean he never made compromises. When there's no choice (*ein breira*), then you compromise. Granted, someone has to decide when *ein breira* applies and when it doesn't. But in the Lavon Affair, as he saw it, the decision was not subjective but objective. His determination that ministers can't be judges was, to him, the objective truth.

The old Mapai comrades were able to pretty much patch things up between them, and Ben-Gurion and Eshkol once again ran at the head of the Mapai list in the elections of August 1961, scoring a respectable forty-two seats. Seeking to put a lid on the rancor and recriminations that still seethed beneath the surface of the party, Ben-Gurion pledged not to bring up the Lavon Affair anymore. He kept that promise until his final retirement from office, early in 1963. But his diaries show that the affair, and what he saw as its profound ramifications for Israeli society, continued to exercise him intensely.

Ben-Gurion's final term was darkened by a pall of internal feuding and media hype surrounding purported plans by German scientists to develop doomsday weapons in Egypt. Nasser boasted in the summer of 1962 that he had in his possession ballistic missiles that could hit any target "south of Beirut."

Mossad agents under Isser Harel, Ben-Gurion's longtime intelligence czar, claimed to have discovered secret facilities in Egypt, headed up by German experts, where missiles, warplanes, and apparently nonconventional weaponry were being developed. Ben-Gurion took the assessments calmly, refusing Harel's advice to ignite a major international storm of protest. His own policy of dealing with the "new Germany" was on the line, but so was the self-confidence and sanity of the Israeli people. He asked Golda and me to work the issue through diplomatic channels. Harel, however, apparently decided to use other channels: Soon Germans thought to be linked to the projects in Egypt were receiving parcels and letters that exploded in their hands. Others disappeared.

A cloak-and-dagger operation that slipped up in Switzerland led to the arrest of Israeli operatives there. Eventually, perhaps inevitably, the issue reached the press in Israel, which outed it in a paroxysm of apocalyptic hysteria. This was predictably exploited by Menachem Begin, who saw it as a dramatic vindication of his own opposition to the gradual reconciliation with West Germany. Ben-Gurion, vacationing in Tiberias when the story broke, was slow to contain the mushrooming crisis. He ordered the IDF's military intelligence to make their own assessment of the danger, and this turned out to be significantly less shrill than Harel's. Ben-Gurion proposed to take it to the Foreign Affairs and Defense Committee of the Knesset in order to try to alleviate the anxiety that was sweeping the country.

Harel, quite properly, submitted his resignation, which Ben-Gurion accepted. He placed the Mossad under the command of the head of military intelligence, General Meir Amit, but the episode eroded Ben-Gurion's standing among his colleagues. There was further erosion when he seemed to overreact to the creation, in April 1963, of an Arab federation consisting of Egypt, Syria, and Iraq. In the summer, the sensitivities surrounding Ben-Gurion's German policy errupted again when Golda clashed forcefully with him over reports that IDF soldiers were training in the use of new weapons in Germany. After arguing with her late into the night in his home, he wrote out a brief letter of resignation and submitted it the next morning to the new president, Zalman Shazar. (His friend Ben-Zvi had just died in April, further depressing him.) This time there would be no going back.

In his diary entry for that day, June 16, 1963, Ben-Gurion wrote, "In fact, I made the decision two-and-a-half years ago, when 'the hypocritical vulture' [Lavon] succeeded in mobilizing all the Parties against us. But at the time I feared our Party would be destroyed if I resigned."

The Mapai Party was in a way destroyed by his resignation now. He immediately returned to the Lavon Affair, stirring up the embers that lay dormant but not extinct beneath the surface of

Mapai. He commissioned Haggai Eshed, a journalist at the Histadrut newspaper *Davar*, to make his own investigation of the whole affair, and Eshed presented his findings in the form of a book, *Who Gave the Order?** Eshed was unequivocal: Lavon did. Ben-Gurion demanded that the official investigation be reopened. Eshkol, the new prime minister, gently but firmly refused.

Ben-Gurion, the bit now between his teeth, refused to take the refusal for an answer. He collected all the material in his possession about the Lavon Affair and submitted it to the minister of justice, Dov Yosef, who sided with him and urged a new inquiry. "I feel it is my comradely duty toward you," Ben-Gurion wrote to Eshkol,

> and even more so toward the Party, and above all toward Israel itself, to prevent a grave mishap—a personal mishap to you, the mishap of the Party's disintegration, and a public mishap to the state—and to tell you that you will be making a terrible mistake if you again attempt to proclaim a "period." There will be no "period" as long as a court does not express its opinion on whether the Committee of Seven was in order or was in error . . . There will be no "period" without a commission of inquiry of the finest judges in the country, in whom the people have confidence . . . Summon up your courage and do the only thing that will end this matter honorably!

Eshkol remained adamant. The inevitable showdown took place at a Mapai Party conference at the Mann Auditorium, the main concert hall in Tel Aviv, in February 1965. The scene there has imprinted itself indelibly on the collective political memory of the Jewish state. Sharett, dying of cancer, seemed to release years of choked frustration and unrequited devotion as he hurled at the former leader, "By what moral right does Ben-Gurion fling this

---

*It was suppressed by the military censor and released for publication only years later, in 1979.

matter at the party? By what moral right does he make this the focus?" Golda demonstratively walked over to Sharett in his wheelchair and kissed him on the forehead. In her own speech she was even more cutting than Sharett, linking the confrontation over Lavon to the underlying battle between the old guard and Ben-Gurion's young favorites. "The first curse lying across the threshold of our home," she asserted, "was when people began to talk of 'favorites' and 'non-favorites.' " Of the Lavon Affair she said, "What does Comrade Ben-Gurion do? He is the accuser and he is the judge!"

Ben-Gurion was scheduled to reply to his traducers, but instead he got up and walked out without speaking. His resolution to request a reopening of the investigation received 841 votes to Eshkol's 1,226 votes opposing it. His followers were jubilant at their strong showing and prepared to fight another day. But he had had enough of fighting within the party and demanded that his followers create a new political entity, which we called Rafi (an acronym for Reshimat Poalei Yisrael, or Israeli Workers' List). We claimed we were still part of Mapai, but Mapai drummed us out after a particularly vicious and heartbreaking proceeding in a "court of comrades," at which Ben-Gurion was accused of "cowardice" and his new list of "neo-fascism." I had stayed on at the defense ministry after Ben-Gurion resigned, working as Eshkol's deputy though never concealing my personal loyalty to Ben-Gurion. Now I had to leave, but I did so reluctantly. I loved my job, but I would never have dreamed of defying Ben-Gurion to his face.

Rafi attracted famous and influential names from the worlds of art, literature, commerce, and science. But in the general election in the fall of 1965, it managed only a disappointing ten seats, while the rump Mapai, running together with Ahdut HaAvoda as the Labor Alignment, scored a comfortable forty-five seats and set up a new coalition with its usual partners, the National Religious Party, Mapam, and the Independent Liberals, leaving Rafi in the opposition.

In 1967, during the anxious weeks of waiting before the outbreak of the Six-Day War, the possibility of Ben-Gurion's return to the nation's helm appeared briefly on the public horizon. People were losing confidence in Eshkol's leadership and, more specifically, in his ability to make the decision to go to war. His uncharismatic personality contributed to this widespread sense of unease (which historians have since concluded was unjustified). Ben-Gurion, brooding anxiously in his home in Tel Aviv, certainly shared that lack of confidence. He thought Eshkol should not be prime minister in wartime, because he believed Eshkol had abandoned a fundamental bulwark of political morality. Eshkol to him was the wrong man at the wrong time. He had originally wanted Eshkol to succeed him, but Eshkol had disappointed him.

As for myself, I'm a Ben-Gurionist, but I'm not Ben-Gurion. I think I've got a sufficient sense of proportion to make the distinction. On the personal level, I really liked Eshkol. But on the plane of principle, I thought he was wrong. In my view, Eshkol should have remained loyal to Ben-Gurion. I think he was wrong to pass the reopened investigation of Lavon on to a committee of cabinet ministers. I'm not rendering a judgment on who was guilty, Lavon or Gibli. The question is, Who were the judges? Judges, by definition, must not have a vested interest in the outcome of their judgment. But that group of ministers simply defended themselves and their interests, just like a trade union. And that is not doing justice.

Ben-Gurion's disillusionment with Eshkol's administration was so intense and unforgiving that, on the eve of the 1967 war, he actually approached his old enemy Begin to collude against Eshkol. I was his emissary. The effort to restore Ben-Gurion as prime minister failed, but the indirect upshot was something of a success: Moshe Dayan was appointed minister of defense under Eshkol, Begin joined the government as a minister without portfolio, and we went to war a united country.

The timing of the war turned out to be perfect. The initial Israeli air strikes were devastating; the Egyptian ground forces in Sinai were smashed within days; East Jerusalem—an unexpected and unintended bonus—was liberated and the entire West Bank brought under Israeli control after King Hussein of Jordan ordered the shelling of West Jerusalem; and finally, the IDF drove the Syrians off the Golan escarpment, from which they had for years been firing down on our settlements in the North.

The dramatic prewar power play, one of the few episodes where I was not in strict agreement with Ben-Gurion, serves as the subject of my final exchange with David Landau. Perhaps there's a message in it for me too. In the end, to be a Ben-Gurion protégé was in fact to think for yourself, to say what you thought—to him too—but never to lose sight of his greatness.

DAVID LANDAU: Ben-Gurion tried actively to oust Eshkol in the run-up to the Six-Day War. Did this reflect his feeling that Eshkol would be inadequate as a wartime leader, or was it also lingering disapproval of Eshkol because he felt he had rigged the outcome of the Lavon Affair?

SHIMON PERES: It began with "truth above all else." The moral factor. He thought the Israeli people had no confidence in Eshkol. He thought the people *should* have no confidence in him.

DAVID LANDAU: But didn't he deliberately erode their confidence?

SHIMON PERES: Okay, so he eroded. Eshkol wasn't actually that pathetic.

DAVID LANDAU: At the end of the day, you stood up to Ben-Gurion and said Eshkol could remain prime minister if Dayan was minister of defense.

SHIMON PERES: Yes. I was less extreme than Ben-Gurion. I thought Ben-Gurion was being unrealistic: We did not have the political power to replace Eshkol. I thought Dayan's entry would be a contribution to the war. I wanted us in Rafi to contribute whatever was possible. I tried to fulfill Ben-Gurion's wishes, but I saw it was impossible. So I did the next best thing.

In the end he agreed with me. Also, Ben-Gurion had given me the task of running Rafi. He didn't know the true state of the party. I knew. Before the war, it was disintegrating. Yosef Almogi* was tired. Dayan didn't want to be involved. I was left almost by myself. Ben-Gurion didn't know this, and it didn't interest him. He was ready to remain alone.

DAVID LANDAU: Which in effect happened at the next election, in 1969.

SHIMON PERES: He carried on with Rafi because he could no longer make peace with Eshkol.

DAVID LANDAU: With Begin he could make peace and with Eshkol he couldn't? There's a famous picture of him lunching with Begin after the 1967 war—

SHIMON PERES: There was something special about Ben-Gurion that I found particularly impressive and attractive: When he attacked someone, it was over his position, not his characteristics. If the man changed his position, he didn't mind. He had no personal gripes. He didn't hate Begin personally. Personal hatred was not a factor at all.

DAVID LANDAU: He had no personal hatreds?

SHIMON PERES: His personal hatreds were the fruits of ideological opposition.

DAVID LANDAU: What had changed in Begin?

SHIMON PERES: Begin supported Ben-Gurion's becoming prime minister before the Six-Day War. He asked me if Ben-Gurion wanted it and if he was capable of it. I replied, capable—yes; wants—I don't know. I told Ben-Gurion; he did not respond. Ben-Gurion didn't order me to make him prime minister. He said, Go and get Eshkol replaced.

DAVID LANDAU: And *was* he in fact capable, as you told Begin? By 1968–69 he was visibly declining.

SHIMON PERES: Well, that's the difference. Then he was capable.

---

*Almogi (1910–91) was a member of the Knesset who also held several ministerial positions and served briefly as the mayor of Haifa.

DAVID LANDAU: To run the war in detail?

SHIMON PERES: To run the war in broad brushstrokes. He had the experience.

DAVID LANDAU: Was Dayan's becoming defense minister part of the package?

SHIMON PERES: That wasn't an issue with Begin. It was an issue within the Labor Party.

DAVID LANDAU: So Dayan would have run the war in practice?

SHIMON PERES: The minute Ben-Gurion was there, Ben-Gurion would have run the war in practice. He was a very powerful personality. He'd walk into the room, and he'd be the man calling the shots.

DAVID LANDAU: Why didn't it happen?

SHIMON PERES: Because Begin became convinced that he couldn't make it happen. He went to talk to Eshkol, and when Eshkol said, famously, "These two horses [himself and Ben-Gurion] can't pull together," Begin understood there would be no majority. The religious parties were against deposing Eshkol against his will. Begin said, If there's no majority, I won't pursue it. So Begin dropped out of the picture.

13

Tomb of the Patriarch

> His essential worldview never changed. He always held
> that not pursuing peace was immoral, and that ruling
> over another nation was immoral. He believed this from
> his very first day in Eretz Yisrael.

After the 1967 war, Ben-Gurion urged extensive Jewish settlement in Jerusalem and in Hebron too, where the Tomb of the
Patriarchs (for Muslims, the Ibrahimi Mosque) is a site second
only to the Western Wall in its historic holiness for Jews. "We
must not move from Jerusalem," he was quoted as saying. He was
against restoring the West Bank to King Hussein, but he warned
against annexing it, with its one million Palestinian Arab inhabitants. "That would be a serious danger for Israel," he said. The
same applied to the Palestinian refugees living in the Gaza Strip.

"As for the Sinai Peninsula," he said, "in my view we should
demand direct negotiations with Nasser, and if he agrees to peace
with us and to free navigation in the Straits of Tiran and in the
Suez Canal, then we should evacuate Sinai." This is in fact what
happened, in stages, after the Yom Kippur War: first in 1975 in the
Israel-Egypt interim accord, and then in 1979 in the full peace
treaty, signed by Menachem Begin and Anwar Sadat. Ben-Gurion
was opposed, during the Six-Day War, to extending the fighting to
the Syrian front, but once the Golan Heights were taken, he was
clearly loath to envisage their return to Syria.

Essentially, the end of the war brought the country back to
questions Ben-Gurion had wrestled with in the days before parti-

tion, when the Zionist factions debated how much of the historical Land of Israel they were willing to sacrifice in exchange for statehood. Some say that he foresaw the dangerous consequences of occupation and that therefore, after 1967, he urged withdrawal from everywhere apart from Jerusalem and the Golan. It is important to stress that his condition for returning the territories was full peace. His essential worldview never changed. He always held that not pursuing peace was immoral, and that ruling over another nation was immoral. He believed this from his very first day in Eretz Yisrael. When we went to war, it was because we had to. We had no choice. Whenever the chance arises, we must pursue peace. That was his permanent position.

After the war in 1967, he asked me to arrange for him to see Musa Alami again. They met in London. He came back disappointed. But why did he want to go? To see if it was possible to make peace with the Palestinians. According to Alami's account, Ben-Gurion said at that first meeting in 1967 that he himself would favor returning all the conquered territories in return for Palestinian recognition. At a second meeting, a year later, he proposed that Israel retain Jerusalem and the Golan. At a third meeting, in 1969, according to Alami, he seemed prepared to revert to his original position.

After 1967 he kept up his fight, increasingly alone, over the Lavon Affair. When he had insisted that "truth is above all else," he spoke as a prophet, no longer just as a statesman. He moved at a certain point from the role of prime minister to that of prophet, of oracle. His deepest belief, constantly repeated, was that Israel's destiny depended on two things: its strength and its moral fiber. And he feared that the morality would be eroded by compromising, by too much flexibility over principle. That was his fight. He believed that to understand Jewish history—and to ensure Jewish existence going forward—we must factor in above all the moral imperative.

Dayan's joining the Eshkol government in 1967 (which became a unity government with the participation of Begin's party) led in time to the breakup of Rafi, the party Ben-Gurion had created in 1965 to protest Mapai's exoneration of Lavon without a judicial review. Most of Rafi's members now voted to join Mapai and Ahdut HaAvoda in the Labor Alignment, and that's how the tripartite bloc ran in the 1969 election, under Golda Meir (Eshkol had died the year before), winning a whopping fifty-six seats. Ben-Gurion and a handful of hard-core supporters—among them, ironically, Isser Harel—refused to go back to Mapai and ran separately as the State List, winning four seats.

Ben-Gurion resigned from the Knesset the following year and retired to Sdeh Boker. There he spent his time writing and reading and receiving an unending stream of guests from Israel and around the world who still sought to pay him homage. Longtime acquaintances found him mellowed and more at peace with himself during those sunset years. One of his last public appearances was at a Zionist congress, held in Jerusalem in 1972, where he surveyed the history of Zionism. He began with Hovevei Zion in the 1880s and covered Herzl and the First and Second Aliyot, but then pointedly passed over the World Zionist Organization's decades of political activism (mostly under Weizmann), picking up the saga again with the foundation of the state. It was his way of confirming one of the central messages of his life: Zionism, for Ben-Gurion, meant leaving the Diaspora and coming to live one's life in Zion.

Granted, this message did not directly influence all Jews everywhere. But it set a direction and a benchmark. Some did pick up and make aliyah from countries where life was comfortable for Jews and there was no pressure to leave. By the same token, his calls to come to Sdeh Boker were largely ignored. But he remained there, and he set an example that affected people in many different ways.

Looking back across the decades at Ben-Gurion's monumental contribution, I distinguish between the nation's needs when creating a state and its needs when maintaining a state. Today half of the world's Jews live in Israel. The proportions are unfathomably different from the early days of the Yishuv, when it was an open question whether the state could come into being at all, whether it had enough people to sustain itself, enough money, enough arms.

It's easy to look at the end of Ben-Gurion's career—when he had grown disillusioned by the Lavon Affair, a scandal that's hard today even for many Israelis to fathom; when he had bolted the very party he had created; and when he lived in seeming isolation in a Negev kibbutz whose culture of asceticism and sacrifice was at odds with the shifting tenor of the growing country—it's easy to look at him in these circumstances and fail to grasp his centrality. But we need to grasp it. What Ben-Gurion did, he did in a heroic epoch, an epoch of great decisions. And yet Ben-Gurion himself was the first to stress that history is built not on repetition but on mutation, on change, and that the changing nature of Israel requires leaders who embody, in their own way, the same grand vision, the same large devotion to Jewish peoplehood and universal justice, the same blend of modern pragmatism and biblical consciousness, that Ben-Gurion exemplified. In an age of ongoing existential threats to the State of Israel, we need that heroic vision as much as ever.

A great lasting image for me of Ben-Gurion, one that captures an aspect of his emblematic importance for Israelis and for Jews everywhere, was in January 1965 when, though out of office, he represented Israel alongside President Zalman Shazar at the funeral of Sir Winston Churchill. Millions watched on that cold, sad January day in London as Ben-Gurion, instantly recognizable by his mane of white hair, walked from the Savoy Hotel (it was the Sabbath) along the thronged but silent Strand to take his place among the world's leaders at St. Paul's Cathedral. Those steps were part of an extraordinary journey. It had begun in Poland in 1886 when Israel, and even Mandatory Palestine, did not yet exist. That a young man from that dream world of Jewish exile should now be a representative of the Jewish state, among the de Gaulles and the Eisenhowers of the world, is a testament to Ben-Gurion's own force of will and to the tenacity and imaginative resilience of the Jewish people. It seems proof of Ben-Gurion's famous observation that in Israel, in order to be a realist, you must believe in miracles.

The world had changed since Ben-Gurion arrived in Turkish-ruled Palestine in 1906, in ways almost impossible to comprehend. Empires had fallen. The European, Yiddish-speaking world that had defined Jewish existence for more than a thousand years had been destroyed, and the Jews of Europe along with it. The Zionists, who seemed a quixotic minority among Jews at the end of the nineteenth century, had, halfway through the twentieth, created a modern nation on the soil of an ancient Jewish civilization. The British Empire, which Ben-Gurion had fought with and against, was gone. It was the pro-Zionist Churchill who, as colonial secretary, had nevertheless sliced off 76 percent of the original Palestine Mandate for Emir Abdullah in 1922. But though the white paper of that year sought to modify Chaim Weizmann's formulation that the Jewish home in Palestine would be "as Jewish as England is English," there was Ben-Gurion in 1965, walking in the funeral procession because it was the Sabbath, consciously embodying the Jewishness of the young national home. Ben-Gurion understood the primacy of biblical consciousness not merely in the creation of modern Israel but in the life of the West.

Churchill has rightly been called "the last lion," and the connections between the two men are worth contemplating. Churchill summoned up a vision of past British glory and valor in order to rescue modern Britain and the West from fascism. The British lion, the sense of England as a sacred place, nourished itself on biblical dreams. Ben-Gurion, who drew on an ancient idea of Jewish civilization to build a modern Jewish nation, understood the power of Jewish metaphors for inspiring the world. He also understood that the days of being only a metaphor were over.

In a letter to Churchill, Ben-Gurion had expressed gratitude for Churchill's fortitude during World War II. The language he used, a fusion of the particular and the universal, the biblical and the modern, might well be applied to his own ideal of the Jewish state: "I saw you then not only as the symbol of your people and its greatness, but as the voice of the invincible and uncompromising conscience of the human race at a time of danger to the dignity of man, created in the image of God. It was not only the liberties and the honor of your own people that you saved."

For me, that somber day in London brought together the three greatest leaders of the last two hundred years: Churchill, de Gaulle, and Ben-Gurion. Despite the differences, there was a certain deep similarity, I felt, in their experiences as leaders of their nations in war and peace. I also thought of Ben Gurion as a latter-day Moses. A great shepherd to his people, he was also their prophet, fighting against all conventions and, like Moses, never fully satisfied. He led them across the desert toward the promised land. In the end he felt he had reached the land but had not yet achieved the promise in its profound moral and noble sense. He died still fighting for the fulfillment of the promise.

As if in acknowledgment of this, he was buried in Sdeh Boker, in a spot of his own choosing, looking out toward the wilderness of Zin, where the Israelites had wandered more than three thousand years before. It is of course more than a reminder of the long biblical journey toward the Land of Israel, offering a breathtaking panorama of the Negev mountains he so loved, whose colors change with the hours of the day.

Paula had died in January 1968 and was laid to rest there. Ben-Gurion survived to suffer, with the rest of his country, the great trauma of the surprise attack on October 6, 1973, which became the Yom Kippur War. He collapsed a few weeks later with a brain hemorrhage and died on December 1. His body lay in state at the Knesset in Jerusalem and was then flown by helicopter to Sdeh Boker.

At Ben-Gurion's request, there were no eulogies, and in its austerity his funeral was the opposite of Churchillian pomp. But the symbolism was just as rich. The entire country stopped at the sounding of a siren. Psalms and Kaddish were recited at the grave, and the cantor who sang *El Maalei Rachamim*, the traditional prayer asking God to gather up the soul of the departed, referred to the deceased as "David Ben-Gurion, son of Avigdor, first prime minister of the State, who effected the redemption of the people of Israel in their land."

That redemption is certainly not yet complete, but it was Ben-Gurion's genius to embrace the pragmatic acceptance of the possible, essential for nation building, without ever abandoning the prophetic yearning for moral perfection. And every year, on the anniversary of his death, the members of the government of the day, whatever its political stripe, together with other civilian dignitaries and military officers, make the pilgrimage to his grave and eulogize the man to whose wisdom and courage they all now agree they owe their country.

APPENDIX

State in the Making, A Reader's Guide

Modern Israel did not spring fully formed from the head of Theodor Herzl—though Herzl did create some of the Zionist institutions out of which the state grew. Herzl's international Zionist movement gave way to the elected executive bodies that ran the pre-state Yishuv, or Jewish community. Together they morphed into the government of the emerging State of Israel. It was this complex and evolving political system that Ben-Gurion navigated—and dominated—with such skill. The following outline is intended to serve as a reference for readers unfamiliar with the pre-state agencies, the labor union that functioned in a quasi-governmental fashion, and the numerous political parties that battled one another in the pre-state era and after the establishment of the State of Israel in 1948. These parties often split and shifted alliances in a rough-and-tumble democratic culture that pitted clashing ideologies against each other, only to come together, tenuously, in times of war.

The **World Zionist Organization (WZO),** created by Theodor Herzl in 1897 as the Zionist Organization, was governed by an elected congress that met annually or biennially and voted on broad Zionist strategy. To be eligible to vote, one paid a *shekel* in membership dues. On the eve of the Holocaust, more than one million Jews worldwide paid their membership dues and were registered as Zionists. Between meetings, an **Actions Committee** or **General Council,** elected by the Congress, would convene periodically to make policy decisions. Day-to-day running of the WZO affairs was in the hands of a small **Executive,** whose members headed the various departments of the WZO.

Before World War I, the seat of the WZO Executive was in Germany, but with the outbreak of war the focus of diplomatic activity shifted to London, where Chaim Weizmann took an increasingly central role. He later became president of the WZO.

With the collapse of the Ottoman Empire at the end of World War I, the League of Nations, in June 1922, assigned the **Mandate for Palestine** to Great Britain. Article 4 of the Mandate provided that:

> An appropriate Jewish agency shall be recognised as a public body for the purpose of advising and cooperating with the Administration of Palestine in such economic, social, and other matters as may affect the establishment of the Jewish national home and the interests of the Jewish population in Palestine . . . The Zionist Organization, so long as its organization and constitution are in the opinion of the Mandatory appropriate, shall be recognised as such agency.

In 1929, mainly at Weizmann's urging, the **Jewish Agency for Palestine** was officially created by the Sixteenth Zionist Congress. It included non-Zionist organizations and individuals—philanthropists and activists not involved in the life of the WZO but interested nevertheless in playing a role in the Jewish return to Palestine. The WZO, however, continued to dominate the Jewish Agency.

The WZO had started out as a territorial-based organization, with delegates to the congresses elected mainly on country-by-country lines ("General Zionists"), but it grew increasingly ideological over the years. By 1939, 386 delegates represented political parties and only 171 delegates represented countries.

By the mid-1930s, the socialist-Zionists, led in Palestine by Ben-Gurion, had become the dominant faction in the WZO, and

Ben-Gurion was elected chairman of the WZO Executive. In Palestine the largest socialist-Zionist party, led by Ben-Gurion, was **Mapai,** a Hebrew acronym for Workers' Party of Eretz Yisrael. Mapai was created in 1930 by the merger of **Ahdut HaAvoda,** the workers' party Ben-Gurion founded in 1919, and **Hapoal Hatzair.** Mapai members also came to dominate the **Histadrut,** or Federation of Trade Unions, which Ben-Gurion created in the early 1920s. The right-wing **Revisionist Zionists,** led by Ze'ev Jabotinsky, seceded from the WZO in the 1930s and formed their own rival Zionist organization and rival trade union federation. The Revisionists returned to the WZO fold after the Holocaust, in 1946.

The Yishuv, as the pre-state Jewish community of Palestine was called, was administered by a **National Assembly** (Asefat Nivharim), a quasi-parliament with authority over socioeconomic, cultural, and religious life. The Assembly was elected every four years in a countrywide vote (using proportional representation) for the various political parties. The Assembly elected a **National Executive** (Vaad Leumi) as its executive arm.

In the period immediately before Israel's declaration of independence, a **People's Assembly** was created, comprising members of the Zionist Executive, the National Executive, and several other individuals; thirty-seven members in all. On independence, its name was changed to the **Provisional State Council** (Moetzet Hamedina Hazmanit), and it functioned as the temporary parliament until elections were held. The People's Assembly created a smaller body of thirteen members, the **People's Executive,** as its executive arm, and this, chaired by Ben-Gurion, became the new state's **Provisional Government.**

The Zionist Movement's pre-state political structure, in Palestine and in the Diaspora, became the basis of the new State of Israel's democracy. The government modeled the British system of government, in which the ministers, including the prime minister, are responsible to Parliament; the Zionist electoral system of proportional representation enabled more than a dozen parties to be elected to the **Knesset,** or parliament. This in turn made a coalition government almost inevitable. Ben-Gurion's Mapai always ruled at the head of whatever coalition it created with other political parties.

Ben-Gurion's coalition partners usually included one or more of the religious parties: **Mizrachi-Hapoal Hamizrachi,** the Zionist-religious group later known as the **National Religious Party,** and **Agudat Yisrael–Poalei Agudat Yisrael,** the ultra-Orthodox group.

On occasion, he aligned also with **Mapam,** a socialist party to the left of Mapai; and with the **General Zionists,** who later split into the **Liberal Party** and the **Independent Liberal Party.**

The Revisionists entered the Knesset as the **Herut Party,** led by Menachem Begin. Herut later joined with the Liberal Party to form the electoral alliance **Gahal.** This alliance later co-opted additional parties to become the **Likud Party.**

A NOTE ON SOURCES

The main source for this book was a series of lively, freewheeling conversations between Shimon Peres and me on Friday mornings over a period of many months during 2009 and 2010 at his residence in Jerusalem. Mr. Peres's remarkable mind and teeming memory made those meetings a treasured experience for me and my research assistant, Shira Philosof.

To help us in our talking and writing, we had recourse to the books and archival material listed below.

—David Landau

1. Beginnings

Quoted material in this chapter comes from
Michael Bar-Zohar. *Ben-Gurion: A Political Biography* (Hebrew, 3 vols.). Tel Aviv: Am Oved, 1977.
David Ben-Gurion. *My Father's House* (Hebrew). Edited by Peter Frye and Amos Ettinger. Tel Aviv: Hakibbutz Hameuchad, 1975.
David Ben-Gurion. *Memoirs*, vol. 1 (Hebrew). Tel Aviv: Am Oved, 1971.
David Ben-Gurion. *The Letters of David Ben-Gurion*, vol. 1, *1904–1919*. Edited by Yehuda Erez. Tel Aviv: Am Oved and Tel Aviv University, 1972.
Achdouth. September–October 1910.

Additional source of reference
Shimon Peres. *Battling for Peace*. Edited by David Landau. New York: Random House, 1995.

2. Young Turk

Quoted material in this chapter comes from
Bar-Zohar. *Ben-Gurion: A Political Biography.*
Ben-Gurion. *Letters of David Ben-Gurion.*
The Ben-Gurion Research Institute for the Study of Israel and Zionism website, http://bgarchives.bgu.ac.il/archives.

Additional sources of reference
Peres. *Battling for Peace.*
Barnet Litvinoff. *Ben-Gurion of Israel.* London: Weidenfeld & Nicolson, 1954.

3. Union Boss

Quoted material in this chapter comes from
Bar-Zohar. *Ben-Gurion: A Political Biography.*
Chaim Weizmann. *Trial and Error: The Autobiography of Chaim Weizmann.* London: Hamish Hamilton, 1949.
Ben-Gurion. *Letters of David Ben-Gurion*, vol. 2, *1920–1928.*
Ben-Gurion. *Memoirs*, vol. 1.
Anita Shapira. *Yosef Haim Brenner: A Biography* (Hebrew). Tel Aviv: Am Oved, 2008.
Shabtai Teveth. *Kin'at David: Chayei David Ben-Gurion*, vol. 2 (Hebrew). Tel Aviv: Schocken, 1981.

Additional sources of reference
The Labor Movement in Israel website, http://tnuathaavoda.info.
The Ben-Gurion Research Institute.

4. Onward and Upward

Quoted material in this chapter comes from
Anita Shapira. *Berl: The Biography of a Socialist Zionist: Berl Katznelson, 1887–1994.* New York: Cambridge University Press, 1984.

David Ben-Gurion. *Talks with Arab Leaders* (Hebrew). Tel Aviv: Am Oved, 1967.

Ben-Gurion. *Memoirs*, vol. 1.

Davar. Historical Jewish Press website, www.jpress.org.il.

Additional sources of reference

Bar-Zohar. *Ben-Gurion: A Political Biography.*

Ben-Gurion Research Institute.

Herut, The National Movement website, www.herut.org.il/hebrew _new/jabo.html.

5. What Could He Do?

Quoted material in this chapter comes from

Shabtai Tevet. *Ben-Gurion and the Holocaust.* New York: Harcourt Brace, 1986.

David S. Wyman. *The Abandonment of the Jews.* New York: Pantheon Books, 1985.

Dina Porat, ed. *When Disaster Comes from Afar* (Hebrew). Jerusalem: Yad Ben-Zvi, 2009.

Weizmann. *Trial and Error.*

Shapira. *Berl: The Biography of a Socialist Zionist.*

Shimon Peres and Robert Little. *For the Future of Israel.* Baltimore: Johns Hopkins University Press, 1998.

Additional sources of reference

Michael Bar-Zohar. *Ben-Gurion: A Biography.* Translated by Peretz Kidron. London: Weidenfeld & Nicolson, 1978.

Ben-Gurion Research Institute.

6. Fateful Hour

Quoted material in this chapter comes from

David Ben-Gurion. *Israel: A Personal History.* Translated by Nechemia Myers and Uzy Nystar. New York: Funk & Wagnalls, 1971.

Moshe Sharett. *Personal Diary* (Hebrew, 8 vols.). Tel Aviv: Sifriat Maariv, 1978.

Bar-Zohar. *Ben-Gurion: A Political Biography.*

David Ben-Gurion. *At War* (Hebrew), vol. 5. Tel Aviv: Mapai, 1950.

7. Birth Pangs

Quoted material in this chapter comes from
Ben-Gurion. *Israel: A Personal History.*

Ben-Gurion. *At War.*

David Ben-Gurion. *When Israel Waged War* (Hebrew). Tel Aviv: Mapai, 1951.

David Ben-Gurion. *Army and Defense* (Hebrew). Tel Aviv: Maarchot, 1955.

Bar-Zohar. *Ben-Gurion: A Political Biography.*

Golda Meir. *My Life.* New York: G. P. Putnam's Sons, 1975.

Additional sources of reference
Davar.

Haganah website, http://www.hagana.co.il.

8. Settling In

Quoted material in this chapter comes from
Bar-Zohar. *Ben-Gurion: A Political Biography.*

Weizmann. *Trial and Error.*

Pinhas Yurman. *A State Starts Up* (Hebrew). Tel Aviv: Gvanim, 2007.

Peres, *Battling for Peace.*

Additional sources of reference
Sharett. *Personal Diary.*

Nir Kedar. *Mamlakhtiyut: David Ben-Gurion's Civic Thought*. Jerusalem: Yad Ben-Zvi, 2009.

9. Jewish People, Jewish Policy

Quoted material in this chapter comes from
Bar-Zohar. *Ben-Gurion: A Political Biography.*

Additional sources of reference
Haaretz.
Central Bureau of Statistics. *Israel Statistical Annual*, no. 4, 1952.
Ben-Gurion Research Institute.
Davar.

11. Defense of the Realm

Quoted material in this chapter comes from
Benny Morris. *Israel's Border Wars, 1949–1956: Arab Infiltration, Israeli Retaliation, and the Countdown to the Suez War*. New York: Oxford University Press, 1997.
Moshe Dayan. *Story of My Life* (Hebrew). Jerusalem and Tel Aviv: Edanim/Dvir, 1976.
Bar-Zohar. *Ben-Gurion: A Political Biography.*
Peres. *Battling for Peace.*

Additional sources of reference
Motti Golani. *There Will Be War Next Summer . . . : The Road to the Sinai War, 1955–1956*. Tel Aviv: Ministry of Defence, 1997.
Mordechai Bar-On. *The Gates of Gaza: Israel's Defense and Foreign Policy, 1955–1957* (Hebrew). Tel Aviv: Am Oved, 1992.

12. Soured Fruit

Quoted material in this chapter comes from
Bar-Zohar. *Ben-Gurion: A Political Biography.*

Additional sources of reference
Peres. *Battling for Peace.*
Haggai Eshed. *Who Gave the Order?* (Hebrew). Jerusalem: Edanim,
　　1979.

CHRONOLOGY

ca. 1882 Members of the Hovevei Tziyon (Lovers of Zion) movement begin to immigrate to Palestine in what will become known as the First Aliyah.

October 16, 1886 David Ben-Gurion, né Gruen, is born in Plonsk, Poland, then part of Russia.

1894 Captain Alfred Dreyfus is wrongly convicted of treason to France. He is sentenced to life imprisonment amid tremendous anti-Semitic sentiment.

1897 Theodor Herzl holds the First Zionist Congress in Basel.

1900/1901 At age fourteen, David Gruen founds his first Zionist group, Ezra.

1904 The Second Aliyah begins; this wave of Zionist immigration will bring 40,000 Jews, mostly from Russia, to Palestine by 1914.

Theodor Herzl dies.

September 7, 1906 David Gruen arrives in Jaffa as part of a group of Plonsk youth who are making aliyah together, settling initially in Petah Tikva.

Late 1907 David Gruen moves to Sejera, in the Galilee.

1908 The Young Turk revolution leads to minority groups gaining representation in the Turkish parliament.

Chronology

September 1910 David is appointed an editor of *Ha'achdut*, the newspaper of Poalei Zion, the Zionist Workers' Party, and adopts the last name Ben-Gurion.

1911 Ben-Gurion moves to Salonika to spend a year studying Turkish in preparation for attending law school.

1912 Ben-Gurion moves to Constantinople to study Ottoman law with his friends Yitzhak Ben-Zvi and Yisrael Shochat.

October 1912 Outbreak of First Balkan War disrupts Ben-Gurion's studies.

Spring 1914 Ben-Gurion spends Passover with his family in Poland.

August 1914 Ben-Gurion returns to Palestine as war breaks out in Europe. He and other Zionists are arrested by Turkish authorities and eventually expelled.

April 1915 Ben-Gurion sails from Alexandria to New York. He will remain in the United States until 1917.

November 2, 1917 The British government issues the Balfour Declaration, announcing that it "views with favor the establishment in Palestine of a national home for the Jewish people."

December 1917 Ben-Gurion marries Paulina Munbaz, known as Paula, in New York.

April 26, 1918 Ben-Gurion joins the Jewish Legion of the British armed forces.

December 1918 Ben-Gurion, as part of the Jewish Legion, arrives in Palestine from Egypt.

November 1919 Paula Ben-Gurion and their infant daughter Geula arrive in Palestine.

April 1920 The San Remo Conference confers control of former Ottoman territories of Palestine and Iraq to the British.

Spring 1920 The Ben-Gurion family temporarily moves to London, where Ben-Gurion runs the office of the World Poalei Zion movement.

March 1921 Ben-Gurion travels with his family to Plonsk to see his father.

May 1921 Arab riots break out in Palestine. Forty-seven Jews are killed. The British high commissioner suspends Jewish immigration to Palestine.

December 1921 Ben-Gurion becomes secretary-general of the Histadrut trade union federation, a position he will hold until 1935.

1922 Britain establishes the Emirate of Transjordan on the eastern part of the original Palestine mandate.

Summer 1923 Ben-Gurion visits the Soviet Union.

August 1929 Arab riots break out in Jerusalem and spread to Hebron and throughout (western) Palestine.

January 1930 Ben-Gurion's Ahdut HaAvoda joins Hapoal Hatzair to form the Mapai Party.

October 1930 British colonial secretary Lord Passfield publishes a white paper restricting Jewish immigration and land purchases. Weizmann resigns as president of the World Zionist Organization in protest.

February 1931 British prime minister Ramsay MacDonald effectively abrogates the Passfield White Paper.

April 1931 Etzel, an independent rightist militia, is founded under the leadership of Ze'ev Jabotinsky, leader of the Revisionist Party.

June 1931 With 29 percent of delegates, Ben-Gurion's Labor-Zionist party is the largest bloc at the Seventeenth Zionist Congress, held in Basel.

March 1933 Ben-Gurion starts tour of Eastern European Jewish communities to gather support for Labor Zionists.

June 16, 1933 Tension erupts among Zionist groups following the murder of Haim Arlosoroff, a rising figure in Mapai who had negotiated with Nazi Germany for the transfer of assets of Jews immigrating to Palestine.

July 1933 At the Eighteenth Zionist Congress, in Prague, Ben-Gurion's Labor Zionists represent nearly 45 percent of the delegates. Ben-Gurion is elected to the Zionist Executive; the Revisionist Party secedes.

1935 Ben-Gurion becomes chairman of the Jewish Agency Executive, a position he will hold until 1948.

April 1936 Arab riots erupt in Palestine. They will continue intermittently for three years.

August 7, 1936 Great Britain appoints a Royal Commission of Inquiry, under the leadership of Lord Peel, to investigate the causes of the Arab Revolt.

July 1937   The Peel Commission recommends the partition of Palestine; the Jewish portion is to include only the Galilee and Jezreel Valley in the north, and a narrow coastal strip. Zionist groups are bitterly divided over whether to accept these terms.

February 1939   Ben-Gurion and Weizmann head the Jewish delegation to negotiations held by the British with Arabs and Jews in London. The talks fail to achieve any results.

May 1939   The MacDonald White Paper, seen by the Zionists as an abandonment of the Balfour Declaration, limits Jewish immigration to 75,000 over five years and drastically restricts land purchase by Jews in Palestine.

September 1939   Germany invades Poland; Britain and France declare war on Germany. Ben-Gurion says, "We must help the British in their war as though there were no White Paper, and we must resist the White Paper as though there were no war."

April 1940   Ben-Gurion travels to London.

May 19, 1941   The Haganah, the military defense organization of Jewish Palestine, establishes the Palmach, a full-time strike force.

May 11, 1942   An Extraordinary Zionist conference in New York adopts the Biltmore Program, calling for the opening of Palestine to Jewish immigration, the placing of Jewish immigration under the Jewish Agency, and the establishment of a Jewish commonwealth in Palestine. For Ben-Gurion this means statehood immediately after the war.

November 1942 The British defeat of German forces at El Alamein, Egypt, removes the threat of a Nazi invasion of Palestine.

May 1944 Antipartition members of Ben-Gurion's Mapai
Party secede and form a separate party, using
the name of Ben-Gurion's original party of the
1920s, Ahdut HaAvoda.

November 1944 Members of Lehi murder the British resident
minister in the Middle East, Lord Moyne. In
response, Ben-Gurion orders the Haganah to
crack down on Jewish militants and hand them
over to British forces.

May 7, 1945 Germany unconditionally surrenders to the
Allies.

July 1, 1945 Ben-Gurion solicits funding from prominent
American Jews in New York to purchase
weapons.

October 1, 1945 In Paris, Ben-Gurion orders the Haganah to
launch an armed uprising.

November 1, 1945 The newly formed Hebrew Resistance Movement, incorporating the Haganah, Etzel, and
Lehi, begins to engage in joint actions, cutting
railroad lines around Palestine and damaging
British ships.

May 1, 1946 The Anglo-American Commission recommends
the admission of 100,000 Jewish refugees and
the restoration of the Jewish right to buy land
in Palestine. The British refuse to implement
these recommendations.

June 16, 1946 The Hebrew Resistance Movement blows up
bridges linking Palestine to neighboring coun-

tries; the British respond with a harsh crack-
down in the Yishuv.

July 1946   Etzel bombs the British administrative headquarters at Jerusalem's King David Hotel,
killing ninety people.

December 1946   At the Zionist Congress in Basel, Ben-Gurion
allows for the possibility of partition in exchange for immediate independence; Weizmann cautions against a violent break with
Britain and resigns from the leadership of the
World Zionist Organization.

1947   Ben-Gurion's concordat with the Orthodox
Agudat Yisrael Party guarantees the hege-
mony of religious law in matters of personal
status in the future state.

February 1947   The United Nations, at the request of Great
Britain, takes on the question of Palestine.

July 1947   The UN Special Committee on Palestine's
visit coincides with the arrival of the ship
Exodus.

November 29, 1947   The UN General Assembly votes for the
partition of Palestine. Violence will escalate
between Jewish forces and Palestinian ir-
regulars, backed by volunteers from Arab
countries.

April 5, 1948   Haganah fighters briefly reopen the road to
Jewish Jerusalem.

April 9, 1948   Etzel and Lehi fighters kill civilians in the
Arab village of Deir Yassin, helping to spark
the Palestinian refugee crisis.

May 13, 1948   The Etzion bloc of settlements south of Jerusalem falls to the Arab Legion.

May 14, 1948   Ben-Gurion proclaims the establishment of the State of Israel. The United States, the USSR, and other key countries recognize the new Jewish state. Israel is immediately invaded by the armies of Egypt, Transjordan, Iraq, Syria, and Lebanon.

May 26, 1948   The Provisional Government establishes the Israel Defense Forces and outlaws any other armed force within Israel.

June 1, 1948   Menachem Begin, head of Etzel, agrees that his fighters will join the IDF.

June 8, 1948   The "Burma Road," an alternate route to Jewish Jerusalem, is opened, bringing relief to the city's besieged inhabitants.

June 11, 1948   A four-week truce goes into effect, allowing the Israeli Army time to bring in arms and train more fighters.

The *Altalena* sets sail for Israel, laden with arms and refugees. Begin insists that the arms be distributed first to Etzel fighters within the IDF.

June 20, 1948   The *Altalena* arrives at Kfar Vitkin, Israel. Ben-Gurion orders his commanders to secure the ship. In clashes at Kfar Vitkin and on the Tel Aviv beach, sixteen on board and three IDF soldiers are killed.

July 8, 1948   Fighting with the invading Arab armies resumes. The IDF achieves successes in the North.

July 18, 1948   A second UN-ordered truce goes into effect.

September 17, 1948   UN envoy Count Folke Bernadotte is murdered, allegedly by Lehi. Ben-Gurion responds by arresting hundreds of Lehi and Etzel members.

October 1948 Ben-Gurion dismantles the separate Palmach command structure within the IDF.

The truce breaks down. Ben-Gurion responds with major attacks in the Negev, forcing the Egyptian Army out of Ashdod and Ashkelon.

January 25, 1949 Israel holds its first parliamentary elections, resulting in a coalition government led by Mapai. Ben-Gurion serves as prime minister and minister of defense.

February 16, 1949 Chaim Weizmann is sworn in as president of Israel, having been elected in absentia shortly after the declaration of statehood.

February 24, 1949 Israel and Egypt sign an armistice.

March 1949 IDF forces reach the Red Sea in the last operation of the War of Independence.

March 23, 1949 Israel and Lebanon sign an armistice.

April 3, 1949 Israel and Transjordan sign an armistice. Israel retains areas in the North and the center of the country not included in the Jewish state under the 1947 UN Partition Plan. Transjordan annexes the West Bank and becomes the Hashemite Kingdom of Jordan.

July 20, 1949 Israel and Syria sign an armistice.

December 9, 1949 The UN General Assembly passes a resolution to internationalize Jerusalem, as per the original Partition Plan.

December 11, 1949 Ben-Gurion leads his cabinet in declaring Jerusalem the capital of Israel and moving the government offices from Tel Aviv.

Chronology

April 4, 1950 Ben-Gurion and the Jewish Agency Executive agree on a plan to build *maabarot*, transit camps, for the massive numbers of new Jewish immigrants.

May 1951 Ben-Gurion establishes the Israel Bonds program at a massive rally in Madison Square Garden, helping to ease Israel's financial crisis.

July 20, 1951 King Abdullah of Jordan is assassinated, putting an end to secret peace negotiations with Israel.

January 1952 Rioting erupts in Jerusalem as the Knesset debates an agreement with Germany over reparation funds.

July 1952 A military-led revolution in Egypt overthrows the Egyptian monarchy.

September 1952 Israel signs an agreement with Germany to accept reparations funds.

November 1952 Chaim Weizmann dies. Yitzhak Ben-Zvi is elected president.

November 1953 Ben-Gurion resigns.

December 1953 Ben-Gurion and Paula move to Kibbutz Sdeh Boker in the Negev. Foreign Minister Moshe Sharett takes over as prime minister, with Pinhas Lavon as defense minister.

July 1954 An Israeli spy ring is arrested in Egypt.

February 1955 Ben-Gurion returns to government as minister of defense under Moshe Sharett.

1955 Egypt, led by Gamal Abdel Nasser, one of the revolutionary officers, announces a major arms deal with Czechoslovakia, signaling a new closeness with the Soviet bloc.

July 1955 Ben-Gurion leads the Mapai to victory in parliamentary elections. A new coalition government takes office in November, with Ben-Gurion prime minister once again.

July 26, 1956 Nasser nationalizes the Suez Canal, hitherto owned largely by Britain and France.

October 1956 Ben-Gurion attends a secret summit in Sèvres, France.

October 29, 1956 Israel, in concert with France and Britain, invades Egypt. Israel conquers the Gaza Strip and the Sinai Peninsula and opens the Straits of Tiran to Israeli shipping.

March 1957 Under pressure from the United States and the Soviet Union, Israel withdraws from the Sinai. UN forces are deployed along the border and at Sharm el-Sheikh to ensure Israel access to the Straits of Tiran.

May 23, 1960 Ben-Gurion announces that Nazi war criminal Adolf Eichmann is in the hands of Israeli security services and will be tried by Israel.

January 1961 Ben-Gurion resigns, in the wake of a government investigation that clears Pinhas Lavon of responsibility for the Egyptian spying debacle.

August 1961 Mapai wins a plurality in parliamentary elections; Ben-Gurion once again forms a coalition and becomes prime minister.

June 16, 1963 Ben-Gurion resigns.

January 1965 Ben-Gurion travels to Britain with Israeli president Zalman Shazar to attend Winston Churchill's funeral.

February 1965 Ben-Gurion confronts Golda Meir and Moshe Sharett over the Lavon Affair at a Mapai Party conference. In June, Ben-Gurion secedes from Mapai and forms a new party, Rafi.

June 5, 1967 Israel launches preemptive air attacks against the Arab armies massed on her borders. In what will become known as the Six-Day War, Israel conquers the Golan Heights, the West Bank, the Gaza Strip, and the Sinai.

January 1968 Paula dies and is buried at Sde Boker.

May 1970 Ben-Gurion retires from the Knesset.

October 6, 1973 Israel is attacked by Egypt and Syria, launching the Yom Kippur War.

December 1, 1973 Ben-Gurion dies.